CW00822461

THE WINNING EDGE 2

Traders' & Investors' Psychological Coach in a Book

by Adrienne Laris Toghraie, MNLP, MCH

On Target Press
100 Lavewood Lane
Cary, North Carolina 27518
919-851-8288

A Division of Trading on Target

First Published in the United States in 1998
Second Printing 2004
Third Printing 2005
Fourth Printing 2007
Fifth Printing 2008

© Trading on Target

The right of Adrienne Laris Toghraie to be identified as author of this work
has been asserted by her in accordance with the Copyright, Design and Patents Act.

ISBN 978-0-9661837-1-9

All rights reserved: no part of this publication, unless indicated may be
reproduced, stored in a retrieval system, or transmitted in any form or by any
means, electronic, mechanical, photocopying, recording, or otherwise without either
the prior written permission of the Publishers or a license permitting restricted
copying in the United States issued by the Copyright Licensing Agency Ltd.

This book may not be lent, resold, hired out or otherwise disposed of by way
of trade in any form of binding or cover other than that in which it is
published, without the prior consent of the Publishers.

PHOTO BY BILL SPURGEON

About the Author

ADRIENNE LARIS TOGHRAIE, MNLP, MCH, is a trading coach, an internationally recognized authority in the field of human development and a master practitioner of Neuro-Linguistic Programming (NLP) for the financial and business communities. She is the founder and president of *Trading on Target* and *Enriching Life Seminars,* two companies dedicated to helping traders, sales people, and other high achievers to dramatically increase profits and success in all areas of life. Using her 20 years of study in the science of Modeling Excellence/(NLP) and numerous other forms of psychological development, Ms. Toghraie has helped her clients to push through their self-imposed limitations to extraordinary and documented new levels of success.

Adrienne's articles and interviews have been featured in most of the major financial trade magazines and newspapers throughout the world. She has authored *Treasure Diary for Creating Affluence* and co-authored *The Winning Edge, How to Use Your Personal Psychological Power in Trading and Investing* with Jake Bernstein and her *Dear Coach, Potty Training for Traders, Brokers & Investors.*

Adrienne's public seminars and private counseling, as well as her television appearances and keynote addresses at major industry conferences, have achieved a wide level of recognition and popularity.

Table of Contents

Section One: *Traders Who Run a Business...*

Section Two: Traders Who Can't...

Section Six: *Traders Who Limit Success By...*

Dedicated to:

Tom Lanny

My Coach From Down Under

A True Gentleman

Acknowledgments to:

Rick Morgan

Who gives the TOT Bull his flair and humor.

Wendy Clouse

Who coordinated the assembly and editing
of this book and is my invaluable right hand.

Antonia Weeks

Who taught me how to write and assisted me every
step of the way by continuously asking,
"So what are you really trying to say?"

Roger Reimer

Who was our invaluable editor.

F. Fox Henderson & Peggy Levine

Who were also a part of the editing team.

Richard A. Shwery, O.M.D.

Who keeps me well.

&

**A special thanks to all of the traders who
contributed their stories, so that everyone
could learn from their lessons.**

Preface

Winning Edge 2, Traders' and Investors' Coach in a Book is a collection of my revised articles appearing in financial magazines and newsletters all over the world. Admittedly, sometimes it was a stretch to include a particular article in a section. But, I felt it was more important to be complete and informative than to be consistent. In addition, you will find certain lessons which are repeated throughout this book. Since these lessons are the ones that traders seem to forget and need to be reminded of periodically, I'm sure you will welcome the repetition.

The stories included in the book are about people who are clients, who have been to my seminars and workshops or whom I have met on the phone. I have changed their names and altered their situations slightly. In some cases, when their story was unusual, I asked permission to write about it even though the information surrounding the story was disguised.

Masculine pronouns are used generically, implying his/hers, he/she, him/her in all cases for ease of reading.

Forward

by Murray Ruggiero

Almost everybody who gets involved in trading does so to make money. Most people also have the dream of becoming such a great trader that they can buy or have anything their heart desires. Some of these people dream of managing money and collecting 20 % of the profits on hundreds of millions of dollars of capital. Others dream of breaking Larry Williams' record of turning ten thousand into over one million in twelve months. Still others dream of taking their small amount of capital and, over the years, turning it into tens or even hundreds of millions of dollars.

Whatever the dream, the question becomes: What separates those who reach that dream from those who fail? Believe it or not, it is the same thing that separates the successful people from the masses in other fields. The successful ones have a plan for success and they follow it. Another important fact is that successful people, in general, have very similar plans and that modeling these plans is the best way to become successful. As a modeler, Adrienne Laris Toghraie, has coached many people in the investment field to high levels of success. She accomplishes this by teaching them success-building models.

In Chapter One, Getting into the Business, Adrienne says that only 10% of all businesses survive more than one year and only 3% of businesses survive more than 3 years. These numbers show that even when you have expertise in the business, your odds of survival are relatively low. A number often cited is that only 5% of traders make consistent money trading the markets. For this reason, many people do not consider trading a viable business. Since the numbers for all businesses are very similar to the trading business, then we would believe that having your own business, period, is not a viable option, which we know is ludicrous. In reality, being successful in trading is no more difficult than being a success in any other business.

In *The Winning Edge 2,* Adrienne sets out a detailed blueprint to realize the dream of success that every trader has. She begins with an overview of a business plan for starting a trading business. The concept of requiring a business plan to be successful for any business is often overlooked by traders who tend to think that just having good trading methodology is enough. But just like a business with a great product, many other factors can cause it to fail. A business plan helps to alleviate many of the problems that result from these factors. That is why many start-up companies will pay tens of thousand of dollars to have consultants develop their business plan.

Next, Adrienne discusses an often overlooked issue: Developing a trading style to fit your personality. Resolving this issue is not as easy as it seems because some traders need numbers and statistics while others are more comfortable working intuitively. Other personality-matching issues are what to trade (i.e. stocks, futures) and whether you should trade your money or someone else's, both of which relate to your personality. Even in this short chapter, Adrienne helps you to open a window into yourself so that you can begin to address these issues. This is important because, even if you had a system that made money consistently, if the system didn't fit your personality, you still may not be able to follow the rules.

One of the chapters that hit hardest in my life is the chapter on managing your time. In fact, I would have been comfortable paying ten times the cost of this book for that chapter alone. This chapter includes not only how to better utilize your time with your clients and how to run your business but also the necessity of keeping your life in balance, both in your business and in your personal life, including your health. Most entrepreneurs do not deal with these issues and with disastrous results (i.e., divorce, heart attack), not realizing how important these issues are until it's too late and they've adversely affected their lives. Just like the ghost of Christmas future, you need to take this chapter to heart.

I've known Adrienne for several years, and we share mutual clients for whom I supply the trading methodology (the rules) and Adrienne supplies the right psychological support to follow the rules. I can say that the traders who come with this kind of psychological support are the best and most disciplined traders. The traders who can follow their methodology and can ask me the right questions are almost always the clients who have had personal consultations with Adrienne. In fact, one of the best traders that I know is one of her lifetime clients.

The important thing about trading is that you can reach lofty goals that seemed impossible. If you have a good methodology that can make you money, you will succeed if you don't sabotage yourself by breaking the rules of your methodology. Traders dream of finding the holy grail, but unfortunately over 90% of the traders that I initially come in contact with would lose money with tomorrow's *Wall Street Journal*. Their problems are what Adrienne calls their psychological gremlins which not only affect a person's life as a trader but all other aspects of his life. *The Winning Edge 2* gives you a plan and covers all of the issues for reaching your dream, including keeping your life in balance. As we enter the 21st Century and computer technology has turned many traders into number crunchers, it is appropriate that this book comes out to remind us that, to be successful in trading, we need a mental edge. And *The Winning Edge 2* delivers a clear path for reaching that success.

SECTION I

Traders Who Run a Business…

Chapter 1

_____

GETTING INTO THE BUSINESS

One of the main reasons that traders fail is not their lack of trading skills, but their lack of business skills. The best education and talent for a particular profession is not enough to guarantee success. If you plan to run a successful business, you must also develop the skills of a businessman. Many professionals make the mistake of assuming that their credentials ensure them of success. If you doubt the truth of this statement, a trip to the bankruptcy court will make you a believer in the importance of having an education in running a professional business.

Business Reality Check

Last year alone, according to a *National News Service*, 883,000 people declared bankruptcy in the United States. In southern California, there were 80,000 bankruptcies. These figures include personal bankruptcies, but do not include the businesses that just fizzled out because of lack of interest, mismanagement or under capitalization. Nationally over 90% of new businesses fail within the first year, and, of the remaining 10%, only 30% continue after three years. So, based on statistics you will only have a 3% chance of creating a business that will survive. To beat these odds you must start with a fighting chance by having the tools necessary for success, the first being a plan of action.

The Great Trader who Failed in Business

Johnny was one of the best floor traders I have ever met. Over the fifteen years he traded in the pit, he consistently maintained steady growth. Eventually, when his pain killers stopped numbing the pain in his back and legs, he concluded that it was time to come off the floor and work behind a computer. Although his fellow traders warned him that this move was the kiss of death for his trading career, Johnny was convinced he could make it in his own trading business.

Johnny realized that the first step in this transition was to develop a new trading style as he could no longer rely on the sights and sounds of the trading floor for his intuitive trading style. Although this learning process was a challenge, Johnny knew how to ask the right questions from the right people.

The second step in the transition, however, became a major problem. Johnny was accustomed to trading institutional money. After years of living a high life style, his savings were only $225,000. The six month transition time to becoming an off-the-floor trader and opening up an office while sustaining his old life style, consumed $100,000 of his savings, leaving only $125,000 in trading capital. At this level, even the optimal profits of 30-50% that he was producing would certainly not be enough to maintain both his life style and his new business. If he were going to succeed in business, he quickly realized that he would have to become a money manager.

Like most new traders, Johnny thought that being a good trader was all he needed to succeed. While trading his own money would require simple business skills, trading other people's money requires sophisticated business management skills. Predictably, Johnny's trading business failed, not because he failed as a trader, but because he failed as a businessman.

Entrepreneurs Always Work for Themselves

Raised in an immigrant family of poor, hard-working shopkeepers, Peter learned very early the lessons of running his own business. By working his way through college, he also learned important lessons in self-sufficiency. From college, Peter moved directly into working as a trader trainee for an institution. He already knew that this was the best way to reach his goal of running his own trading business. Unlike his peers, as an institutional trader, he thought like a businessman. Although he operated within the guidelines of the institution, Peter felt that he was making his own business work. This type of thinking was responsible for his rapid promotion to manager, and then to department head. After carefully saving his money and creating a business plan, Peter knew he was ready to go on his own. Here is an outline he developed of skills and resources which you will need if you want to increase your odds for creating a successful business.

TRADING BUSINESS PLAN

The purpose of a business plan is to provide a realistic and systematic process and method of action in order to make a profit.

I. **Creating a Business Plan**

      A. **Philosophy**   beliefs which establish the parameters for the business and its personnel

      B. **Mission**   primary focus of the business

C. **Objective**   where you want the business to go

D. **Goal-Setting** the big unit steps for accomplishing the goals

E. **Tasks**   methods of delegating and using resources toward getting goals

F. **Resources**   knowing your existing resources, creating others needed, e.g., licenses, sales and marketing skills, equipment, professional services

G. **Contingencies** planning for everything that could go wrong or right

II. **Office Management**

A. **Organizing an office and having a time management plan**

B. **Maintaining information files and retrieval systems**

C. **Hiring and supervising professional services and employees**

D. **Negotiating for best prices**

E. **Dealing with vendors and creditors**

F. **Buying equipment and maintenance services**

III. **Money Management Skills and Other Factors**

A. **Budgeting and risk control** - startup capital and a minimum of six months operational capital

B. **Accounting principles**

C. **Tax planning**

D. **Investing principles** - (non-speculative) for personal savings as well as company profits

IV. **Banking and Money Connections**

A. **Developing banking connections**

B. **Locating investors**

C. **Creating credit and maintaining credit** - both for business and personal life

V. Trading Skills

A. **Modeling top people** - in the area of trading that you want to pursue

B. **Trading criteria**
1. Which markets do you want to trade?
2. Which timing fits your personality, lifestyle and budget?

C. **Trading rules** - for
1. Evaluating signals
2. Entering a trade
3. Managing profits

D. **System testing**

E. **Money management rules**

VI. Marketing Skills

A. **Developing marketing tools**

B. **Advertising and promotion**

VII. Sales Skills

A. **Presentation** - of yourself, your office, and your products

B. **Maintaining clients**

C. **Motivating others**

VIII. Interpersonal Skills for Business

A. **Effective communication**

B. **Telephone skills**

C. **Handling business transactions**

D. **Socializing**

E. **Interviewing techniques**

F. Positive attitudes, beliefs and values

IX. **Personal Skills**

     A. Self-discipline, motivation

     B. Time management

     C. Emotional balance and control

     D. Stress and health management

This outline is brief. I would recommend a more detailed plan with an explanation written by those who have succeeded in the investment field such as Sunny Harris' best seller *Trading 101, How to Trade Like a Pro* and *Trading 102, Getting Down to Business*, also Joe Ross' classic *Trading is a Business*. Reading about the skills it takes to run a business and coming up with a plan is a beginning, but developing the actual skills takes experience. If you do not have the experience, you will save money and time by finding someone who does. Sales and marketing are skills that will make or break a business.

Conclusion

As you will notice, only a few of these planning and management skills relate directly to trading. Successful traders learn that they need to master this range of skills before they can apply their specific professional training to be successful in running a business.

Chapter 2

———

MAKING THE RIGHT INITIAL DECISIONS

Traders use many different criteria in determining what to trade and what particular system or methodology to use. But probably the most important single criterion in making these decisions should be: Is the choice a good psychological fit for the trader?

When a brand new, "money-eyed" trader comes into the business, all he can see is the joy of future success. The process of succeeding is secondary. However, when the new trader goes against his psychological nature, the trip to success can become a bumpy ride, with the obstacles, coming from his own personality, being often too great to overcome.

The Right Fit

The process of getting the right fit begins with the way traders get into the business. When we visit someone in a new state or country, we feel comfortable at first, knowing someone who knows the place. Soon, however, we often find ourselves wishing that this person had not met us at the airport because he does not really know about his home. Traders can fall into this same trap by starting out under the advice of an Uncle Ned, the floor trader, or an Aunt Tilly, the money manager.

Because of this casual, unsystematic introduction into the trading business, the new trader has instant familiarity with an area of trading and usually feels that he has a direction. The underlying problem is that instant familiarity can become a trader's nemesis. By not going through the normal process of self-assessment, a trader may make decisions that result in a poor psychological fit.

I.   **Personalities**

Many of the systems that are currently available work but do not produce results for everyone who uses them. The principle reason for this failure is that everyone

9

has different levels of tolerance for working within certain time frames, volatility, risk and draw-downs. Some systems are generally acknowledged to bring in solid returns if traders can follow them. However, while assessing the facts and figures in selecting a system, the bottom line question is, "Does this system fit me?" For example, some traders have the personality to tolerate 70% draw-downs while trading 15 minute time frames, while others need to trade at low risk in long-term time frames. There are systems with 70-80% draw-downs that make money. But imagine if you were to hold ten thousand dollars in your hands and be required to give away eight thousand of it in order to ultimately or potentially make an $18,000 profit. Could you handle it? What kind of personality can?

A. The Mathematician Trader

This personality type totally believes in the rule of mathematics and will view money as numerical figures, without attaching any emotion to it. For the true mathematician trader, money has no value except for the ultimate outcome in a probability equation tested over a time period. These traders know that they will make money just following their signals. This type of personality disconnects from the excitement of the game of trading and from the emotion of the rewards. Because he is mainly interested in the win of the numbers, this trader can trade a trend following or oscillator type of system.

B. The Intuitive Trader

This personality type is the opposite of the mathematician trader, although these two personalities can be equally intelligent and interested in the mechanical/research aspect of trading. However, the mathematician personality is predominantly directed from the left brain, which promotes precise, unemotional, linear thought. The intuitive trader is predominantly directed from the right brain, which promotes illogical leaps of understanding, intuitive knowledge, and emotional/sensory awareness. These traders learn to use their intuitive signals to make money and are able to harness their emotional power to trade more effectively. These traders can and often do use a mechanical system but add to it an intuitive indicator.

C. The Gambler Trader

This personality type suffers from a confusion of signals from either the right or left brain. He is too excitable to maintain an emotional distance from trading, on the one hand, and too excitable to detect the subtle intuitive signals, on the other hand. This type of trader is able to tolerate systems that are loaded with high risk, high volatility, brief time frames, and high draw-downs. Although the gambler trader is capable of extraordinary moments of trading brilliance, this personality type is usually unsuited to the profession of trading because of his lack of inner discipline and his need to create enormous wins rather than a steady stream of moderate gains. All traders can fit into this category for short periods of their trading life which often leads to their demise as traders. No system is the right one for this trader because he is undisciplined.

Not only does a trader have to have the right psychological fit for the system he trades, he also needs to check that his personality, including his habits and tolerance levels, match what is required for the type of trading he does.

II. Instrument Vehicle

A. Futures Traders
The futures trader is someone who is usually willing to assume a higher level of risk than most other people. The futures trader likes the fact that he can get leverage on his money and, therefore, can trade with more money than he actually possesses. The fact that losses are proportionately higher to his investment is not a problem in his thinking. He is willing to assume this level of risk because he feels that he will not lose. In other words, $25,000 in margin on a $100,000 contract could mean, in a fast-moving market, that a trader owes more than $25,000, etc. An exceptional futures trader has an extremely high level of self confidence and feels that no matter what happens he will always be okay.

In addition, futures traders usually have more imagination for trusting in paper and ink value than equity traders, because they are trading something that really does not exist until some point in the future. An equity trader is trading a piece of paper that represents a share of a company's physical assets right now. However, a futures trader is trading on the future delivery of a particular commodity with the assumption that it can be delivered.

B. The Equity Trader
An equity trader who introduced himself at one of my seminars said to the audience of futures traders, "I really don't understand you guys. As far as I'm concerned, what you do is really weird. The idea of looking at wiggly lines, bar charts, candlesticks and all of the other patterns you look at to make a trading decision is beyond my comprehension."

The equity trader likes to feel that he has a piece of something. Instead of dealing in abstraction, he needs to deal in what he thinks is concrete reality. In equities, he can visualize the property of a company and feel that he is holding something that has value. Equity traders are often people who love to do the research on the detail of what makes this particular property have value. They like to be able to go out and look at a *McDonald's* or at an aircraft and know it has a connection to something concrete. They like to get into the history of a company and know that their decision is based on solid evidence that this particular company or product has a tangible value.

11

While there are decisions to be made on the different types of instruments to trade, there are also decisions to be made on the logistics and time frames of how to trade these instruments.

III.   The Upstairs/Downstairs Traders

A. Upstairs

The individual trader who trades at a desk behind a computer screen must be a self-starter who enjoys working by himself. Unlike floor traders, upstairs traders are people for whom the idea of standing closely next to others makes them feel claustrophobic. The extroverted experience of the floor-trading environment would be painful for the upstairs trader. Instead, he likes the idea of working on his own and enjoys watching the activities on the screen. He must be able to handle details and the day-to-day monotony of successful trading. As a businessman, he must be able to maintain organization and self-discipline.

B. Downstairs

While an equity trader needs a connection with the specific vehicle, the floor trader has to feel that he has an immediate connection with what is happening. Floor traders trade by a connection to the rhythm and emotion of the crowd. They need instant gratification, but have to be disciplined enough not to get caught up in a case of gambling fever. They have to have the patience to wait for a signal and not try to push action that is not there.

IV.   Time Frames

Generally, all time frames can be traded regardless of whether you are an upstairs or a downstairs trader.

A. Day Traders

Day traders need to have a feeling of control over the day-to-day activities of the market. They do not like the feeling of leaving positions on overnight. They need quick profits and lots of activities to sustain them, although their need for instant gratification and activity is not as great as that of the average floor trader.

B. Position Traders

The position trader is often someone with a lot more confidence than other traders. He is also, generally someone who is trading with more money. Position traders are willing to go through the ups and downs of long-term trading and have an opinion about the market. These are usually trend-following, moving-average, or oscillator traders.

V.   Source of Money

The question of where the trading capital comes from is a major decision that must be addressed in relation to individual personality. Based upon a person's values, beliefs and comfort zones, he feels differently about his various sources of money. It is a mistake to trade with money with which you are uncomfortable trading because the guilt, fear and discomfort can limit or damage your trading results.

A.   Your Money
Traders who only feel comfortable risking their own money must wait until they have enough capital with which to trade. They must think of their capital as inventory for their business and cannot relate it to personal funds. If you cannot disassociate from your own personal security issues, then perhaps you should consider trading other people's money.

B.   Other People's Money
While it is important for a trader to be responsible, you cannot become emotionally involved with your client's money and what they plan to do with it. A money manager must disconnect himself from the stories behind the investor and only deal with the task of following risk averse money management rules. Other people's money can come from various sources, and these too can come with emotional associations for traders:

1.   Individual Investors
A trader must feel comfortable dealing face to face with an individual whose money he is trading. He must be able to deal with the prospect of bringing bad news to this individual. The money you agree to manage for others should have the least emotional attachment in order for a trader to feel comfortable in trading it.

2.   An Institutional Investor
A trader must feel comfortable dealing with a large and/or powerful institution or company with large sums of money. While a trader should trade responsibly knowing that the dreams and lives of people are being affected, he also needs to disconnect himself from the stories attached to the investors' money so that he doesn't get emotionally involved.

3.   Your Employer's Money
Few people are capable of trading for an employer. Trading in a company can mean dealing with social, political and ethical issues that you would not have to deal with when trading on your own. Also, you always face the possibility of losing your job if you begin to lose money in your trading.

No matter whose money you trade, you must not become emotionally attached to that money or you will face sabotage issues.

VI.   Other Investment-World Careers

Aside from being a trader, someone who is interested in participating in the trading world has other options if he decides that he is psychologically unsuited to trading, per se.

A. Stockbrokers
Most brokerage firms are more interested in hiring a salesman than a stock analyst-trader to work as a stockbroker. For this reason, the extroverted, right-brained, people-oriented qualities make for a good psychological fit. You will have to deal with the fact that most institutions care only about their bottom line, not the customers. Very often you are put in a position to sell, knowing you are going to lose the customer's money.

B. Money Managers/CPO's and CTA's
All types of money managers must possess not only the selling personality of the stockbroker, but the tough left-brain qualities of a businessman to deal with regulators and to maintain a squeaky-clean operation that can be inspected at a moment's notice. In addition, they must be able to control the excitability of their clients by trading within a 10-20% range with no larger than a 10% draw-down.

With Three You Get Eggroll

Obviously, in order to make the decisions you need to make to be successful as a trader, you have to correctly match a combination of factors. The more of these factors you fit to your psychology, the more you limit the scope of the psychological problems you will have to handle. To help you make these decisions, you need to ask yourself certain questions:

1.   **What is my personality type?**

2.   **What instrument vehicle am I interested in and best suited for?**

3.   **Am I an upstairs or downstairs trader type?**

4.   **What time frame am I comfortable with?**

5.   **Should I actually be trading, or would I be better suited to managing money or working as a broker?**

Conclusion

"To thine own self be true" was never truer anywhere than in the trading world. Doing an honest self-assessment is a relatively painless way to avoid the potentially high costs incurred when a trader is mismatched with his trading decisions. The best time to do this self-assessment is before you take the leap into trading. However, if you realize that you have made a wrong decision and that you are psychologically ill-suited to the type of trading you are doing, the best time to do the self-assessment is now.

Chapter 3

———

MANAGING YOUR TIME ASSETS

Not having enough time is one of the biggest complaints I hear from traders. The bottom line is that you only have a 24 hour day. Your goal should be to use that time effectively and efficiently, while enjoying the process.

Because time usage is such a major problem for traders and because of the incredible demands upon my own time, I have devoted considerable thought and energy, over the last decade, to developing time-saving strategies. Having compiled a list of helpful observations about the source of time-wasters and effective ways to eliminate or control them, I would like to share this information with all of you who want to take control of your time.

The Time Plan

If you want to get more out of the time that you have, you must plan your time and stick to your plan. Too easy, you say? Then you would be surprised to see how many people do not make a plan. But, for those who do, it is equally amazing how difficult it is for them to keep to that plan. The problem is all of those unscheduled, unplanned interruptions and temptations, which I call the Time Gremlins.

Before we look at handling the "Time Gremlins," let's put together some basic rules for a Time Plan:

1.   A plan starts with goals - What is it that you want to accomplish? Remember the old saying, "If you don't know where you want to go, any path will take you there."

2.   Once you know where you want to go, a time plan needs a monthly plan, which is then broken down into a weekly and then a daily plan.

3.   Next, you need an overview of what goes into a yearly plan.

4.   This overview then needs to get down into the nitty-gritty detail, which requires that you decide on the following:

- What you want to get accomplished - your goals.

- What you would really like to do beyond what you want to get accomplished.

- What you have to do, specifically, in order to accomplish your goals.

5.   Then, prioritize. Your goals, as well as your list of tasks that will help you reach your goals, must be prioritized, so that you know what is most important. If you start your day by doing the most important things first, you will be saving time and moving rapidly toward the achievement of your goals.

It is important that you have fully addressed each one of these areas for a plan to be complete. For example, you know that you need to spend a certain amount of time in your career expanding your education. At the same time, you need to spend a certain amount of time with your family and friends as social activities are important to your well-being. Health is important to your physical maintenance and your spiritual time can be the most important part of your life. Then, there are the repairs, cleaning and maintenance of all of the parts of your environment, or, in other words, what some people call chores. Below is a list of the major areas of your life which must be addressed in your time plan in order for your plan to work:

1.   **Career:** including the specific elements of your career such as your career goals, sales and presentation skills among others, networking, business associates, resources, and a business plan.

2.   **Education:** broadening your horizons in all of the areas in your life is not limited to what you can learn in a classroom, although that is an important part of it. It also involves changing our thinking, your habits, your beliefs, your values and acting as if it were so.

3.   **Health:** involving the routine maintenance of your body including: diet breathing, exercise, relaxation and vitamin and herbal supplements. Other areas of health maintenance can include: acupuncture, massage, dental treatment, and periodic medical exams.

4.   **Financial:** involving a set of financial goals, a mind-set about money and prosperity, personal money management, and financial contributions to the world around you.

5. **Social:** playfulness and its various outlets such as your adventures, sharing experiences and social activities, special moments and events, trips, dining out experiences, etc.

6. **Relationships:** including all of the relationships and interrelationships which form the fabric of your existence, the loves, the family, friends, coworkers, etc. The communication, intimacy, agreements, and feelings that are part of these relationships.

7. **Emotional:** the world of feelings motivating you to take the actions you take. The people and things you have in your life are reflections of your attitude about yourself. Important areas of your emotional world are your self-esteem, your mental state resources, your emotional discomforts and your nurturing thoughts and experiences.

8. **Spiritual:** the world of religious dogma and rules, of traditions giving us a sense of belonging, of practices giving us focus, and of the spiritual truths showing us the meaning of our existence.

9. **Action:** manifesting into reality our goals, ambitions and dreams and the discipline which is necessary to take action. Effective action requires these elements: organization, time management, balance, resources, planning, emotional control, and rewards.

All of your activities need to be balanced against all of the outcomes you want to achieve in your life. It is very important to prioritize while keeping in mind that if you neglect any of these areas which must be addressed, you could wind up sabotaging the very things you want as an outcome.

The Time and Energy Gremlins

People Gremlins
The people in your life, regardless of how much you like them, are often your major time gremlins. The more you try to accommodate their feelings, however, the more of a problem they are likely to become. In order to simultaneously satisfy their needs while not wasting time for you, you must train them. They must regard you as a person who gets things done and respect you for it. And they must also know that you have their best interest as well as your own, in mind with regard to time. People, in general, feel comfortable when they know what to expect with regard to another person's time availability.

Controlling Clients

One of the major time wasters is when people need your attention, which generates a volley back and forth of conversation whether in person or on the phone. This situation often develops with clients unless you train them from the very beginning to know how much time you are willing to give them. Once you have established an understanding about the amount of time you will spend with them, if there is any more time available, they are very happy. It is very important to set up these personal interactions in advance by FAX, email, or post. Once made, however, you must keep these appointments.

Family and Friends

With family and friends, you must set up a parallel arrangement. However, your approach to the subject of your time availability must not make them feel that they must make appointments with you for a small piece of your time. You want them to feel that they are so important to you that nothing or no one will interfere with special time together. At the same time, you need to establish in your mind which relationships you really want to maintain in your life. Are you spending time with people you are not really close to at the sacrifice of time with the people you really love and enjoy?

When people are not fighting for your time because they know that a specific time is set aside for them, they can fill their time with productive activity rather than constant attempts to gain your attention. The following strategies for time management will turn people gremlins into time friends:

1. Let everyone now what is and is not appropriate with regard to your time.

2. By very consistent.

3. Reward your spouse and children for allowing you to get a project done without interruptions.

4. Assure those people who take a long time to express themselves or who love to tell unending stories, that you are very interested in what they have to say. Then, set aside for them an appropriate time to have these conversations.

Talking on the Phone

Phone conversations require a special set of strategies. When you are on the phone, you need to let the other party know that you value their time. If you do not have the time to talk, give the person you are addressing a specific amount of time in which the conversation can take place. For example: "Jack, I have only four minutes to talk. Can we handle the subject in that time, or can we talk at 3:00? I have fifteen minutes free at that time." For those people who normally talk a long time on the phone, you will be amazed at how quickly they can come to the point when they know the limits of the time they have to speak with you.

On some occasions, it may be necessary to let them know that you have a meeting, a task or an appointment in a certain time frame. For example, "I have to leave for an appointment in five minutes." You may need to use a fictional time frame for those people who love to talk when you do not have the time to do so. The wonderful thing about talking on the phone is that the other party cannot see you and cannot confirm what you are saying - at least, not yet. But, some people do not seem to pick up cues or hints. For them, you must do a "pattern interrupt" which literally interrupts the flow of your "time gremlin's" unconscious behavior and suddenly wakes him up. You can do this by changing the inflection of your voice in a very dramatic way and adding to that a dramatic halt, such as, "Oh, wow! I didn't realize the time. I need to go right now" or "If I don't go right now..." such and such will happen. Surprisingly, there are still people who will not willingly let you go, in which case you can open the door, ask them to see themselves out and give them a task to complete their leaving. "On your way out, will you please put that ----whatever---on the other side of the ----what ever." If the person is a good friend, do what I do and say, "Goodbye already! Remember: I'm from New York."

Time Gremlins in Trading

Traders have limited time during the day in which to place and monitor their trades. After hours, traders can do research and return calls, but that time between when the market opens in the morning and closes in the afternoon is terribly finite. For this reason, traders are more concerned about saving their time than most people.

Phone Solicitors - Smile and Dial

During the trading day, traders are constantly bothered by people who call you to sell them things. Phone solicitors have an expression, "Smile and dial." They know that it takes a certain number of calls to make a certain amount of sales. Each individual call is unimportant to them, except that it brings them closer to the next sale. For that reason, they appreciate you honesty in saying, "This call is a waste of your time. Goodbye and better luck on your next call." "I never give money over the phone." Or a simple, "No thank you," will do the job as well. Then you hang up. Telephone solicitors appreciate that more than the person who wastes their time.

Meetings

When you go to a meeting in which the person in charge is not really in charge, the conversation will keep going around and around, never reaching a conclusion. In this situation, you will be saving your time and everyone else's if you summarize what has been said, succinctly listing the pros and cons of each of the ideas presented, and then asking for consensus from the group. If a decision cannot be made by the group, clearly state the decision you would prefer, but add that you will abide by whatever decision is reached by the group. And then leave.

Although you want to make the most effective use of your time when it comes to dealing with other people, it is vital to remember that you may have to spend a little time to save a lot of time down the road. If your job depends upon the cooperation of others, you may have to make time to gain their cooperation. One trader, in a large and successful partnership, was so driven to use every precious moment of his day to get his work done, that he walked out of meetings while other people were talking to him. He was reviled by all of the people who associated with him and was eventually left out of the loop except when it was absolutely necessary. As a result, much time was wasted and effort duplicated for everyone involved in the partnership.

Business Luncheons and Dinners

When you are invited to attend a business luncheon or dinner which will take longer than you are able or willing to stay, let your host know in advance how long you are able to attend. Notice how people are willing to accommodate you and how pleased they are that the business part of the meeting is conducted in a timely fashion.

Chores that Take you out of the Office

Lists will save you time when you go out to purchase things or to perform errands. Make certain that you have a list. And go one step further: bring the list with you. Another effective way to save time is to map out the stores or stops you have to make in the most effective order, and then follow your shopping or errand plan.

The Right Equipment

When you don't have the right equipment or your equipment breaks down frequently, an enormous amount of your time can be wasted. A simple job can take much longer than it should when the equipment is inadequate. More time can be wasted in waiting for expensive repairs to take place. Important trades can be lost as well as other business opportunities for lack of working equipment when it is needed. For these and many other reasons, it is important to research the equipment you need so that you purchase the very best you can afford. Simple office equipment like electric hole punchers, paper cutters and postage equipment as well as more expensive equipment like shredding machines or FAX machines, telephones, printers, copying machines or computer hardware are all worth the initial effort to get the best you can afford.

Worry - A Major Time Gremlin

Notice how easy some days are and how different others are. What's the difference? Worry. You can learn the best lessons from yourself.

**There is nothing in this world that wastes more time
(and gives no benefit to anyone) than worry.**

Worry saps energy. A good night's sleep is impossible when you are in the midst of worry. The next day, you will feel tired and lifeless. Everything takes longer to do and you will make mistakes that will also waste time to correct.

Worry dulls the senses and makes it harder to make good decisions. You are more prone to accidents when your mind is focused inwardly on your worries. One small accident can rob you of months of precious time.

One effective way to reduce worry is good planning. Planning involves identifying problems, setting goals for their resolution, listing your resources, forming solutions, and then laying down the specific steps which must be undertaken and the time frames in which they are to be done. This process takes the wind out of worry's sails. Action is the best antidote to worry.

The Pressure Gremlin

When people feel that they are under pressure, they often react the same way that they do when they are in the throes of worry. They tend to lose focus and start to waste time. However, pressure need not be a time gremlin for you.

Taking care of your emotional stability will certainly save you a tremendous amount of time in the long run, and that involves whatever it takes to enjoy the process of everything you do. Contrary to the belief of many that getting things done under pressure is the fastest way of getting things done, if you translate pressure into stress, you will pay with time either now or later. But, a lot of pressure can actually mean that you are enjoying the process if you translate pressure in the following way:

> **Pressure -** a consolidated time in which to get something done so that your entire being is taken over by a state of <u>passion and excitement</u> for the task at hand.

Another effective way to reduce pressure is to listen to cassette tapes in the car. By listening to relaxing or motivating tapes while you are driving, you can help to reduce the pressure that often builds up when you start to talk to yourself about what has to be accomplished in your life.

Health Gremlins

When you stop spending time on maintaining your health, you run the risk of expending untold hours or days in doctors' offices, in hospital emergency rooms and in your own bed. Your grandmother's old saying, "a stitch in time saves nine," was more than applicable in this situation. A maintenance program that includes a good diet that is balanced with rest and exercise will not only save you time in the long run, it will give you the energy to do more in the same amount of time than you were able to do previously.

Eating processed foods or eating at fast food restaurants can actually waste your time in the long run. It takes more time in the short run to have to cook a dinner, but if you keep eating processed foods in the long run, you are going to waste your time dealing with health issues, such as obesity, heart disease, etc. There are many ways of preparing food in a healthy way with fresh foods that require very little time. If you are not creative or a natural cook, just go to the local book stores and look for healthy cookbooks.

Another health-related long-term time saver is taking the time to exercise. Exercise gives you energy which saves you time. But, you must do at least 20 minutes of sweating each day for the real benefits of exercise to pay off for you.

Addiction Gremlins

Addictive behavior such as smoking cigarettes, drinking alcoholic or caffeine-laced drinks, taking drugs, gambling, or overeating will rob you of an excessive amount of time because:

ANYTHING THAT WILL TAKE AWAY ENERGY WILL TAKE AWAY TIME.

Yes Gremlins

The "Yes Gremlins" are your own gremlins. If you have great difficulty or a fear of saying NO, you will find yourself being stuck with time-wasting activity and demands. You will also have far too many interruptions. Other people will then assign you tasks that you do not have the time to work on and which have much less priority than the tasks you already have to complete.

The Perfectionism Gremlins

If you are not able to move on to the next task until the one you are working on is perfect, you are caught in the perfection trap. You will be wasting time creating perfection where it is not needed.

Time Savers

In the previous paragraphs, along with the "Time Gremlins," I have included many time savers. Here are some additional ones:

Doing Two Things at Once

If at all possible, perform two tasks at the same time if one or both tasks can be done automatically. The ability to perform two or more time-consuming functions at the same time is a valuable tool for busy people. For example:

- Drive to work while listening to educational or motivational tapes or making phone calls which require a minimum of concentration.

- While on the phone, organize your rolodex, open your mail, clean your desk, do dishes.

- Exercise while watching the news in the morning.

- When commuting by train or plane, use the time for planning, reviewing goals and tasks and other paperwork.

- Meet with business contacts while waiting for your children at various activities.

"Wasting Time to Save it Later"

Sometimes the best way to save time is to "waste it." Many busy people avoid all forms of socializing with their associates and employees because they perceive spending five minutes asking after the health of their assistant's wife to be a waste of time. However, when you are in a world class rush to get something done, who will be willing to go the extra mile for you or find a creative solution to your problem? Secretaries are often the most important people you know, but they are often overlooked as if they are invisible. When the minutes count in your business, they may be the very people whose help you will rely on the most. So, time you "waste" developing a trusting or friendly relationship with associates may turn out to be your greatest time saving strategy.

Training New Employees

This is often perceived as a waste of precious time. "He'll catch on eventually," is a common attitude. New employees, however, are capable of making fatal mistakes which can cost their employers precious time and money.

Taking Over

If decisions need to be made, you can save yourself a lot of time by being the one to organize the process and make certain it is done in a timely manner.

Read Instruction Manuals

Often, when you do not read instruction manuals very often tasks have to be redone several times, or you are forced to hire others to fix what you haphazardly put together. Maybe hiring a person is a good place to start. For instance, many people find computer manuals too difficult to understand, while others would find them interesting and fun. You really should consider what your time is worth.

Dealing with Customers

Considering how long it takes to bring in a new customer, it would be a tremendous waste of time if you did not service them correctly. Unfortunately, many people in business feel that once a new customer is signed, anymore time spent is wasted. Customers like to feel that they are valued. When they begin to feel taken for granted, most of them will quickly take their business elsewhere. To service your customers, you need to have a staff that is trained to provide service, or your time needs to be managed to give them the kind of service they want. Once again, this may feel like a large expenditure of time, but it really is a time saver in business.

One valuable way to save time is to give good service to clients and then ask them for referrals. Referrals are the best source of new customers.

Delegate, Delegate, Delegate!

Many traders find it difficult to delegate because it takes time to explain what needs to be done. Then it takes time to supervise the efforts of others. HOWEVER, until you learn to delegate tasks that you should not be doing yourself, you will never take control of your time. If you are failing to delegate because of control issues or an aversion to asking for help, you may need to address these issues.

What is Important to You?

A waste of time to some people is a special moment to others. While I would find it a waste of time to mow my lawn, others find it a meditative experience which relaxes them and gives them a needed release. While I find it enjoyable to plan a party, others might find it a tremendous waste of time. For some traders, the most enjoyable part of becoming a trader is developing their own system, and for others it is a big chore and a waste of time because they don't know what they are doing.

Letting go of Time-Wasting Clients

Sometimes, it is better to let a client go because he consumes too much of your time and does not bring in any money. The 80-20 rule often becomes a 90-10 rule as it applies to many clients who take up 90% of your time and provide 10% of your business. Eventually, you may have to give up 90% of your clients, but I suggest you give up 10% at a time. As a result, this will give you time to bring in and service more profitable business.

Ask, Ask, Ask

One of the great time savers is to ask for help in solving problems. Just pick up the phone and start asking people if they know how to solve your problem. People love to solve problems, so let other people help you save time.

Organizational Time Savers

This is a list of time-saving, organizational strategies that I have developed over the years that I do not have to think about. I just do them:

Everything that is broken:

- Fix it
- Give it away
- Throw it away

Clothes and items that you have not used for 2 years (no sentiment):

- Throw away
- Give away

Paper flow - accounting in order and papers organized:

- "In-Basket" - complete everything you put your eyes on that can be handled in 10 minutes
- DO IT - DELEGATE IT - DUMP IT
- Pending immediate - have files set for areas of your life, in order of importance
- A next action statement should be on top of each task
- Long pending - have 12 files for monthly delegation
- Out basket - to whom, with action statement.

Clean out

- Drawers and closets
- Basement and attic
- Any space that you occupy

Conclusion

We each have a finite amount of time in which to accomplish the things we want to complete in our lives. You can gain control over your time when you start out with a plan and respect your time. Without a sense of your priorities, you will wind up wasting time because you will focus your energies outside of your self-interest. Once you decide what is important to you and plan for it, time-saving strategies will come easily to you.

You can fail your way to success in pain,

or model your way to success

and enjoy the process.

Tip from the Coach

Chapter 4

LONG-TERM DECISIONS

Life is a smorgasbord for traders: there are so many tempting options from which to choose that the process can be exciting and rewarding, or confusing and disappointing. Unfortunately, it can also be filled with hidden dangers. So, I've decided to provide you with the risk/reward content of your trader options. Then, you can make more educated choices that will fill your needs, not only for the moment, but for your entire career.

Life Options

What are the life options from which a trader must choose? Once you have made your general and logistic decisions, such as:

- What criteria to use for making decisions about trading

- Whether to trade for yourself or for someone else

- Whether to trade from a home office or outside the home

- Whether to day trade or position trade

- Whether to be a mechanical or intuitive trader

- Whether to trade on or off the floor

Following these decision, come the life options which will support or take away from your performance. The options are the ones that have to do with your personal decisions, actions, thoughts, feelings and beliefs. The choices you make from these options determine how you will conduct yourself, and how you will feel about life:

- Whether to have rules or not for your trading and your daily conduct (I've never met a successful trader who did not have rules)

- Whether to follow your rules or not

- Whether to break your agreements with yourself and others when they become difficult or inconvenient to keep or whether to do whatever it takes to keep those agreements

- Whether to work relentless, long hours or to live on a schedule that allows for breaks, vacations, rest, time with family, etc.

- Whether to ignore, neglect, or otherwise fail to nurture the relationships in your life or to commit the time and energy required to nurture the relationships in your life

- Whether to ignore, neglect or otherwise fail to sustain the spiritual needs in your life or to make the commitment to keep that flame alive in your life

- Whether to abuse your body with bad food, inactivity and stress or take the time and effort required to feed yourself properly, get adequate exercise, and practice stress-reducing activities such as meditation

- Whether to indulge in addictive gratification such as smoking, drinking, gambling, taking drugs, loading up on caffeine or to forego the pleasurable rush, the instant energy boost, the temporary relief from stress or pain or sadness offered by these addictions for long term health benefits

- Whether to ignore all negative feelings and emotional problems or to face them, work on them, seek help in resolving them

- Whether to jump into trading unprepared or take the hard road of study, preparation, and testing

Paying the Piper

If you look at these options carefully, you will see that they each come with positive or negative consequences. Most, if not all of them, also require you to choose between immediate gratification (with long-term sacrifice) or immediate sacrifice (for long-term advantage.)

These choices are the hardest ones to make because we must pay the piper now or later - a little now or a lot later. Unfortunately, many of us are extremely good at deluding ourselves that we will never have to pay up. This inevitable reckoning is the risk/reward factor each trader faces when he decides how he will handle these options. The problem is that we are making these decisions daily, unaware that we are making them. If we could be more conscious of the fact that we are making choices, perhaps we would choose differently.

Bundling Options

Once a trader has made his selection from this first list of behavioral/psychological options, he finds himself linked to a new set of options or "option packages" which bundle together many of the day-to-day life decisions made by the trader. The results of these options have a far greater impact than any single choice he may have made because they reflect a trader's general approach to life:

Option Package Number One: Abuse Now, Pay Later

I don't know how many times I've gotten calls from traders who say to me, "Adrienne, why are you asking me to behave like a Boy Scout and do all of these good things for myself when Jack does everything wrong and he's getting great results?" Jack is always a trader they know who smokes, drinks hard alcohol and consumes tons of coffee, diet cokes, and fast food. He never exercises, rests, relaxes or spends time with his family. In fact, Jack is a miracle of self-abuse. The problem is, unfortunately, what these "Jacks" are indeed doing is all wrong, yet they are still making lots of money!

What my frustrated traders cannot see is the picture of Jack over time: abusing now, paying later. While some traders have the ability to seriously abuse their bodies over a period of time with no ill effects, others find themselves seriously harmed by far lower levels of abuse of the same vices. Take Ted, for example, who led a pretty straight life except for the relatively innocent vice of drinking four cups of coffee a day. It is true that caffeine is a powerful adrenal stimulant, but many people seem to function well after consuming it in quantity all day long. And with all the advertising of coffee as a refreshing stress reliever, it is hard to believe that something so innocent can effect you in a very negative way. Yet, each individual's body has its own unique sensitivities. In Ted's case, four cups of coffee had the effect of damaging his focus, memory and performance outcome. When it became obvious that something was creating a problem in his performance, Ted was surprised and dismayed to discover the source of his difficulty. Once he had given up coffee and had gotten his body back on track, his performance level rapidly returned to normal. So, while there are some people who can indulge themselves in many addictions over a period and not be affected, there are others who can be negatively affected by something as seemingly benign as a combination of the wrong foods.

So, which kind of trader are you? Are you the one who can abuse yourself and get away with it or not? In the Middle Ages, when the Bubonic Plague swept across Europe, one out of every three humans perished in its wake. Not only is the fact astonishing that a third of the population of a continent was wiped out, but the other astonishing fact that anyone survived. Obviously, the immune systems of the survivors were strong enough to resist the exposure. This is the human condition: some of us are strong enough to resist the exposure and some of us are not. The problem is that we do not know our category until it's too late: Hence, the policy of avoiding exposure developed as a respectable survival strategy.

Let's say that you are one of those people who can take many of these negative elements into your body and still manage to get good performance. The question to ask yourself is: How long before I reach the point of no return? If you think that you can go on forever in your present mode of operation, think about all of those times that you have been to a funeral for someone whose friends kept saying, "I can't believe it! He was a guy who loved life. I thought he would go on forever." Then, suddenly, he keeled over from a stroke, a heart attack or a fatal disease.

As a trader, you have many options from which to choose regarding how you are going to treat your mind and body. Trading is performance; and when you realize that very few people get a positive result on a consistent basis over a long period of time, you might start to make better choices if you want to be one of those traders.

Option Package Number Two: Up or Down - the Seesaw Trader

In addition to deciding if you want to pay now or later, you can also choose whether you want to be on the seesaw or not. If you choose the seesaw, however, you must then choose whether you are going to be up or down, remembering that the seesaw always keeps moving. The only way to stay off the seesaw is to maintain consistent performance through positive physical and mental habits. But, if you choose not to take the hard road of self-discipline, you will certainly find yourself on the seesaw.

Al, an exceptional trader, rides the emotional and physical seesaw. He cannot maintain his brilliant results consistently because he drinks too much, smokes too much, carouses late into the night and finds all manner of ways to abuse himself. Then, his wife puts him on the wagon for his sake, and for the sake of his children and marriage. Every few years, I check in with Al. Some years he is living in a mansion on the North Shore and, some years, he is crowded into a small apartment, licking his wounds and drying out. After each new round, however, Al's ability to rebound seems less and less spectacular. The extremes of his ups and downs take more out of his family and health, as well. And frankly, I think he enjoys the drama of the ride less and less each time.

If, you have opted for that same breathtaking ride up and down, perhaps you are getting as frayed around the edges as Al is. Perhaps you are also like Al in that you resist the notion that you have to give up the self-destructive binges in order to bring happiness into your life. In Al's case, a deeply dysfunctional childhood is the cause of his antipathy to stability. What is the cause of your own?

Option Package Number Three - Samson - With or Without the Ponytail

Samson was not obsessed with his strength (at least he wasn't in the movie version.) Like most of us, he took his gifts for granted. However, once he lost his strength, he was well aware of its absence. For many traders, the issue of strength is translated into a real need for a substantial and continuous supply of energy. As long as a trader has access to his supply of energy, he is unaware of its value to him. But, as soon as his source begins to dry up, he suddenly becomes obsessed with getting it back. When your energy supply begins to dry up, the underlying cause may be so serious that there is no return or the road back may be as long as the original journey. The best option is one that nurtures, respects and conserves energy all along the way.

Recently, I presented my advanced *Intuition Seminar* for professional traders who are actually making money. I knew that I would receive the same old hemming and hawing from the group when I began my presentation about the foods that are negative for most people's bodies. This year, I decided to do something different, however, by giving a demonstration of applied kineseology. This technique, which has been studied extensively for several decades, is used increasingly in medical circles to test for the body's response to various foods, vitamins, minerals and other substances. Studies have shown that within 30 seconds of putting salt on your tongue, your kidneys have already dropped the rate of urine production by 50% in anticipation of the salt eventually appearing in the bloodstream. Other substances placed on the tongue will immediately result in the brain signaling the body to anticipate their arrival. The body, in turn, reacts as if the substance has already arrived. If the substance is needed, the body will become stronger in seconds. If the substance spells trouble, the body will instantly react by becoming weaker. This relative strength can be demonstrated by using the muscles of the arms and legs to show the different responses of the body. The person who has this minute portion of a substance placed on his tongue is unaware of what the substance is, so that he has no idea of how his body will react.

In my demonstration, one of the traders sat down with his arm in an elevated side position, with his forearm in a bent-forward position. I then applied downward pressure on his forearm while instructing him to resist the pressure at the same time. This first demonstration established a baseline for his natural level of strength at that time. Next, I applied minute samples of different foods onto his tongue, which included sugar, coffee, spirulina, blue-green algae, and B-complex vitamins. In addition, we blew cigarette smoke in his face to see what effect this substance would have on his strength. The result was that the sugar, coffee and smoke all demonstrably weakened his muscle strength so that it was easy for me to push his arm down with one of my hands, while the remaining substances strengthened his arm so that I was not able to push it down.

A wide range of muscle tests reflect the effect of different substances on various glands of the body. This particular test reflects the effects of substances on the adrenal glands. The strength of your adrenal glands is particularly important because traders rely on their adrenal glands to keep them going at peak performance all day long. After the test of the different elements on the tongue, we also tested the results of negative and positive thinking and how they affect the adrenals. And as you might have suspected, positive thinking brought a strong forearm and the negative thinking brought a weak forearm. So, even if you are a person who can tolerate high substance abuse, just think of how much stronger you would be and how much more focus you would have if you made better choices.

Option Package Number Four - A Party of One or Two?

Everyone knows how much fun it is to go to a fine restaurant and eat at a small table set for one. We all try to avoid this experience, but sometimes we have made so many poor choices that we run out of options. The experience of feeling alone when you are surrounded by people is the same life condition. Unfortunately, traders who make the wrong choices over time eventually alienate their families, friends and associates. Traders need emotional support to sustain successful trading over time.

Recently, I completed the consultation on a trader's 15 page evaluation. Mike had been a strong floor trader for fifteen years, but was having trouble maintaining focus. On the evaluation, two areas of concern were Mike's personal and emotional life. Mike had been divorced for several years. Since that time, he had had limited contact with his children and even more limited contact with his old friends. In fact, Mike's circle of relationships was collapsing on itself. Once an outgoing individual, Mike was rapidly becoming socially isolated. This decline in social and emotional outlets was running parallel to a decline in Mike's performance on the floor. Mike's commentary on his situation was, "I don't need anyone."

Conclusion: Options and Choices

Every day, traders make choices about the kind of life they lead. These choices relate directly to a trader's emotional and physical well-being, but the ripple-effect eventually determines their trading performance. And contrary to the evidence of all of the successful, self-destructive traders who are doing it all wrong and still winning, there are no real short-term advantages in this game of options when you weigh those advantages against their long-term costs.

Chapter 5

_____

SWITCHING TO OTHER TRADING MODES

The Fork in the Road

Transitions into another area of trading can be career suicide for many traders or fun and even easy for others. What makes the difference?

Know-how - Preparation - Resources

Before we consider the necessary elements of success in each area of trading, let's first look at the kinds of transitions many traders have to face or choose to face:

FROM:	TO:
floor trading	off the floor
broker	own account
own account	money manager
institutional	own account
one system	another system
short time frame	long time frame

Scalped to Change

Burt, a successful floor trader for over fifteen years, believed that you did not have to be young to work on the trading floor. He thought trading in the pits would always reward an exceptional scalper like himself; so he never planned to leave.

One day, he was standing in his usual spot and turned backward to complete a fill just as another trader was pushing forward. Burt ended up in the hospital in serious condition after hitting his head on the corner of a step. With partial paralysis in his right arm and frequent fainting spells, he spent the next year in recovery as well as most of the family's savings. The good news was that he overcame the paralysis; the bad news was that he could not trade on the floor anymore. As a result, Burt began the transition from floor trader to off-the-floor trader. For him, the most difficult part of the transition was the lack of control. He said, "Trading off the floor is like giving up the pilot's seat in an aircraft and becoming a passenger. The passenger makes a decision where he wants to go, but the pilot has control over reaching the destination."

Basics to Specialization

Basic knowledge of the markets is necessary to be successful in any area of the financial business. To be a good trader, you also need a system you believe in, money management rules with which you are comfortable, and the discipline to follow your own rules. Each type of trading requires its own unique know-how, preparation and resources in order to maintain positive results. Let's look at each particular area of trading with its advantages and disadvantages.

Banking Institutions

Most banks are looking for trainees who come from ivy-league universities, preferably with an economic, financial, or mathematical background. When looking for a seasoned trader, they want someone with a good track record for trading, a long term employment pattern , and a college degree.

As a trader for a bank, you need the ability to deal with office politics. Very often you must follow rules which are not conducive to good trading. Institutional aversion to draw-downs limits the ability of a trader to take appropriate risks. Much of a trader's time is consumed with excessive paperwork, management duties and the training of other traders. When dealing with clients directly, selling skills are necessary. The skills of a poker player are useful to market makers.

The benefit of trading for an institution are: they very often allow you to trade with large sums of money, even if you don't know what you are doing; you do not need your own start-up capital; you are usually given an allowable sum to lose each year, and the extensive on-the-job training is a definite asset when you are looking for more lucrative opportunities.

Brokerage Houses

Advanced education is usually required by the top brokerage firms and is helpful if not necessary in the remaining firms. The reality of working for a brokerage firm is that you often have to sell investments in which you do not believe. In addition, more often then not, you must focus your efforts on a winning situation for yourself and the brokerage house and not on your clients. For example, when a brokerage house buys millions of dollars worth of bonds at auction, the brokers are required to sell the inventory even though they know their clients will not make a profit.

Similar to working for a banking institution, you have the advantage, as a stockbroker, of working with investors' assets, while having to build their trust in your ability to make them profits. Many brokerage houses provide exceptional sales training. Once you have developed the ability to sell intangibles on the phone, you have a skill that can be utilized in many areas of business.

Floor Trader

As a floor trader, you must develop a listening sensitivity to the rhythm and heart beat of the markets. When you trade on the floor, you must become one with the passion of the crowd and know how to translate that oneness into winning trades through hand signals and a loud voice. You must watch out for false rumors created by big players. You must be willing to be bitten, kicked, and shoved, to lose your voice and your hearing and to suffer from back, kidney and foot disorders. The cost of purchasing, leasing and main-taining a seat can be very expensive. There are opportunities, however, in some of the smaller pits, such as grain options, where start-up costs are substantially less than that of a full membership. Once established, you only need about $30K with which to trade in order to earn substantial gains.

On the floor, you feel an instant connection with your results. The high pitch of passion that builds up in the pit is a totally exciting and addictive experience.

Trading Your Own Account

You need enough start-up capital for your basic business needs and enough trading capital to carry you through the highs and lows. You must view the trading capital as your business inventory. Business and trading capital, however, must not be linked with the basic needs of your personal life. If you do not have another source of income other than your trading, you will also need money to sustain you through your learning period. The skills needed to run your own business and the ability to be a self starter are also essential for running your own account. To succeed, you must consider the cost of each trade. You must establish an agreement with your broker that if he allows you to break your rules, he is fired. In many ways, trading your own account is the most emotionally challenging trading option because it is so difficult to let go of the idea that your trading account is not connected to your personal account.

Having the freedom to make your own decisions without answering to an institution or a customer is very attractive to many traders and affords you the luxury of making your own trading decisions.

Money Manager

Being a money manager requires all the skills of trading your own account as well as the sales skills of a broker. The start-up capital which is required, however, is higher than for trading your own account. You need at least ten million under management before you begin to earn enough to maintain your office and a moderately comfortable life style. For your clients to be comfortable, you must be consistent about what you tell them, you must earn a minimum of 15% and never have more than a 10% draw-down. When trading your own account, you can conceal your trading record. However, you are a money manager, your trading record becomes a part of the public records. In addition, your record keeping must be perfect. However, the most challenging aspect of this career path is that you are subject to the very stiff rules and regulations of the regulatory agencies.

The principle benefits of being a money manager are that you trade with other people's money and that you do not have to risk your own money. But, if you do decide to risk your own money with the money you are managing, you have more leverage and less risk due to having more capital with which to trade.

A Piece of Cake Gone Bad

While it is important to have a positive attitude, Lenny's "it's a-piece-of-cake attitude" got him in serious trouble when changing from a broker to a money manager. Lenny only knew success in his life. He was an honor student at Yale, a star football player and a "mean" lasagna-maker. Lenny made the millionaire's club on Wall Street as one of the top producers in his brokerage firm. However, he had always felt uncomfortable working as a broker and wanted to be "a real trader." In addition, Lenny thought that if he were going to earn money for his clients, he would have to be a money manager.

Armed with his confident attitude and his exceptional ability in sales, Lenny acquired the necessary licenses, developed a business plan and started to look for the best people to assist him. Positive feedback from investors gave him even more confidence in his prospects. Soon, however, he was settled in his office, having depleted half of his savings. Lenny had not accounted for things going wrong. Investors wanted to give him money, but only after he provided proof of profits. He was in a catch twenty-two situation.

While Confidence is Essential to Success, You Must Look at all of the Realities:

1. Verbal promises and words of support are not money in the bank . You have nothing but good words until the money is actually in your account.

    Only count on what you actually have.

2. Your present life style consumes your capital while you are in the learning, developing stages.

    Budget into your expenses one year without an income.

3. Just because you had what it took to be successful in one area of trading does not mean you have the ability in another area of trading.

Whenever possible, prepare yourself with the appropriate knowledge before jumping into a new business. Start a new business with a "beginner's mind." Assume that you have to learn everything from the beginning rather than coming with the assumption that you are an expert. Otherwise you may limit your ability to learn a new field. And wishful thinking will get you in trouble.

4.   Associates can be your greatest assets, or your worst nightmare. You must know how to hire and manage people so that everyone feels that they are participating in a win/win outcome.

In order to be a good leader you must have self confidence, be able to organize and delegate, and most importantly, have the ability to create an atmosphere in which associates want to do an exceptional job: i.e., they like and respect you and know that you have their best interest at heart.

5.   A business plan is not solid until it is written down.

A business plan is the road map of the direction you want to take in life. It does not matter whether you are working for someone else or for yourself. You still must have a detailed business plan written down. You must also be prepared for the worst-case scenario. It is best to go over your plan with an accountant and a lawyer who are experienced in developing a business plan.

6.   You must have an ability for sales, if only to motivate yourself.

No matter how talented you are, sales ability will make you a more successful person.

7.   Time is money and you must make the best use of it.

There must be someone in the office who knows how to develop and maintain organization. Time must be managed like money with the end result being the most profit gained.

8.   The basics take time:

Education   without the best education, you will waste time.

Licenses   it might take you more than once to pass, so account for that in your plan.

Office   **all office needs, e.g., installation of phones and other equipment always takes far longer than you planned for and can be very frustrating. Computer set up time takes three times as long as most people plan for. If you are doing it yourself, it is better not to trade during this period.**

Burt, our floor trader who overcame the results of a bad fall, is finally earning a living after two years of transitional struggle. He had not been prepared for this change, but he adapted to the requirements of his new trading career. Lenny, on the other hand, made two fatal mistakes that traders make in moving into a new area of trading: he failed to make a realistic plan and he consumed most of his capital in living expenses. Lenny was unable to adapt rapidly enough to the requirements of his new career and washed out of trading. Eventually, he bought a restaurant franchise where he's using his ability to make his mean lasagna and is doing exceptionally well.

Conclusion

Whatever type of trading you are presently doing, it would help you to prepare for the possibility of going into another area of trading. Naturally, the more preparation you have for a change, the easier the transition will be. All trading transitions, however, will require a realistic business plan, the careful monitoring of personal and business finances, a commitment to learning the new trading business, and the ability to adapt to the personal and professional demands of the new field. Transitions which are carefully planned and executed result in successful trading business changes.

_____

Chapter 6

TRADING FROM HOME

Discipline is a Major Challenge When Trading from Home

"Free at last!" Mike shouted as he flung open the front door of his home. With a dozen long stemmed roses in hand, he swept his astonished wife, Julie, in his arms and swung her in the air. Mike did have something to celebrate. He was leaving behind the dictates imposed upon him as an institutional trader to become a trader who worked from home. He would now have control over his career and set his own rules. But this unsuspecting trader was about to find out that working at home has its own set of rules that must be followed in order for a stay-at-home trader to become successful.

Freedom Requires a Trader to be Highly Disciplined

Once Mike found himself home alone with no one to set the rules, the greatest challenge to his success suddenly became time and how to use it. Ironically, although traders want to be in control, their new-found freedom often results in an actual lack of control. Mike kept making excuses for why he was not making bigger profits and saw the cause of his problems in all of the people and circumstances of his life. For Mike to take control, he needed to ask himself, "Am I willing to give up excuses and do what it takes to run a successful trading business at home?"

When Mike came to a seminar, he discovered that other traders faced many of the same problems he faced. He was no longer home alone with his distractions. He now had lots of company.

What are the Most Common Reasons why Trading from Home is Difficult?

1. **Self-Motivation**

Self-motivation is challenging, especially when you have been externally motivated for a long time. When you are the one to dictate policy for your business, it does not feel as important to stick to policy as when you have other people to whom you must answer.

Bill had worked for an engineering company where there was no question about what to do, when to do it, and how to do it. He could not wait to get away from the constraints of that business. What he did not realize was that one of the main reasons that his engineering company was successful was that those policies gave employees a structure for being disciplined.

2. **Loneliness**

When you are working by yourself, the lonely business of trading can get even lonelier. For many traders, however, it is hard to admit to actual loneliness. What they tell themselves is that they need to make calls and be in contact with others for business reasons.

John was a floor trader who could not wait to leave his screaming companions. Although he was in his own world in the pit, John discovered, after being alone at home for a while, that he began to miss the snarling traders bumping and shoving him in the pit.

3. **Chores**

If your spouse is at work outside the home and he or she does not understand your business, you may be expected to perform household chores during your working hours.

Gerald's wife Mae said, "What does it take to put a few loads of laundry in the washer while you are trading?" What it takes is broken focus and momentum. "The problem is that my wife thinks that because I'm home, I should be helping around the house," Gerald complained. "She doesn't believe I'm doing something important unless I'm gone." As a result, Mae was continually calling him from her job and asking him to help her with the responsibilities of maintaining their home during his work hours.

4. **Helpers**

Help from your spouse can be costly and not the expense saver you intended. If a spouse is not totally involved in specific tasks of trading or assisting, the over-the-shoulder emotions he or she adds with each tick of a trade will also add stress and distraction to the working day.

Carol and Bob were honeymooners with stars in their eyes and a passion for each moment they experienced together. Bob decided to trade at home and have Carol assist him in setting up the trading business. Setting up the business was fun, as the couple shared a kiss with every encounter. When Bob finally started trading, Carol wanted to bring out the champagne and caviar whenever the markets were going in their direction. Her reaction to losses, however, progressed from, "it's okay" and 'it's just part of the game" to "are you sure you know what you're doing?" It was not long before they realized that trading and honeymoons don't mix.

5. **Distractions**
Unlike being in an office far from home, when you are home by yourself, you are surrounded by so many distractions pulling at you, such as your avocations, the television, the refrigerator, and any other escape away from the task at hand.

Jack decided to become a trader because trading, for him, translated into having many toys and playing at all the sports he loved in exotic places in the world. What Jack was not prepared to do was the work that was involved in supporting his pleasures. Working became a distraction from daydreaming. He wanted to take any easy way towards success. His workday was occupied by trading other people's advice while using every distraction as an excuse not to work.

6. **Work Life**
Because your working hours are not set, they tend to take over every part of your life so that there is no home life, only a work life.

Drake believed hard work would get him whatever he wanted in life. Because he worked from home, he set no limits on the amount of time he put into his trading. Soon, work consumed all of his time. He did not pay attention to his family's need for his participation in their lives. In addition, he believed that living a healthy life was a waste of his time. Social activities were not interesting for him. Eventually, after a series of painful lessons, Drake began to realize that he had become successful at the cost of losing out on life. He did not know how to play. Eventually his hard work actually began to sabotage his trading.

7. **Interruptions**
Family and friends do not consider your time at home to be work time and they interrupt you constantly.

Ralph's father and mother retired close to their children and grandchildren. They had three sons: a doctor, a lawyer, and a trader working from home. Guess who got the calls during the day? "Just one little favor," Ralph's dad would say. "What! You can't take the time out to talk to your own mother?"

8. **Day-care Provider**
   The stay-at-home trader can be viewed as a day-care provider by the spouse who works outside the home.

   Molly and Jerry just had a baby. Molly's income as a real-estate broker paid for their comfortable lifestyle. Jerry had been testing his system during the entire time Molly was pregnant and was now ready to trade it. Since he was home, they decided that Jerry would take care of the baby, rather then hire someone to do it, since he was trading from home. Little Peter was a colicky baby....(and you can fill in the blanks.)

9. **The Web**
   Computers, with all their software, and a world ready to talk to you can all be seductive attractions.

   Charley was a successful institutional trader by day and a web-site junky at night. Finally, Charley had enough reserves in his bank account to work as a trader on his own, at home. The only problem was that, once home, more and more of his day was distracted with his addiction.

The Solution to Working at Home: GAINING CONTROL

The major issue for the trader at home is control. The trader must be able and willing to assert control over his work time in such a way that the interruptions in time and concentration are kept to an absolute minimum and that they relate exclusively to work. Otherwise, like many traders who have given up in defeat, they will be forced to move into an office outside of their homes.

The only way to regain control of the work situation at home is to take assertive action. This step requires a trader to decide what he wants in the situation, identify those conditions or people who are blocking his path, and then take constructive action to stop the problem. In the case of family members or friends, one of the most effective ways to stop their interruptions is to explain to them what your expectations are and then gain their agreement.

The best way to gain agreement and cooperation from those around you is to convince them that it is to their advantage to help you. When Gerald sat down to talk with his wife, Mae, he started by asking about her goals for their family. Mae realized that her own goals could not be achieved if she distracted Gerald's trading with her constant demands that he do household chores during trading hours. She promptly hired a part-time house-keeper.

Most importantly, in order to take control of your working time at home, you must establish a set of simple, effective rules that you are willing to follow. Listed below are some guidelines for the home-alone trader that will allow him or her to conduct a successful trading business without the stress and frustration that accompany a loss of control:

Guidelines for the Home-Alone Trader:

1. When possible, separate your work space and home space.

2. Define very specific working hours and keep to those hours.

3. Meet with your family and let them know what your office policies and rules are as though you are working at an office outside your home.

4. Have a separate phone line for your business and only give the number to those whom you would be talking to during the day. Use your personal line for screening your calls.

5. Ask cooperation from family members and friends to qualify calls: "Emergency" means stop everything you are doing and take care of the call; "Important" means get to the phone as soon as possible; "It can wait" means that you can call after working hours. You can handle those who abuse these particular messages like the boy who cried wolf.

6. Clearly defined rules with regard to those activities which have nothing to do with business and use them as rewards for specific tasks accomplished.

7. Take regular breaks by setting an alarm clock. Have a stairmaster or walking machine in your office for those times when you cannot leave. Have a pot of herbal tea and/or water available in your office so you can sip it all day, as well as fresh fruit, energy bars, and music, preferably upbeat instrumental music that has a soothing effect on the psyche; for example, baroque music and light jazz.

8. Leave coffee, cigarettes, alcohol, sugar products and salt products for non-working hours, if at all. These products will distract your focus from your trading.

9. Give yourself special rewards for accomplishments. These rewards can include a reflexology massager under your desk, a massage chair in your office, or a back vibrator.

10. All of your computer screens should be eye level or higher because you continually access an emotional state when your eyes are focused down-ward.

11. The lighting in your office should lift you up. Full spectrum lighting from the outside is best. Also, vegetation within view will add to a warm environment that is conducive to your trading.

12. Prepare a list of all household chores, and after getting agreement from your family members, divide the chores up among them, setting a specific time for completing those tasks that are not during office hours. If you are by yourself, either make the schedule for yourself or, if and when possible, hire someone to do some of these tasks.

13. It is best to stay away from conversations about winning and losing on a daily basis. On a daily basis the only thing your wife should ask is: did you follow your rules and your response should be you have? Any other conversation should be about the lessons you have learned. Anything beyond that should not be discussed, unless your wife is specifically in-volved in all phases of the business and understands all phases of the business. Then conversations about business should only be conducted during office hours.

Conclusion

Many people enter the field of trading and work from home because they want inde-pendence, freedom, and the control they do not feel in working for an organization. However, if they approach trading from home without the kind of preparation it takes to run a business, they soon discover that working from home can mean a loss of control. All businesses require a plan that includes time management, organization, specific tasks, and rules. Finally, you need the self-discipline it takes to follow those rules and the cooperation of the people in your life to respect and support you.

When Mike, our home-alone trader, began to follow the set of guidelines listed, he turned his life around. He suddenly experienced the sense of freedom and control over his life that he had always wanted. In the meantime, his relationship with his wife and family reached a level of mutual respect and support that he had never experienced before. And best of all, Mike is now making the profitable trades that allow him to feel like a successful trader.

When you have a conflict within yourself,

the emotional side wins.

When you have a conflict within an

organization, no one wins.

Tip from the coach

Chapter 7

————

TRADING FOR SOMEONE ELSE

When everyone is in conflict within an organization, no one wins. These conflicts can be on the surface or hidden in the basic foundation of the beliefs, attitudes and behaviors that top management bequeaths to each new generation. Even when large budgets are allocated for hiring the most capable individuals and the best training is available, the system's patterns of bureaucracy will not support success taken to a higher level. Status quo feels safe, because no one has to take responsibility for being wrong about innovative decisions. The attitude of the management often is, "Let the other institutions try it first and if it works for them, then maybe we will try it." By the time those ideas are proven to be a standard for success, the innovative organizations are on to the next idea, keeping ahead of the pack.

Justin - Looking for the Pearl

Justin was headed for a top position trading in the financial world. As one of the top ten graduates in economics from a prestigious northeastern university, he worked hard to be considered for the best entry level positions offered. Several recruiters from major firms approached him before graduation with many attractive offers. Justin chose a major, international banking institution based upon the training package it offered. Having done his research, and knowing how many traders fail, he was going to make sure he would take the necessary steps to become one of the best in the field.

Justin polished up for his first day of work, which he expected to be filled with meetings with his new colleagues and beginning the foundation of good trading. He imagined his colleagues would show they had a sense of camaraderie and company allegiance. Justin found himself sadly disillusioned. What he did experience was apathetic and overworked traders welcoming him with unfocused eyes and saccharine smiles. Justin was disappointed further when Dick, his so-called trainer, threw him a reading list and told him that he would be attending seminars in a few weeks to learn about technical analysis and the fundamentals of trading. By speaking to a new recruit who had been hired six months before, Justin found out that the training package that was offered to him was full of empty promises. The new recruit said that most of his training came from a self taught "hit or miss process that was mostly misses."

Justin watched and listened as he waited two hours for his new supervisor and trainer to give him further instructions. Dick was juggling the phones and screaming out for prices. Between the myriad of interruptions, coffee gulps and cigarette puffs, Dick managed to bellow out some instructions. "Here's your desk and set up. Basically you are allowed to lose two hundred fifty thousand over a period of a year. If you lose more than twenty-five thousand in any one month you're out, so cover your behind. But, he laughed, "I wouldn't worry about it. If you get canned from here, there will be other institutions interested in hiring you and paying you more money just because you're already trained." Throughout the day, Justin continued to listen to the negative remarks from the traders about everyone in any authority and about the institution as a whole. The accepted mode of conversation seemed to be that the person who complained the most about the organization won the popularity prize.

Howling with the Wolves

By the end of Justin's first day on the job, he realized he would have to make the decision to either fight the system, leave the system, work within the system, or beat the system by becoming outstandingly good. He chose the last alternative.

When Justin became a client, he told me, "This place has given me the motivation to want to trade on my own. From the first day, I knew I needed to get out of this negative environment as soon as possible."

Facing a Losing Battle

The trading department was facing a financially critical setback that could not be ignored. The management knew they had to do something fast because the very existence of the institution was being threatened. Our company was hired by the head of the trading department to do the *Trading on Target Seminar* and private consulting for the top traders of the organization. The goals the company established for everyone participating in this training were to create teamwork, a less stressful atmosphere and better performance.

It was important to make sure that there were private sessions with each individual attending the seminar in order to be the most effective for everyone. By having the individual sessions, the root cause of the problem could be established. From these sessions, a typical scenario emerged. The main problems of the institution appeared to stem from top management and worked their way down to the trading department. This conclusion was arrived at by listening to what individual traders and managers had to say about the company they worked for and from observing the networking of the environment and comparing it with other institutions. The very people who set these noteworthy goals for the institution, were the same ones who set up roadblocks to sabotage them. It was part of the system of the environment they inherited.

Four out of the six traders in private sessions revealed they were planning to leave to trade on their own. One trader was planning to turn in his resignation the following week. Only one trader said he would stay. He was one of the few who felt comfortable adapting to the environment and he was also the least successful trader of the group. This information created a precarious situation. The company knew that confidentiality was an integral part of the interview process and agreed to abide by it. In reality, they expected loyalty to be directed towards the people paying the bill. At the beginning of our private sessions, each trader was asked to come up with a list of goals for the group session. The problem was, most of the goals the traders set for themselves had to do with gaining the confidence and knowledge necessary to trade on their own.

TRANSFORMING MANAGEMENT

Everyone had to be willing to take the responsibility to make changes. Here were some of the recommendations made to management:

1. **Hiring Strategy**

    Good grades from top universities do not necessarily ensure that the individual is capable of becoming a good trader. Turnover is one of the most expensive problems institutions have. If you have a large turnover problem, you know something needs to be changed.

    Hire someone based upon a modeling study done of what it takes to be a top institution trader. Some examples are:

    - Have a psychological profile (Myers Briggs) of people who enjoy the institutional setting or working with others. If you want independent thinkers who would be the type to run their own organizations, you must set up an environment that includes their needs.

    - Have a top performance model transferred to each new recruit by a modeling programmer. (Management must support this model in order for it to work.)

    - Ask prospective employees about their childhood activities as well as their present activities. A key to the future of an certain individual is how he has conducted his life from childhood through adulthood.

    - Open opportunities to self-taught traders who have spent time and money and have persevered to develop themselves as good traders. They might not have the college background normally required, but they do have what it takes to be

55

a good trader. Many of them are looking for opportunities in an institution because they do not have enough money to trade on their own.

2.   Building Trust

Institutional recruiters and managers must carry out offers and training as they are represented. This builds respect and trust and sets the right tone for getting the best out of each individual. A business plan and structure encouraging all employees to be more creative, must be devised and carried out by all managers, and supported by employees. In other words, "practice what you preach." All people need to know what they can rely on from their trading group and the organization itself. Where there is no trust, there is no solid foundation on which to build.

3.   Plan to Manage and Train

When a manager's time is divided between trading and managing and he has a personal trading quota to meet, both the training and trading will suffer. There must be a structured plan with a specific time given only to training. The manager should not be penalized for dealing with the added stress of having to meet the same quota while most of his or her time is spent in training. It is important to note that just because someone is a good trader, does not make him a good manager. A manager has to love training people in order to be effective.

4.   Objectives and Goals Should be Set and Reviewed

It is important that everyone know the institution's goals and objectives, because this creates the working cooperation necessary to build a happy, fruitful environment. These goals and objectives should be in alignment with each department as well as each individual. Excitement and passion for the success of the institution and fellow colleagues must be in the hearts of each individual. This can only happen when there is an atmosphere of trust and respect, in addition to incentives.

5.   Offer Incentives That are Within Reach

There must be incentives for both individual and team efforts often enough to stimulate excitement in the trading room on a monthly basis if possible. Rewards are the best way to encourage the passion necessary for top performance. Managers should have available funds to give smaller incentives in recognition of exceptional days or individual achievement (i.e., a bottle of wine, theater tickets, dinner for two). It should also be noted that incentives for many employees come as words of praise and recognition for a job well done. Establish an environment of noticing, admiring and praising when deserved.

6. Give Real Support

Managers must communicate to the top management and board members about the needs of each department and the individual employees. Money allocations need to be distributed to those areas that will serve the organization in the most effective way. Each trader's individual talents must be used to serve the organization in the best way possible. This can be accomplished by having all employees write down their job descriptions, duties and goals after their managers have explained them.

Expect traders to develop their own systems and money management rules before allowing them to trade. The progress forward, goals and outcomes must be monitored and rewarded with verbal or monetary recognition when they are reached.

Managers must also manage the stress levels of each individual. It is not in the best interests of either the company or the individual to have traders who work in too many hours, or work too long between breaks. Good trading comes from being at top performance level.

7. Tell It to the Person Who Can Do Something About It

There should be a set of agreements among colleagues in which they agree to end all gossiping and complaining. If they do not like a situation or the way things are, they will agree to tell it to the person who can do something about it. All problems must be responded to and given appropriate consideration within a certain designated time frame. If this can't be done, a reason should be given to the people who are involved or to the individual involved.

8. Create a Healthy Environment

If the people in your organization are continuously stressed because of the environment, everyone loses. An unhealthy environment is not conducive to top performance. Some suggestions to decrease stress are:

- **Clean Air**
  Prohibit smoking in the workplace.
  Use air purifiers - most air conditioners are not enough. This purification will also cut down on sickness.

- **Soothing Sounds**
  Use sound absorbers on walls or wherever possible to cut down on noise. Music in the background where possible with a rhythm that is conducive and to stimulate and soothe such as Baroque (chamber music) will increase production and make people feel good.

- **Adequate Space and Clean Surroundings**

  Keep work areas very organized. Create work areas with enough space to be organized and require cleanliness. Space should be adequate so there is not too much intrusion on colleagues' conversations. Clutter, dust and shouting are not conducive to good performance.

- **Healthy Food**

  Prepare tasteful, gourmet, fresh, fast foods low in fat, sodium and sugar. (This is when lunches are provided or available).

- **Rejuvenating Facilities**

  Use a quiet room for resting and meditation. Breaks in this area should be encouraged. Have an exercise room with equipment for stretching and aerobics.

9. Transforming the Trading Room and the Traders

Confidence and respect were developed during the seminar because the participants believed in the material presented. As a result, they were willing to make the changes, but they felt they needed the support from management. Everyone was looking to everyone else to take the responsibility for making the changes possible.

The next step was to encourage traders to take the responsibility for making the changes themselves. This step was made easier by having two days with each of the leading traders, two of whom were trading room managers.

Here are a few of the recommendations for the traders:

1. Business Plan

Develop a personal business plan. You must work within the confines of the institutional rules. Remember, rules are necessary, even when working on your own.

2. Trading Plan

You must have a system and good money management rules that you believe in before you perform your first trade. Even if a specific system is given to you, you must make it your own. Ask yourself if you would be willing to invest your own money in the system. Next, handle any psychological issues you may have, preferably with a professional. It is better to work with someone who has worked with traders. If you do not handle your psychological issues, they will show up in your performance.

3. Prepare for Opportunity

Act as if it were your own business. When you project this kind of thinking, your behavior will be the most responsible and, as a result, you will get the highest performance out of yourself. Make yourself the best trader you can be. Be prepared for a promotion or start promoting yourself within the same position. When you outshine your own expectations and those of your friends and family, everyone starts relying on the enhanced version of your position. In this way, you automatically train yourself to be prepared for a higher position and/or an increase in salary. Make sure you are noticed for your extra efforts. Write down what you plan to accomplish and what you have accomplished and give this list to your manager. This way, both you and the manager have a record of why you deserve recognition for your exceptional efforts.

4. Good Environment

Starting with yourself, create the environment you want to work in. Here are several ways to ensure a good environment:

- Don't talk negatively about others or the institution. This is a reflection of how you feel about yourself.

- Support and give praise to others and they will start supporting and praising you.

- Go to the person who can make change happen if there is a problem. If there is no change, learn to live with the problem so it does not affect you or your work. If this is not successful, consider moving on to another company.

- Work within the best part of the system and encourage change in the areas that are not working for the good of the entire company.

- Become a leader and innovator. Even if you lead only yourself to success, you will feel good about yourself and others will feel good about you.

- Know whether something is reasonable or possible. Think from the perspective of a responsible leader.

We devote one-third of our life to work. If you do not enjoy the process, it will negatively affect all other parts of your life. Whatever position you are in, take responsibility and do whatever it takes to enjoy the process of your life. Your life depends upon it and so does your profession.

Here is a simple test which will indicate whether an institution or a trader needs to consider making a change:

For Institutions and Traders

1. Are you making the returns that you should be making based upon the resources available?

2. Is there camaraderie between colleagues and departments?

3. Is there an atmosphere where people feel comfortable expressing ideas and problems?

4. Does management make and keep promises to employees?

5. Are incentives within reach and do they inspire healthy competitiveness and motivation?

6. Is there a healthy environment that supports top performance?

For Institutions Only

7. Do you have a lot of turnover?

8. Are you considered the kind of organization with which people take pride in being associated?

For Traders Only

9. Do you enjoy the process of making money?

10. Do you trust the organization's promises to you?

11. Do you take pride in being associated with this organization?

12. Do you look forward to coming to work every day?

13. Do you want to stay with this organization?

Conclusion

When everyone personally takes the responsibility to create a winning environment in an organization, everybody wins. Very often this goal requires giving up the patterns that worked in the past and taking calculated risks on new ideas. Unfortunately, the management from many organizations will not do what it takes to make changes until they are in a desperate situation.

By Justin's company taking action to make winning changes, costs went decreased because fewer people were leaving. Production and profits increased because everyone wanted to contribute to the success of the organization. Most traders who were planning to trade out on their own stayed. The one who left called me up recently and said, "I wish you could come over and throw some magic dust on the institution I work for now." And finally, Justin is now head of the trading room.

Chapter 8

_____

TRADING WITH OTHER PEOPLE'S MONEY

To run any business, you must wear many hats. But, to make a business successful, it is important to decide which of these hats fits you so that you know what your contribution is and you know the gaps you need to fill. Let's look at some of the roles which need to be filled in your trading business venture:

1. Managing the business
2. Acquiring and maintaining the licenses to operate your business legally
3. Secretarial and administrative work
4. Sales and marketing
5. Dealing with clients
6. Research
7. Trading
8. Money management
9. Legal and accounting

While there are those CTAs who are able to handle all of these roles and become successful from the ground up doing everything.. If you are not one of these people, you have to look at your own skills and see if your business is best served by you performing tasks for which you do not have the talent. For instance, if you are an extremely good trader, but are very bad with people, you are going to do the CTA a disservice if you don't learn how to be a people person or have some kind of agreement or partnership with someone who has these skills. If you are a person who is more suited to business or bringing in clients, and do not have the trading skills, you are not going to be able to keep those clients unless you show a profit.

So, in the very beginning, you must do a balancing act by taking all of these roles and deciding what you are good at and what you need to farm out. One helpful idea when you are working with a very small budget is to delegate certain functions of the business to other people who have their own offices and equipment, such as a business management firm to help start up the business, or a marketing consultant to develop an initial marketing plan, or a secretarial service. Another option is to find people who have the needed skills who do not want to work full-time, or are willing to work for less than the going rate. Examples are college students majoring in business management who can come up with a business management plan or law students majoring in corporate or contract law. Working with students on a part-time basis and giving them an opportunity to use a very high level of skills for a small amount of money can be a winning strategy for both parties. Hiring a retired person through the organization SCORE can be an added resource. Another possibility is hiring a woman who was once an executive but is now at home. With a family she would enjoy the opportunity to perform a highly skilled job part-time.

How to Raise Trading Capital

A CTA business cannot run without trading capital. This capital, unless you have a very rich uncle that is willing to give you money, will have to come from other people. Therefore, one of your major responsibilities will be to raise capital. This new responsibility means you'll be wearing the salesman hat. "Excuse me?" You say, "I'm just a trader, not a salesman."

Not if you are going to run a CTA, you're not! Raising capital is all about selling. What you'll be selling is your money management services, and you'll need to be able to persuade people that you're the right person to increase profits on their money. And once you have their capital, you'll need to be able to convince them that they have made the right decision so that they keep their money with you. The selling never stops.

So, now let's talk about selling. The word selling comes from the Norwegian word, *selje*, which means to serve. Those people who fear selling or approaching other people with the intention of persuading them are attaching a different meaning to the original idea of what selling is supposed to be. If you approach selling as taking something away from the other person (unless you are a charlatan), you are going to be uncomfortable selling a person anything. However, if you approach other people with the understanding that you are presenting them with an opportunity and that you have every intention of making it a winning situation for them, your neurology will respond differently. So, when you are coming up with a product line, you must develop it with the idea that the buyer is going to benefit tremendously and believe that this is so. The buyer must see the belief and the passion in you before he can start building the passion in himself that is needed for him to say, YES.

However, we are getting ahead of ourselves. Before we can even get to the point of approaching someone to sell them on the idea of anything, we need to look at our-selves and how we perceive ourselves. The major issue that prevents one person from approaching another person is self-esteem. How you feel about yourself will be reflected in the face of a potential client. If you doubt yourself, doubt is what you will see in his face.

Let's Talk About Whom to Target

Speaking of mirrors, time and how you use it will be reflected in your income. Everyone has the same number of hours in his day. It's how you use those hours that counts. Are you using your time as productively as you can? If not, consider an overview of your time. Using your time productively applies to raising capital as well. If you go for only the small accounts over a period of time, how long will it take you to actually bring in enough capital so that you can make a living off your CTA business? A money manager needs to manage at least ten million dollars before he can bring in an average salary.

When Dr. Robert Schuller was trying to figure out how to build the Crystal Cathedral in California, the budget he came up with off the top of his head was ten million dollars. He was doing this from the vantage of the rented drive-in movie theater where he was presenting his weekly sermons. After he thought about the prospect of raising ten million dollars, Dr. Schuller said to himself, "I could get one person to give ten million dollars, ten people to give me one million dollars each..." and he kept scaling down the line. What he decided to do was to put a certain amount of energy into each group of people, people in the one million category and people who were in the fifty dollar category and everything in between.

Most CTAs have told me that ten million is what is needed to begin to operate a successful CTA business. Remember, both Dr. Schuller and I are talking about the same goal of raising ten million dollars. Now, if you're going to raise that kind of money, you need the right kind of mind-set. Dr. Schuller believed deeply in what he was trying to do, and he believed just as deeply that he would be able to do it. However, if you are starting out to raise ten million dollars with the mind-set of who's going to give me that kind of money since I don't have anything to show for it, you'll have nothing to show for it. If Dr. Schuller had thought that way, he wouldn't have raised ten dollars, much less ten million dollars. So, when you're first starting out, you have to determine what you have of value for which another person would be willing to give you money.

If you can't come up with what you have of value, and why a person should give it to you instead of to someone else, then no one will give any money to you.

The first step in putting together a successful strategy for raising trading capital is to find out what you have to offer. To know what you have to offer, you need to know what the people you are selling to actually want and need and how they live. So, let's first look at the psychology of wealthy people.

1. Wealthy people enjoy good sales strategies because most of them are salesmen themselves. Like CTA's, they don't call themselves salesmen, but in order to accumulate capital, you must have been able to persuade other people to give you their money.

2. Wealthy people have cash flow cycles. Wealthy people are not salaried. They buy and sell and this is done on a periodic basis.

3. They have a need for business referrals and contact if they are interested in expanding their economic influence, which they always are if they want to stay wealthy.

4. Wealthy people are always interested in increasing their capital base, but they do not like to put their money at any significant risk to do so.

5. Wealthy people like to align themselves with winners, which are usually perceived as other wealthy people or people who are successful or recognized in some way. This makes them feel good about themselves and safe in associating with you or investing with you.

With these factors in mind, what could you possibly have to offer to wealthy investors?

1. If you have already demonstrated that you have the ability as a trader to bring in a substantial income or that you are aligning yourself with traders who can bring in a substantial income, this could certainly get their attention.

2. If you come from the business world and you have a record of always having success in business, this would be attractive to them.

3. If you are the kind of person who is a leader in the community, who has created a name for yourself such as a philanthropist, or someone who has achieved some recognition in sports, scholastics or any area in life, that would be attractive to them.

4. If you are useful to them in another area of business or in their personal life or if they feel an obligation to you in some shape or form, this would be attractive to them.

5. And finally, naturally, they're going to be attracted to someone with all the skills to put together a good presentation package.

The most effective relationship you can have with a wealthy investor is to position yourself as a friend, as an advisor or as a professional peer of the wealthy. You or someone who represents you, such as a partner, must speak the language of the wealthy and address their concerns and their needs, which are:

1. They need recognition for their achievements.

2. They need or, at least, are vulnerable to sales appeals each year during the months when they received most of their annual income.

3. They need referrals for their business.

4. They need sales professionals who are willing to become part of their affiliation groups (trade association, professional organizations, etc.) and will organize programs and seminars for members of those groups.

5. And last, not first, they need what you are selling.

They need, more concisely, salespeople who are in tune with the rhythm and flow of their business needs, accomplishments, cash flow cycles, and professional orientation.

One of the largest concentrations of wealth are among the owners of privately held businesses. These businesses are growing in this country at three to four times the rate of the population – And these people are driven to be recognized by their peers.

How to Find Whom to Target

The names of potential investors are actually easy to uncover. All it takes is a willingness to do some research.

1. Scan local, regional, and national newspapers for clues, which include:

   - personality profiles of successful people
   - news of a major contract
   - mergers
   - consolidations
   - buy-outs
   - negotiated sales of privately held businesses
   - trade journal advertising

2. Identify major advertisers. Companies or individuals who are doing a lot of advertising have capital. Call these advertisers for information about their products or services. This information will give you the names of the principals involved.

3. Attend trade shows where there are going to be major purchasers of any kind.

4. Become an authority on a subject and write articles so that people find out who you are. Be sure to give a number or address so that people know how to reach you.

5. Get involved in community activities such as politics, civic improvements, civic organizations, etc. This strategy will introduce you to the influential and wealthy people in your community.

6. Go to events and meet people who are involved with horses, and you will start meeting the wealthiest people in the community. Then start attending the *Kentucky Derby* where the wealthiest people in the world congregate for one weekend.

7. Attend art galleries and other events where wealth people congregate.

8. Find a way to meet the new people in town. When people move to a new location, they are more likely to be open to new friendships and to be needing advice.

9. Target people in sales and marketing. You can find these people in trade organizations, in church, in your neighborhood, etc. Six of the top eleven households that earn more than $100,000 per year are headed by someone who works in the sales/marketing area. Members of this group are also the most sensitive to persuasive presentations.

10. Look for philanthropic donations. Find out who gave the largest donations to an organization. These people are usually on a committee for making decisions.

11. Get to know some purchasing agents for local employers. Find out from them the identity of the best sales people they have encountered.

12. Call or write the corporate information department of large businesses in your area requesting a list of award-winning suppliers, and then ask those companies for the names of their top salespeople.

13. Join your local country club and learn to play golf and tennis. Work out in the gym and eat in the club restaurant periodically.

14. Develop a passion for boats and buy yourself one, even if it's a small one. Like the "horse-set," the "boat-set" is often well-healed.

Conclusion:

Being a successful CTA either requires you to wear a lot of hats or to delegate the jobs you do not do well. Unfortunately, the job of raising capital with which to trade is one hat you will have to wear. In order to wear this hat successfully, you will have to learn how to sell your services to wealthy investors. To do that, you will have to possess the self-esteem that is needed to approach people and to believe that they will want to place their money in your able care. In addition, you will have to be able to find potential wealthy clients in order to approach them. These are not daunting tasks if you approach them with the following deeply held beliefs: first, that selling is an honorable, win-win arrangement in which you provide service and opportunity; second, that you have something valuable to offer; third, that you have the willingness and desire to track down potential investors; and fourth, that a fair number of prospective investors will positively respond to your approach. This is the hard part of raising capital. All of the rest is just leg work.

Team synergy is exponential in its results.

Tip from the coach

Chapter 9

_____

RUNNING YOUR OWN INSTITUTION

Is the Main Goal of a Financial Institution to Earn the Greatest Amount of Profit?

Before you answer this question reflexively, stop for a moment and consider this: Who are the people creating the flow of money in this institution? How do these employees spend their time? How could they make better use of their time in regard to profit? What motivates them, and what are their attitudes towards their jobs and their employer? These questions are often not considered by financial institutions when they are making budget cuts.

Surprisingly, the evidence seems to contradict the assumption that the goal of every financial institution is to generate profits for that institution. All too often, the company's board of directors and top management are disconnected from the dynamic group which creates the company's actual profits. Operating without this vital connection, decisions made by the company's top echelon, are often so counter-productive to the long-term bottom line that the company might as well be run by its competitors. At this point, the main goal of the institutions appears to be survival instead of making profits.

Killing the Golden Geese

Within each financial institution is a cadre of brokers, traders and sales reps whose sole activity is generating profits. Unfortunately, when it is necessary to trim budgets, these highly productive people, the "golden geese," are often not taken into consideration.

For example, a major international bank had a sales team of six brokers, individually averaging $60,000 per year and collectively generating $15,000,000 in profits. An hour of each broker's workday was worth $ 1,250 in profit to the company. Yet, unbelievably, a third of their time was spent doing clerical work that was necessary to maintain his client accounts, i.e., recording transactions, filing, typing, client follow-up, etc. This is time that could have been dedicated to generating more profit.

If a secretary, earning $20,000 a year, worked full-time for three of these brokers, she would have cost the company $10 an hour, but would free up a third of each broker's day, thereby increasing the profit of the company by $3,500 per broker per day. If the company hired two secretaries, relieving all six brokers of clerical duties, the annual increase in revenue would be $5 million dollars, less the $40,000, plus fringe benefits paid in secretarial salaries. Does this sound like a company with its eye on the bottom line?

Management sometimes gets jealous of its top salespeople when they make as much or more than the management does. The notion that a sales rep will be motivated to do even better if the commission rate is cut or the territory is reduced is just as bad. The thinking behind this is that the rep will work even harder to make what he was making before he was penalized and in the meantime, another salesperson will be mining for gold as well. This attitude often backfires and does so with a vengeance.

Many years ago, I worked with a brilliant rep who was disenchanted with the small financial institution where he worked. When he started, the company had a sales team of five reps who generated a $10 million income per year. He found his customers were very unhappy with the service and product the company was offering. So, this innovative rep went back to the staff and began to educate them. He overcame a lot of resistance, but he got an agreement from his company to redesign their service and product so they met the actual needs of their top customers. As a result, his own revenue for the company increased to $50 million annually, while the other five sales reps still produced $10 million.

What happened next was tragic. His bosses became jealous of the fact that this industrious rep was now making much more than they were. So, his commission rate was cut in half. He was very hurt, but worked twice as hard and brought his production up to his former level. The company's next move was to cut his customer base. They did this four times. Each time, with Herculean efforts, he increased his productivity to the same approximate level. Surprisingly, the productivity of the other reps did not increase significantly. The innovative rep was so overworked and angry that he finally quit in disgust and found a new institution in which to work. He told me, with bitter satisfaction, that shortly after his departure, the annual revenue fell to its previous level of his former employees. I have seen this scenario repeated many times, but never so graphically.

If the management of this institution had kept its eye on the bottom line, it would have taken steps to insure the valued golden goose plenty of happiness and provided for his support and motivation. Unfortunately, like the husband who is afraid to complement his wife for fear she will think too well of herself and leave, many companies seem to operate from the same misplaced insecurity when it comes to their best employees.

The Unhappy King

These days, we read about how the customer is king and that we must keep the customer happy if we are going to make money. But, if the customer is truly king, why are so many kings looking glum these days and changing their allegiances whenever the opportunity comes along? The problem often results from management's trickle down indifference to the people who are generating the flow of capital.

How much does it actually cost to keep a customer satisfied? The damage that one unhappy customer can do to a business is a very serious matter. In one survey, it was shown that each unsatisfied customer is responsible for 225 people knowing about his bad experience. People like to share their good experiences, but they *love* to share their bad ones. Recently, I attended a party where a guest brought up the subject about service given at a particular institution. The general reaction stirred so much sentiment that twenty people were trading horror stories about the terrible treatment they had received in their dealings with this company. No one listening to this conversation would have considered taking their business to that company.

It is much more difficult to overcome bad publicity than it is to take care of your customer from the start. One of the biggest problems facing a salesman is handling the paperwork necessary to complete the transactions in an efficient time frame. When dealing with a product or service that is roughly equal in quality and cost to others in the same industry, customer service is what makes the difference. Everyone from new customers who receive bad follow-up service to long time customers who feel taken for granted, is perilously close to taking his first step toward the closest exit. Loyalty can only stretch so far before it gives out.

The three most effective and cost efficient ways to correct this problem are:

- Back-up support for the sales force

- Training of the sales force

- More immediate incentives and motivation for the sales force

The Little Engine that Could, But Didn't Have the Time. The Importance of Backup Support and Training

Just as it was profit-efficient to add two secretaries to the sales team at the major bank, it is always more profit-efficient to give salespeople the clerical and technical support they need. Remember, the question I asked in the beginning of this chapter: Do you know how your most productive people are spending their time? Are they making money for you or pushing around paper?

You may not need a larger sales force if you are properly supporting and training the one you have. Peter Drucker, the grandfather of business management theory, once wrote that a manager gets the people he gets, not the ones he chooses. But, he contends, you can turn any group of people into a highly productive and smoothly functioning machine by simply identifying each person's strengths and building on them. Unfortunately, many operations focus on weaknesses and force people to try to do better at what they naturally do poorly. In the case of our sales force, clerical and technical activities often fall into the category of what they do poorly. Selling and bringing in clients are what they do best.

Marley and Scrooge, Ltd.: Are There No Workhouses...?

Many financial institutions, especially in Europe and Asia, fail to consider the physical conditions and/or equipment necessary, for maximizing day to day productivity. Some sales teams work in such cramped, poorly ventilated, noisy and electronically polluted environments they fight just to stay alert and well to make it through the day. The people working in these environments feel tired, sick and frazzled from air-conditioning systems which recirculate the same stale air polluted with fumes from carpet and building materials, cleaning fluids, and cigarette smoke. In addition, bright fluorescent lighting can also play a part in creating a stressful environment. Their level of productivity is severely restricted by the unhealthy conditions in which they operate. It is difficult to find confidence to deal with important people and large sums of money when you are working from such a position of weakness.

A Stitch in Time...

When institutional cost-cutting is called for, it is often supplies and equipment used by the producers which are suddenly in short supply. When these shortages force the people who service customers to make excuses about delays, mistakes and poor service, the bottom line will ultimately suffer.

Recently, I did some work for a financial institution which decided to send out promotional campaigns to a select list of potential borrowers with outstanding credit lines. As an added inducement, a time limit for the promotion was printed on the mailers. This company has a policy of severely limiting the cost of supplies. Instead of having electronic stamp machines, they purchased cheap hand stamps which broke in the middle of the mailing effort. Suddenly, the job was taking four times longer than predicted. Management pulled its sales force into the clerical area and made them hand stamp thousands of these mailers. The result was very expensive to the company. The golden geese spent days doing clerical work instead of bringing in revenue for the company. Many of the mailers arrived after the deadline for the response, which compounded the loss of revenue to the company.

If an institution hires a top salesperson, the initial cost of hiring and training to that institution could range from $50,000 to one million dollars. This figure is not frightening if you amortize it over an extensive life expectancy of that employee. But, what is the life expectancy of a top employee? If he is very good and he is treated well, it could be twenty-five, possibly thirty-five years, during which time you will get good work from him. On the other hand, if he feels unappreciated and unsupported, it could be as long as it takes him to find a better position, or approximately two years. During that time, he will look for as many ways as possible to get out of working. He will dissimulate so well that you will think he is being productive. After he leaves, however, you will discover how little he actually did.

In many European institutions, employers and long-time employees form loyal relationships where both parties will do anything to avoid confrontation. In this climate, poor performance is unlikely to be discussed openly and will persist over a lifetime. Similarly, if an employee can see a more productive or efficient way of conducting business, he will feel unwilling to challenge the authority of his superior. Change or transformation, which is the lifeblood of an institution in a competitive world market, is then inaccessible to the very people who need to be putting it into operation.

A Tale of Incentives: The Sales Force that Killed Itself for a Root Beer Float

The expensive, highly trained employee is both an asset and an investment. If he is very good, he will be bringing in far more money that he is consuming. For him to maintain a high level of productivity, you must identify his motivations and support him through the proper incentives.

Unfortunately, banks are notorious for ignoring the importance of incentives. In some corners of the globe, incentives are considered to be in poor taste, which seems to be a culturally related prejudice. After all, the reasoning goes, banking is a gentleman's game and the reward of having done a good job is reward enough. This position flies in the face of the very nature of the work being done. In sales, the rep or broker must face potential rejection, embarrassment or humiliation with every call. I have seen stockbrokers in their fifties, with over twenty years at the job, approach the phone with their palms sweating. For most people, the job does not get easier. Here is the problem: The rewards are usually in the pay check which may not come for another three weeks. Even the excitement of making a commission on a weekly basis becomes humdrum. Meanwhile, the rep feels tired and overwhelmed with reasons not to pick up the phone. What he needs is an immediate incentive, something that will help him to overcome that great wall of resistance.

I worked with a sales team which lived strictly from their commissions. One would think that having no base support would be plenty of incentive to stay at the phones. But, by Friday afternoon, all the salespeople could think about was playing. They were tired and did not care anymore. However, the manager of this sales team had come up through the ranks and understood what was needed to pump life back into them. The manager would announce that if the group brought in a certain amount in sales, he would shut down the office and everyone would go home early. Suddenly, the incentive was immediate and meaningful. The office was energized and the goal was reached in a short time.

Periodically, this same manager would burst into the office at the low point of the afternoon holding a cold, luscious root beer float high above his head and would yell out, "The next person to make a sale gets this!" Even the excitement of making a commission could not compare to the excitement generated by the prospect of the immediate gratification offered in the root beer float. The office was so electrified by that cold, sweet incentive that it re-ignited the entire selling state of mind for everyone. Each salesperson was a winner because everyone made a sale and sales increased many times over the normal for that afternoon.

That root beer float, as inexpensive as it was, fit the description of the perfect, immediate incentive. You could see it, taste it and imagine it. It was instant gratification and it satisfied an immediate appetite. No one found it demeaning. It was fun, and to win it was considered an enviable achievement.

Other possible incentives are bottles of wine or mystery presents wrapped up brightly with huge bows or you can simply use your imagination. The important thing is that the incentive can be accepted immediately.

Other, less immediate rewards for top work can actually increase individual performance by providing training and motivation, i.e.: books, tapes and seminars.

As important as it is to develop the individual broker, rep, or salesman, it is also important to build the team. By focusing on the team, a manager will be creating a positive atmosphere in which the individual can flourish. For example, some managers reward their teams by bringing in pizzas at lunch. As an exciting way to treat this sales team, one creative manager I know rented a truck, filled it with oranges from a local farm and filled a room with fresh oranges. Each sales rep was invited to take out as many oranges as he could in one trip. The scene was exciting and funny as reps rushed into this room with empty shopping bags and scrambled to fill them. For the remaining oranges, the manager installed a juicer in the kitchen which produced a constant reminder of the event. This manager had one of the most productive and loyal sales teams I have ever seen. He told me his secret: "I hire the best, pay the best and give them the best incentives."

Not By the Hair of My Chinny-Chin-Chin: Ownership as Incentive

The benefits of home ownership versus renting has been clearly demonstrated to a community. People generally work harder and care more about that which they own. Can you imagine the third little pig fighting the big, bad wolf over a rented apartment? This principle operates universally. Can you imagine what would happen if an employee owned his job? We know that people who own their businesses generally work harder and longer hours than people who work for someone else.

Suppose you owned your job, but worked within the parameters of an institution. When you outgrew your job, you would do the same thing you would do if you owned your business: You would create within that position a much bigger position, or you would find another position within the company that allowed you to grow. You would be highly motivated to have your job working for you to have and you working for your job. However, if you were unmotivated because you felt no ownership of your job and no reason to stay, when you outgrew your job and you did not see room to grow, you would move on to another employer. In any case, it is better to work for yourself, even when you are working in an institution. If you are a part of the team, you want the team to work because those people in your team will make your position work better and that in turn will make life better.

The King is in the Counting House, Counting All the Money: The Curse of Tradition and Indifference

Conclusion

No evil witch could cast a more terrible spell than the one that seems to have attached itself to those financial institutions which cling to tradition and the status quo. In these companies, where a privileged few work very hard in their early years in order to get on the express track, progress toward the top becomes assured. Once they reach a certain level, this group of beknighted leaders can comfortably relax and talk about "the little people." They are rarely required to justify their existence since they are their own judge and jury. Tradition becomes an excuse for lack of vigor and accountability because things have always been done that way. In the meantime, highly motivated and productive employees who bring profits to the organization, either become indifferent, or take their golden touch elsewhere where there is a policy of support and reward.

SECTION II

Traders Who Can't...

Chapter 10

FINISH THEIR SYSTEM

"How's your trading?" I asked Ted when he called recently. "Well, I'm still working on my system," was his answer.

For the last four years, I have gotten the same status report from Ted. Like many novice traders, Ted is stuck in a pattern of trying to create "The Holy Grail Trading System." This is a system which will only allow for high returns and no losses. As a result, his system is never quite right. Instead of trading with a simple system that is well tested and brings back a reasonable return, his standard reply is "it should be ready in two months." The underlying reason for his never-ending delay is masking the real reason, which is fear. Like the performer who continually practices to get on stage but never actually does, preparing to trade can become an avocation. When that happens, a potentially good trader will set himself up for being more anxious if and when he ever does start to trade.

Why was Ted so Afraid to Take the Plunge?

The answer lay with Ted's relationship with his family. Coming from a long line of farmers, Ted worked as a professional wheat farmer while educating himself as a Certified Public Accountant. His dream, however, was to become a trader. Although his family had always been supportive of his dreams, this particular dream was met with apprehension because Ted's family had always equated trading with gambling. Strangely enough, even farmers, who are in a very risky business themselves, find it difficult to support a family member trading in the markets. One reason is that they hear so many devastating stories about their fellow farmers who failed despite their attempts to hedge their crops.

We can learn a lot about the common problems traders have in getting started from Ted's situation:

1.   **It is not easy to take action when you are fighting with yourself.**

Ted's battles are all internal ones. He feels a lot of inner conflict about trading. On one hand, Ted wants to trade, while on the other hand, he is afraid to risk his family's money until he is certain he can earn money as a trader.

2. **You can never prove your system unless you use it in real time.**
   As long as Ted continues to paper trade and back-trade his system, he will never know how good it is, what its problems are, and whether or not his solutions work. While Ted feels he needs to prove to his family and himself that trading is a viable business in which he can profit, he will never be able to do so until he takes the plunge.

3. **The more complicated you make your system, the longer it takes to complete each step and the less useful it becomes.**
   Ted has fallen into the trap of believing that the more sophisticated and technical he makes his system, the more he will reduce his risk. According to the best traders in the business, however, the reverse is true. Simple is best.

4. **The transition to a high-risk income from a well-paid, secure career is difficult without a start-up capital base that does not have an emotional attachment.**
   Ted was afraid of losing the comfortable life he had lived as a farmer. At the same time, he did not have a capital base without using his family's money. It is easy to justify not starting to trade under these conditions.

5. **Once you commit to action, you risk losing a dream.**
   In Ted's case, his dream was to become a successful trader. As long as he can use "working on his system" as an excuse not to trade, he does not have to commit to trading his system and risk losing his dream.

Henri's Story - A Lesson in Taking Action

In stark contrast to Ted, Henri is a model for traders who want to successfully get off to a good start. Henri is not afraid to take action because he feels assured of success. Therefore, he does not place self-imposed obstacles in his path, such as an unfinished system. Why is Henri so sure that the actions he takes will result in success? The reason is that Henri learned a secret early on in his life about how to create success by modeling successful people.

Although Henri graduated with high honors in his economics major at the university, he was not only talented scholastically, he was good at everything he attempted to do. The key to Henri's success was not so much innate talent but his ability to model people who were exceptionally talented in a particular field of endeavor. He learned this skill at a young age by assisting his uncle, who was a successful international manufacturer's broker.

The most important lesson Henri learned was that successful people simplify their actions.

When Henri completed his studies, he was recruited by a major European institution into its training program for traders. Although Henri's new employer had the reputation for hiring some of the top traders in the industry, the training program overwhelmed and confused new traders with too much information at one time. The result was that the young traders did not start out with effective skills, and the turnover rate was very high. Instead of focusing on the difficulties of the program, Henri decided to side-step the training and use his skills in modeling successful achievers. With his charismatic personal qualities, Henri was able to develop close friendships with several top traders. Soon, Henri was learning what made these great traders successful directly from them. Here are the steps Henri used for modeling on successful people:

1. **Identify and analyze mental resources**
   The first thing Henri did was to identify and then analyze the mental resources of the individuals he was observing: their beliefs and attitudes, the way they think and solve problems, and how they develop resources.

2. **Identify and analyze decision-making criteria**
   Henri watched how his subjects made decisions. What criteria did they use?

3. **Identify and analyze decision-making actions**
   Henri carefully studied the specific actions and steps his subjects took when making decisions in order to model them.

4. **Identify and analyze their rules**
   Each successful person has a set of rules by which he runs his business or profession. In the case of traders, the important business rules are their money management rules, which Henri carefully studied and modeled.

Once Henri had defined these models of successful behavior, he was ready to take action. These are the steps he took:

1. **He created a time frame**
   Henri set himself a time frame in which he expected to put his plan into action and achieve a definable set of results. Without this step, he had no way to measure his progress and no concrete goal.

2. **He set risk parameters**
   Henri then decided how much risk he was comfortable assuming.

3. **He defined his style**
   Henri developed an overall style based upon his own personality, needs, goals and philosophies. One of the things Henri learned about modeling

was that he did not have to be a clone of another person. He could take the best features of his model's attitudes and behaviors and fit them into his own style of living.

So, what did Henri learn about successful trading? As Henri studied the great traders in his company, he found that they all shared the following approaches to their trading.

1. **Follow your rules**
    The one major philosophy they shared was: Follow your rules precisely while trading. The truth of this statement was demonstrated to him over and over again as he began to trade on his own.

2. **Keep your system simple**
    Henri's simple rules were:

    - Enter a trade when two indicators cross.

    - Trade 2% of the total core equity (total money you have at each new level of gain or loss).

    - Always put on a stop.

    - Manage the profits.

3. **Making profits means handling the exit**
    Henri's interest in learning how to be a great trader was in making large profits. What he learned in his modeling study was that **the secret to making profits was how you handle the exit, not the entry**. Using this knowledge, Henri developed the following rules for exiting:

    - Either be stopped out or,

    - Let your system put you into the next trade.

4. **Handle your emotions**
    Henri discovered that the most successful traders followed their rules while remaining emotionally detached from the outcome of their individual trades. They told Henri they learned this after hard lessons of losses. It was through those losses that they made the commitment to learn how to handle their emotions. Henri found top traders agreed that the secret to being consistently profitable was in handling the psychological issues standing in the way of following their own rules. Here are some of the lessons they taught him to increase profits by using psychological strength:

    - **Have the patience to only trade the best trades.**

Just because you are a trader, does not mean that you have to be in the markets all of the time. One of the biggest mistakes traders make is to wear themselves out by trading all of the time. Most profits are earned from only ten percent of the trades. **There is always going to be another trade.**

- **Prevent stress from accumulating.**
  Stress is the predominant reason why traders do not follow their rules. Traders need to learn how to manage stress and how to reduce it.

- **Handle psychological issues.**
  Psychological issues will sabotage your best performance. For this reason, successful traders follow a maintenance program for handling stress. To handle these issues a trader should apply the material from books, tapes or seminars on the subject of trading psychology, and, if necessary, seek professional help.

By comparing Ted's and Henri's situations, we can learn a lot about the most successful ways to get started trading without falling into the unfinished system trap.

1. **Model the best**
    If you are not in Henri's position to directly model from great traders, there are many other resources you can use:

    - Read books like *The Mind of a Trader* by Alpesh B. Patel, *Market Wizards* by Jack Schwager and *Market Masters* by Jake Bernstein,

    - Listen to interviews of top traders on tape, such as my *Trading on Target* Tapes series.

    - Attend gatherings of top people in the investment field like the annual *Futures Conference* and The TAG Conference.

    - Network with other traders who trade in a similar style.

2. **Develop a business plan for trading**
    Like Henri, you need to have a plan that includes setting objectives, goals, required actions, and deadlines. This plan helps you to discipline yourself into a pattern of keeping commitments and sticking to your own rules.

3. **Educate family members**
    What Ted needed to do to gain the support of his family was to let them know what it takes to become successful in trading. By engaging them in the part of the process that is not involved in making the actual trading

decisions, you are more likely to get their support. People are only afraid of what they do not understand.

4.   **Build your strategies from the bare-bones rules of entry, stop and exit. Leave out the unnecessary**
Write down all of the trading rules you can find that apply to your particular style of trading. Then, put them in order of importance. Next, trim them down to those which are absolutely necessary. The less complicated your rules are, the easier it will be to follow them. It is important to note, however, that you must have all the rules you intend to follow written down on paper and back-test.

Conclusion

A system that constantly needs to be perfected before it can be traded says less about the value of the system and more about its trader. The problem in the unfinished system syndrome is that the trader does not have a successful strategy for taking action, which fills the trader with fear and anxiety about the outcome -- and with good reason. To make matters worse, the result of continually reworking a system is a complicated system that has too many things that can go wrong.

The solution to this problem is for traders to learn what Henri learned in modeling the most successful traders: Simplify. After gaining a good trading education, a trader who wants to be successful should always seek to simplify all of his actions. Starting with a good plan of action, he should stick to specific actions in the plan, and complete actions within a predetermined time frame. Instead of creating the perfect system, traders should start with a simple system and put more emphasis on managing their money and maintaining the discipline of sticking to their rules. The system will evolve over time as a result of periodic reviews. By keeping the system simple, fewer things can go wrong, which results in less emotional involvement. The less emotional involvement you have, the more likely you will be to maintain discipline. Following this model of successful action from the very beginning will make it easier for you, as it did for Henri, to start trading your system.

And What About Ted and Henri?

Ted's call inspired me to write this chapter. As a result of our conversation, I recently received a call from him, shouting triumphantly, "It's done!" While four years after Henri started trading, he is the undisputed leader among all rookie hires. His next goal: to be the best trader in his institution. I'll place a buy order on that one.

Chapter 11

PLAN OR TAKE ACTION

One of the reasons so many people fail to become successful traders has to do with whether their approach to trading is proactive or reactive. Which approach is better? Do successful traders plan for and anticipate everything or do they jump in without a plan, react to events and go with the flow? The answer to this question may appear self-evident to you, but is far more complex than most people realize.

The Obvious Choice

Bill and Jerry are clear examples of proactive versus reactive approaches to trading. Bill was a successful lawyer who decided he wanted to switch professions and become a trader. Starting out with a careful business plan, Bill contacted several top traders and asked them for strategies that would expend minimum time while producing the maximum results. These traders suggested several seminars, books and tapes. From this list, Bill was able to create a substantial library, selecting only the resources which would help him become the kind of trader he wanted to be.

Based upon the advice he received, Bill hired a systems designer to develop a system and someone in the trading profession to work with him as a colleague as well. Then, he hired a trader's coach to assist him with his psychological issues and a trading coach to teach him the techniques of trading, so that he felt supported at every step. By this time, many of you are shaking your heads in disbelief at the time and money Bill spent starting his new business. His total start-up time was thirteen months and his start-up costs were roughly $100,000. This left Bill $200,000 with which to trade.

While Bill's investment represents a great deal of money, it was the typical amount necessary as start up costs for the first year in a new businesses. Consider how much it costs to lease office space and to purchase inventory and other items necessary for a new business. The costs also seem modest when you consider the losses which new traders usually experience without this kind of proactive approach. Needless to say, Bill was quickly out of the gate and ahead of the pack from the very beginning.

Jerry, on the other hand, plunged headlong into trading like a walrus into the sea. As soon as he made the decision to become a trader, he promptly quit his lucrative job as a manufacturer's rep. Like Bill, Jerry had approximately $200,000 to start his trading. Unlike Bill, who studied and prepared for each step, Jerry was the kind of person who would buy a new mechanical toy, fail to read the instructions, and somehow, haphazardly, put it together and eventually return it, broken. Jerry hated to plan, to work with details and to organize. What he liked was action and immediate gratification, which his selling career provided him. Jerry was also very good with people, and he instinctively understood their needs, their weaknesses and their feelings.

Regarding the business of trading, Jerry possessed the same level of information and technical resources as the ordinary man on the street. In other words, Jerry put money into an account with a broker whose trading advice he eagerly followed. He then shared the same unhappy fate as many others who have taken this approach; he lost more than half his money. Barely wiser, Jerry decided to go to one of the trading conferences where countless "professionals" offered to lead him to every possible path to success. Unable to make a reasoned decision, Jerry selected the advisor with the most polished line who promised, "Follow my analysis and you will make millions, the same way I do." So long to more of Jerry's money. In the end, Jerry's reactive approach led him back to where his real talents lay, in the sales profession.

By the end of their first year, both Bill and Jerry had expended nearly $100,000 in their trading businesses. However, Bill had earned over $100,000 during that time in his law practice, so that he came out even for the year. At the end of two years, Bill had made back his $100,000 investment in trading, while Jerry was down $100,000 with nothing but aggravation to show for it. In this comparison, the benefits of a proactive approach are obvious. However, that is not always the case.

The Other Side of the Coin

In fact, **PRO** does not necessarily mean **progressive** and **RE** does not necessarily mean **regressive**. Take, for example, the case of Randy and Jeff. Randy, who planned for every contingency, was certainly proactive in his approach to life. He was highly organized in everything he did, and was cautious about leaping into something before he was prepared with information, backup systems, and technical support. When Randy decided to become a trader, his approach was nearly the same as Bill's approach to setting up his business. They both anticipated, planned, and spent money on the development of their respective businesses. They both held off full-time trading until they were fully ready to do so.

The big difference between Bill and Randy was that, armed with the same resources and information, Randy made all of the wrong decisions. He and Bill read many of the same books, but Randy found it difficult to hone in on one type of trading. He interviewed many brokers but could not decide whether he wanted to go with a full-service broker or save money and go with a discount broker. When he finally decided to become an options trader, he was not sure whether he wanted to trade long-term or short-term options. Five years have gone by and Randy is still taking a proactive approach to trading although he has never put real money on a trade.

Having the Right Moves

Randy used "planning, preparing and organizing" as a means of preventing himself from having to make decisions, take action, and deal with risk. While he has fooled himself, everyone around him has his number.

Jeff, on the other hand, is a person who goes with the flow of life. He does not make long-range plans, although he knows generally what he likes and wants in his life. Instead of focusing on his goals and forcing them to become a reality, he lets life present opportunities and then deals with them as they occur. In other words, Jeff attends to whatever is in his immediate focus, whatever comes up next.

The extraordinary thing about Jeff's approach to life is that it has served him very well. This kind of reactive, seemingly non-goal directed approach to problem-solving and life-planning works very well for Jeff. He decided to become a trader while sitting in a cocktail bar in Chicago, talking with a group of floor traders and listening to their stories. When he said to them, "I'd like to do that," someone in the group, equally spontaneous, offered to take him on as a runner. Soon, Jeff was recognized for his efficiency and willingness to go the extra step for his traders. After a few months, someone offered to train him as a broker. Jeff continued to follow the bouncing ball of life and found that each step led him to the next level of success.

While Jeff does not write a plan of action down, there is a plan. Jeff is an exceptional chess player. He thinks four to six moves in advance and has a contingency plan for every possible outcome. He daydreams about the possibilities in life and usually the ones that are the most dramatic manifest themselves into his reality.

Place Your Bets

If the informal results of my own observations are to be used in this process, I would have to say that, by and large, those traders who approach the business of trading from a proactive posture tend to be the successful ones, rather than the reactive traders. Too often, traders who are motivated by greed, the need for excitement and immediate gratification use a reactive approach to trading out of laziness and not through natural inclination.

Either approach, whether it is proactive or reactive, requires attention to the process. In order for Bill to be proactive, he must work very hard and continually ask himself what the next step is and then follow through. His so-called luck comes the old-fashioned way;

through hard work and attention to detail. He takes full responsibility for his outcome, either way. Bill's proactive stance is the result of a conscious self-discipline that he has cultivated since his high-school days.

On the other hand, most people are certain that people like Jeff, who are successfully reactive, are just naturally lucky. But, Jeff also attracts opportunity to himself through a process of focus and discipline, that is not as obvious to most people. In order to be able to go with the flow, Jeff has to stay calm and focused. As a result, intuition plays a big role in his success. He cannot fill his mind with endless details and anxieties about the outcome. He has trained himself to be very trusting of the universe as well as his own intuition and instincts. If you were to study Jeff's day-to-day encounters, you would discover that he passes up most of the potential opportunities which come his way. In fact, he attracts all manner of people, a fair number of whom are eager to exploit his easy-going and open disposition. Yet, Jeff seems to steer his way clear of these land mines with a highly accurate internal radar.

The difference between our two reactive traders is that Jeff sensed that trading was the right career for him, while Jerry fell into it for the wrong reasons. Jerry was drawn to trading because he felt that he could make a lot more money trading than he could selling. Although Jeff was willing to go with the flow, he was also willing to work hard at whatever he did. Unfortunately, Jerry did not sense that trading would require a serious commitment of time and energy. He did not really understand who he was and where his strengths lay.

A Strategy

In order to use the right approach for you in trading, whether proactive or reactive, start by discovering your own strategy for completing tasks. Ask yourself about these three areas of your approach to successfully completing tasks:

1. What are your beliefs about completing tasks?

2. What specific tasks or actions do you undertaken?

3. How do you prioritize your tasks?

You might also ask yourself if you are faster than average in completing tasks. Which tasks did you like and which ones did you dislike? If you do not have a successful task strategy, you can model on someone who is successful. What is this person's strategy, and how does he set about accomplishing goals?

Optimizing Your Approach

Both proactive and reactive traders can be successful, if they are willing to optimize their own approach to decision-making and problem-solving. This is accomplished by doing what each strategy requires to be successful.

Both successfully proactive Bill and successfully reactive Jeff instinctively knew what worked for them. Unfortunately, many people have no idea what works for them. The first step, of course, is to decide whether you are best at anticipating each step and planning and working out the details, or whether you are best at intuitively sensing what is best for you in each situation. If you are naturally proactive, you must make a commitment to go all the way in planning and anticipating each step. At the same time, you must also make a commitment to taking action and following through on each step.

To go forward with this proactive approach, a trader must have a mind that is cleared of the doubt and confusion that waylaid poor, indecisive Randy.

If you lean toward the reactive approach to life, you must make a commitment to learn how to listen to the intuitive messages that your brain sends you. But, in order to use the conclusions that are drawn from this experience, the reactive trader must work on himself, like Jeff did, to clear his mind of the self-destructive motives that sent the reactive trader, Jerry, back into sales. It does not matter what direction you are coming from if you know who you are and where you want to go. The commitment to making the journey in the best way you can is what matters..

Which are You?

Take a moment to answer these questions, and determine for yourself whether you are proactive or reactive. Answer each question and then add up the total.

Question: Would you rather:

1. Learn something new by the "hands-on experience, learn from your mistakes" school? Or learn something new by reading about it first and doing your research before attempting any hands-on experience?

2. Be recruited? Or do the recruiting?

3. Allow the team to make the decision and live with it? Or actively campaign for your position?

4. Tell the barber to do his thing? Or give him instructions so he gets it right?

5. Get to the ticket window at the cinemaplex and see what's available? Or buy your tickets in advance and show up early for the best seats?

6. Have the Thursday night basketball team selection done by lottery? Or have the team selection done by choice?

7. Find your own way when you're lost? Or ask directions?

8. Be content to let life guide the right mate to you? Or set out to find her/him for yourself?

9. Go to a doctor when you are sick and let him/her be responsible for your recovery? Or research the problem yourself so that you can take control of your own health and not be dependent on the advice of your doctor?

10. Follow the teachings of your religious faith without question? Or search for the religious and spiritual truths for yourself?

11. Trade by intuition? Or trade by a purely mechanical system?

12. Read the want ads to find what's available? Or advertise for what you want?

13. Vote for whoever is on the ballot, but otherwise avoid politics? Or work for the candidate of your choice?

14. Complain about the problem? Or create the solution to the problem?

15. Let your employees design their own work schedules? Or present them with the schedules that you want?

16. Spontaneously go on a picnic today and take your chances with the weather? Or watch the five day forecast and plan for the day with the best weather prediction?

17. Allow your angry spouse to ventilate his/her feelings and see what develops? Or anticipate your spouse's angry reactions and prepare your own defenses in advance?

18. Take a trip to a foreign country without making plans so that you can stay where you like when you get there? Or carefully research your trip, making your reservations and itinerary before you leave?

19. Go grocery shopping with no list and no menus planned for the week and see what strikes your fancy? Or take inventory of your supplies and prepare a menu and needed food list before you shop?

20. Go to a bookstore and browse the shelves for books on trading? Or read up on the best books in the field and order them?

Conclusion

As you can see, in some areas of life there are times when it is more appropriate to be proactive and times when it is more appropriate to be reactive. It is important to know which outlook works best for you under which circumstances so you can get the best results from each situation.

The markets and professional traders

welcome those without a proven system.

Tip from the coach

Chapter 12

———

TRADE RESPONSIBLY

Are you gambling with your money? Before you answer, consider this statement: You probably are gambling if you are consistently getting bad results. "Wait a minute," you say. "A gambler is someone who takes uncalculated risks." While this is certainly the case, I know many traders who spend their lives taking what they consider to be calculated risks and whom I would still categorize as gamblers. Why? Because their ends define their means. When a trader loses money consistently, regardless of his intentions, skill-level and money-management rules, the level of the risk he is taking has exceeded the parameters of his advantage and he has entered "The Gambling Zone."

Wearing Many Hats

When you look at the functions most traders perform in order to be traders, you will find that they wear many hats, such as systems designer, businessman, salesman and trader. Fortunately, a trader does not have to perform all of these functions himself. He can hire someone else to perform any one of these functions to make up for what is missing in his background. While a businessman has the skills to operate a trading business and a system designer has the skills to design a trading system, these abilities only make it easier for you to be a trader. However, they do not necessarily make you a trader. A trader is someone who has a set of rules that he believes in, who follows those rules, and as a result, gets a positive outcome. In trading, a gambler, on the other hand, is someone whose outcome is not positive. Naturally, draw-downs are part of the overall success of a good trader.

If it Doesn't Work

Rob was a brilliant student of math and science whose heart was set on becoming an exceptional trader. He was confident that he could come up with a unique system which no one else had devised to give him the tools to become this type of trader. Using his computer programming skills, he believed that he would be able to design this system in a three or four month period. More than two years later, Rob was finally at the point where he said, "Now, I have a system." With his natural abilities in selling, Rob was able to persuade several investors to invest money with him, based upon his prospectus, his education, and his father's influence. Enthusiastically, Rob entered the business, calling himself a trader. When I asked Rob, "How is your system going?" He replied, "The system is doing exactly what it is supposed to do." When I pressed him for exact details, however, it turned out that his system was consistently losing. Rob was not trading. He was gambling.

System Design

System designing is an art form. If it were an exact, ever-reproducible science, you would not see this disclaimer with every system's ad: "Past performance does not guarantee future results." While you might have computer and mathematical skills, there is a key ingredient in becoming a successful professional systems designer which surpasses these two skills. The key ingredient is intuition. When a systems designer starts designing a system, he has absolutely no proof of whether or not he is going in the direction of a positive outcome. He may believe he is, but, in fact, no one really knows if a system is going to be a good system until it has been exhaustively tested. So, while it is absolutely necessary to have the mathematical, logical, left-brain skills to design a system, it is also imperative that you have the vision, the creativity and spontaneous intuition of a right brain thinker to point yourself in the right direction.

With this much talent required to produce a working system, it is not difficult to understand how easily a trader can create a poorly functioning system which can create significant risk in a trader's business. At a certain point, that risk can exceed the parameters of a trader's advantage so that the trader is gambling by using his system.

The best system can still be overly risky to use if the trader does not consistently follow it. Even the most profitable systems will produce a level of acceptable losses when followed to the letter. These losses, however, will reach unacceptable levels when the system is not followed exactly.

Following a system is like baking. As an avid cook who is noted for her creative dishes, I am still unable to bake a cake that is light, delicate and edible. The reason is that I am too creative to just follow the recipe. I want to add a touch of this and a touch of that and use all of my creativity in baking the same way that I do in the rest of my cooking. Unfortunately, the smallest deviation from a baking recipe will often bring the entire project to ruin. A significant proportion of traders are gambling with the outcome of their trades in the same way.

If You Don't Work

Joe is typical of all of the gambling traders with whom I have worked. As a serious trader, Joe has read most of the major books on systems development and taken countless courses on the subject. With a background in math and engineering, he has developed and tested a good trading system which should be making him a solid income. Then why is his system not making him any money? The answer is simple. Joe just can't follow it. Joe is dealing with psychological issues which get in the way of his being disciplined. He cannot always enter the market when his system tells him to enter, and if he does get in, he cannot exit when it tells him to exit. As a result, despite the fact that Joe is doing all of the right things he was trained to do in the traditional approach to trading, he is not a trader. He is a gambler.

Discipline

What Joe is missing is the discipline necessary to pull the trigger. Like most of the traders who are in his situation, what is holding him back and preventing him from being disciplined is fear. In his case, the reason Joe is afraid is that he does not trust himself, and as a result, he does not trust his system to work. At one critical point in his life, Joe made an unwise decision which resulted in the loss of a great deal of money. From that point onward, he has been sabotaging all of his efforts to make money because he fears that he will lose it. The result is that Joe is carrying around emotional baggage which must be opened, examined and disposed of before he can get on with his trading. Until he deals with this emotional baggage, he will not be able to deal with the risk-demands of trading, and he will remain a gambling trader.

If You Don't Believe You Deserve It

Fred was also a gambler trader who was not able to consistently follow the rules of his system. In Fred's case, his fear came from the fact that he did not believe that he deserved to make money. This feeling was so deeply imbedded in his unconscious mind from years of poverty as a child, that he was not even aware of it. Nevertheless, this feeling produced a crippling fear each and every time Fred made a trading decision. As Fred's losses mounted, he assured himself and his family that he wanted to make money, and he fervently believed that he would do so, while at the same time, his level of fear continued to increase. One of the strategies Fred used to deal with his problem was to seek out books on trading discipline and to read them over and over again. While this strategy has helped many traders, the issues in Fred's case were larger than just poor trading habits. Fred needed professional help.

Beliefs

If your beliefs are not in alignment with the goal of creating success and abundance, you will create a drama to sabotage your efforts, such as a pattern of winning, only to give it back. By working with Fred using Neuro-linguistic Programming techniques to transform his beliefs to more positive ones, we moved Fred out of the gambler category and into the real trader category.

If You Must

John did not have the background and training necessary to develop his own winning system and test it properly, but he did have the determination to keep trying. Like many traders, he had been steeped in the trading tradition which said that a trader had to create his own system. John was not the kind of person who could admit defeat, or worse yet, admit to a weakness. Although John was normally cautious about most things, his ego had been piqued by this challenge to his abilities. The results were continual losses. John fiddled with his system endlessly, but the outcome was the same.

Buying What Works

The great difficulty in transforming John from a gambler trader to a real trader was in convincing him that he was not a failure if he were to use a system designed by someone else. Once I was able to do that, John found a system that he now calls his own and that works for him.

Just as a dancer does not have to be a choreographer, a great cook does not have to create his own recipes, and a great actor does not have to write his own script, a great trader does not have to design his own system.

The Excitement Junkie

No other group of gambling traders is as easy to spot as the excitement junkies. These traders enter trading for the excitement, for which they need a high level of risk. This group of traders ride the emotional roller coaster of the highest highs followed by the lowest lows. These traders are people who have become addicted to experiencing the emotional extremes, to the adrenaline rush of great joy and excitement and great fear and anguish because it allows them to relive old emotional traumas through their trading. These traders are using unacceptable levels of risk because of deep-seated emotional problems which must be addressed.

When you and your system work, then you can call yourself a real trader.

THE GAMBLER'S EVALUATION:

1. Are you consistently losing money?

2. Are you afraid of the responsibilities you would assume if you were to become rich?

3. Do you give yourself excuses for why you are consistently losing money?

4. Do you feel uncomfortable when you have experienced a long spell in which you are disciplined and have made solid profits?

5. Do you feel that you lack the consistent discipline necessary to become an exceptional trader?

6. Do you believe that people who have a lot of money usually have unhappy lives?

7. Do you believe that if you make a lot of money, something bad will happen to you?

8. Do you believe that you honestly do not deserve to make a lot of money?

9. Is there a part of you that is afraid of each new level of success?

10. Do you risk more than you are willing to lose?

11. Do you fail to use stop losses consistently and it gets you into trouble?

12. Are you inconsistent with how much you are willing to risk?

13. Do you fail to limit your risk to a percentage of total equity?

14. Are you spreading yourself over too many markets and calling it diversification?

15. Do you stay in the markets when they become too volatile?

16. Are you undercapitalized for successful trading?

17. Are you always trying new markets which then get you into trouble?

18. Are you over-stressed or depressed most of the time?

19. Did you come from a dysfunctional home in which your family life was filled with emotionally negative scenes?

20. Are you unwilling to or deeply resentful of the need to make changes in yourself in order to succeed?

21. Do you need excitement, drama, a sense of danger or unpredictability in order not to feel bored with life?

22. Do you scoff at the idea of taking care of your health, eating right and exercising?

Now, take a look at the number of yes answers you have given to this evaluation. Each yes answer represents an increase in the risk levels you are assuming in your trading. If you have more than three or four yes answers, you are definitely gambling in your trading. If that is the case, you have four options:

1. You can continue to do what you are doing. Just remember the old adage: If you do what you have always done, you will get what you have always gotten. When unacceptable risk is carried long enough, it will eventually defeat you.

2. You can make a commitment to correct the situation. The first step is to become aware of those areas in your trading which are the sources of unacceptable risk. Remember, the unacceptable risk can be coming from either you or your system. If it is your system, then you need to be testing it more carefully and perhaps, reworking it. If the source of your problem is in you, then you need to make a commitment to working on your issues.

3. You can hire people who can give you support in the areas where you are deficient.

4. You can seek out professional help. If the issues you need to address are deep-seated, you will need outside help to work on them.

Conclusion

A trader does not have to openly exercise irresponsible risk in the market to be a gambler. Unacceptable risk exists whenever a trader is consistently losing. This outcome means that either a trader is not following his system and money management rules, or his system is not worth following. In either case, the trader is assuming too much risk with his money or his investor's money. Many traders continue to trade successfully for awhile carrying too much risk. The problem with unacceptable risk is that, over time, it will eventually end trading careers. For that reason, traders need to distinguish trading from gambling in their own professional lives and make a commitment to reduce or eliminate the causes of unacceptable risk in their trading.

Chapter 13

SUCCEED WITHOUT SELF-SABOTAGE

Are You Limiting Your Profits Because of Poverty Consciousness?

Poverty-Conscious Traders are those individuals who, limit the amount of profits that flow into their lives because of a particular type of negative thinking. This negative thinking occurs when a trader's attitudes are fogged with thoughts and feelings of lack and limitation. This "limited thinking" becomes a self-fulfilling prophecy that can lead to limitation and loss in the real world.

The Echo that Created an Avalanche

Trading brought in a steady, average income for Rick. By combining his income with his wife's, Rick's family lived an upper middle class lifestyle. However, any unexpected bills put a strain on their budget. Despite this delicate economic balance, Rick had promised to support the dream of their second daughter to attend an expensive European school.

Rick got the flu. Foggy from the effects of the virus, Rick let a mental stop get away from him. Then, instead of packing up for the day as he normally would have done, he increased his risk in the next few trades, trying to make up his losses. And you can imagine the results.

When he arrived home that evening, he was met with excited, expectant faces. His daughter, by taking advantage of winter discounts, had purchased a new wardrobe for school. She modeled for her father, unaware that this made him feel even more guilty for going against his rules. In addition, he was overcome with fear that he could not make up the losses.

Rick was angry at himself and the markets. He could not stop the chatter of negative dialogue in his head. The markets were against him, life was against him, and the future looked bleak. He believed that he couldn't possibly make up the losses which meant he would have to face the disappointment of his wife and daughter. These thoughts eventually became the reality.

Not all traders react the way Rick did to a temporary loss. Some traders rise to the challenge and make up losses in a brief time, and others simply take these losses in stride as part of the game. However, Rick's psychological pump was primed to react to such a temporary setback with anxiety and guilt. He was raised in a family that struggled financially to meet the basic needs, and harbored a deep fear that he would not have enough. In fact, the level at which he was living was out of his comfort zone, increasing his anxiety and stress.

Tidal Wave Over the Economy

Just as a family can be negatively affected by one trader, negative thinking in the trading community can affect the entire world. When the trading community is in a state of worry, trading becomes erratic. Traders either hold back from trading at their normal levels of activity, or buy and sell wildly, thus creating a negative impact on the world economy. There is less money in circulation, thereby limiting the activity in the markets, which in turn makes traders even more restrictive in their activity.

The poverty consciousness in traders that results from activity in the marketplace is a temporary but self-limiting reaction. However, beyond the normal reaction to external forces and circumstances in a trader's life, he can have many forms of poverty-conscious thinking. This thinking can start at any point and time in life, although the roots of it are most common in childhood. For instance, if a baby cannot get his basic needs met, the longing for fulfillment of those needs can last a lifetime. Even if a trader has the appearance of affluence, his choice of behavior can sabotage his full potential.

Fly in the Ointment

When Ronald was two years old, his mother suffered a serious case of postnatal depression after the delivery of his brother. She never left him and did what she could to care for him, but from his point of view it seemed that his mother had abandoned him. This feeling of loss lasted after his mother's return to emotional health and everything in his home was normal and happy.

As an adult, Ronald went on to manage over $20 million. His deep longing for something missing in his life would bite into his trading money when things felt too good to last. A large loss would immediately follow a large profit or the opening of a substantial new account. Deep inside Ronald's unconscious mind, he did not trust his good fortune to last and since he expected it to be taken away from him, he took control of losing it himself.

Here are some specific kinds of poverty-conscious thinking, how they might affect you as a trader, and solutions to these mental impediments:

1. **The Unworthy and Undeserving**

   These traders find it difficult to reward themselves, no matter how much money they have. They live as though they are poor because they feel that they still are poor. In some cases, they are afraid to find joy in their success for fear it will cause it to end.

   Effect

   Traders in this category put a cap on their potential earnings by failing to reward themselves when they succeed. The unconscious mind needs to be rewarded for successful behaviors and attitudes in order to be motivated to repeat them.

   Solution

   Set realistic goals to accomplish and attach a small reward. It is important to follow through and enjoy this reward.

2. **Self-imposed Notions of Lack and Limitation**

   These traders buy into the notion that there is not enough to go around. This usually starts in childhood when the environment cannot support the child emotionally and/or materially. As adults, these individuals become pack rats because they feel that someday their garbage will be useful. Many people who grew up during the *Great Depression* display this behavior.

   Effect

   Traders in this category are often very disorganized. This disorganization results from a deep conflict within. Their conscious minds tell them that they have a goal to reach and they must get into action. But, their unconscious minds, controlled by fears of poverty, tell them that their goals are unreachable and hopeless. As a result, they never have enough time to complete anything, and they find a way to create lack and limitation in their trading. In the event they do create abundance, they are very uncomfortable with it.

   Solution

   Make your garbage useful now by giving away all of the items that you have not used in the past two years. It is a good idea to have an organized person help you. List the things you want to accomplish and a time frame in which you can complete the tasks. Put them in order of importance and either delegate the rest to someone or give up the tasks that are least important.

3. **Doomsday is on its Way!**

   These people live in the shadow of impending disaster: "You never know when you're going to lose it all so plan as if disaster is on its way." Unfortunately, for many, this fear is based on the reality of past, traumatic losses in their lives. As a result, they expect these losses to recur and feel a perverse sense of fulfillment and vindication when they do.

Effect

These traders are perpetual bears. They often miss the obvious upward movements because they are so focused on an impending downward trend. Traders in this category will take profits too soon if they overcome the fear of entering a trade in the first place.

Solution

Expand your present level of risk by 10%. When it feels comfortable to trade at this new level of risk, expand it again by another 10% until it becomes comfortable at that level, and so on. You can deal with "Doomsday" when it arrives, but act as if you are anticipating more affluence with each new day and notice the difference in your life.

4.   The Taker: I Deserve it, You Don't

These people always look at every situation by thinking, "What's in it for me?" This position comes from a great insecurity and a sense of lack. These traders often resent the fact that they have to work hard and do not necessarily see the value in other peoples' contributions. At the heart of their world view is the notion that there is not enough to go around. Life for them is a struggle for survival. The root cause of this syndrome is often a childhood in which the child's basic emotional and physical needs were either unmet or attended to with indifference. As a result, they are willing to toss the scraps of overflow to their family, friends and society. They expect family and business associates to put out equal effort, but they do not believe in equal rewards.

Effect

Traders in this category fail to see that success is greatly influenced by the willing cooperation of people around them. Their insensitivity to the feelings of others and their eagerness to point the finger when things go wrong creates stress and bad feelings all around. The negative environment created by these behaviors ultimately affects trading performance.

Solution

If you live by the motto, " You only have what you give," you will find that your life will prosper as your generosity increases. This strategy invokes the power of the "ten-fold principle" which multiplies abundance through prosperity. The people around you will then want to help you become more successful instead of begrudging you each success and looking for ways to sabotage you. As a result, trading will become less stressful and, as a result, more profitable.

5.   Hitting the Poverty Tolerance Level

We all have a level at which we begin to feel insecure financially. For some traders, insecurity is reached when they lose their job, with no prospects and no money in the bank. Then there are traders who are financially secure, but have a temporary losing streak and feel deprived from being able to enjoy frivolous spending.

Effect

When poverty consciousness kicks in, opportunity checks out, because you are entering a victim state of mind. When you see only problems, you will not find solutions and performance will suffer until you take control.

Solution

List a group of actions which would take you toward the success that you want and start with the easiest first. This puts you back in control and will pull you out of a victimized state of mind.

6. **The Guilt Ridden**

    These individuals feel they should not have what other people do not have either. Regardless of their efforts and their successes, they feel guilty in reaping the rewards. A childhood in which praise is absent and criticism is abundant is often the reason for this viewpoint.

    Effect

    These traders sabotage their efforts to become successful so they do not have to face the problems of feeling guilty about having too much.

    Solution

    Work with the idea of putting yourself in a position of abundance to help many people and share the joy of your successes. At the same time, examine the relationships in your life for friends and family members who are critical and unsupportive. These relationships feed your low self-esteem and need to be either corrected or eliminated if you are going to feel worthy of success.

7. **The Success Comfort Zone**

    Everyone has a comfort zone of success. If a trader grew up in a poverty, he may feel uncomfortable in an expanded comfort zone of success. Some traders sabotage success just to stay in their comfort zone.

    Effect

    The best case is that your level of success stays the same or your growth is very slow. The worst case is that you create major losses whenever you are feeling anxious about being too successful and outside of your comfort zone.

    Solution

    In order to have a quick transformation to higher success you must transform your limited beliefs. Dwell on beliefs that would bring you enormous success, e.g., "By the creative actions I demonstrate, I deserve to enjoy affluence and abundance."

Visualizations of yourself in a new life of abundance can help your unconscious mind accept comfort at each new level of success.

Outcomes for Rick and Ronald

For Rick and his family, downsizing their lifestyle was not an easy transition, but it was a necessary step to take in repairing the situation. As a result of this downsizing, the family is no longer under the constant strain to make ends meet. Rick's trading performance has never been better. Life is less stressful and toys are more abundant in their new townhouse. Their daughter is doing well in a local state college. This summer, Rick is taking his family on a trip through Europe and will be dropping his daughter off to enjoy her sophomore year at the *Sorbonne*.

Ronald and I worked at discovering and overcoming the sabotage problem. He now feels confident that he will not have to go through the trauma of those periodic large losses.

Conclusion

Poverty consciousness can affect any trader and the results can range from a dampening of profits to large losses. Most traders come by this sense of loss as a result of external and temporary forces. For those traders who have an underlying sense of optimism about the future, they move through this phase and go on to recoup their losses. However, those traders whose psychological pumps are primed for neediness and privation can find themselves permanently stuck in poverty consciousness.

Pulling out of this psychological state is often difficult because the first step out is to acknowledge the existence of these feelings of neediness and low self-esteem. These feelings, buried deeply in the unconscious mind, must be accepted for what they are and how they affect personal success of the trader. Once this is accomplished, the trader can begin to take positive action which can transform the outward reality and reshape the internal, motivating feelings.

Perfection in trading is

being able to follow your methodology.

Tip from the coach

Chapter 14

GIVE UP CONTROL

Is your goal to be a perfect trader? To do everything right? To make no mistakes? If so, you have a lot of company. You may believe that in order to maximize your profits, you need to do everything as perfectly as possible. The interesting thing about most of these traders is that they are the people who fail to do the very things that are necessary to obtain the best possible outcome.

Nose to the Grindstone

Rick was raised with the belief that the more you do, the more you will have. It is true that hard work is an important ingredient for success as a trader, but hard work must be tempered with other ingredients. Unfortunately, one of the other ingredients in his mix was a fear of failure, which came from his critical parents. Rick was desperate to do everything perfectly because when he made a mistake, his parents attacked him with derision. After a childhood of verbal assault, Rick had internalized their voices so that now he was his own worst enemy. The result was that Rick became a procrastinator. He put off doing important things and making important decisions for fear of the consequences.

Understandably, his fear of failure made trading a nightmare. He was unable to follow his own rules or stick to his system for fear of losing money. All successful traders experience losses. The goal is to win more than you lose. But for Rick, the level of risk that is built into trading and the need to act on his rules nearly paralyzed him. He spent most of his time frantically designing systems and back testing them, only to find that he could not trade them.

As an adult, Rick was plagued with not knowing what he really wanted in life. He tried many professions, including accounting, real estate, and multilevel marketing. He thought trading might be the right choice. With the belief that anything he did would ultimately

113

result in failure, he created a self-fulfilling prophecy. In actuality, he created average results. Because of his need to be perfect, he spent a good percentage of his time working hard to be average.

Compounding his problems, Rick felt that it was not okay to reward himself for his achievements, and it was not okay to accept compliments. Once more, his critical inner voice demanded higher standards than he could possibly meet. Rick was driven to work hard without rewards for his efforts. Consequently, the only incentive to work was criticism.

Beak to the Goal-line

Robin, on the other hand, is a successful trader who is also exceptional at organization and time management. She is able to get twice as much done in half the time it takes Rick, and her profits reflect her focus. Instead of fearing activity, she was raised with the belief that you should enjoy the process of producing the best possible outcome. Robin learned these important life lessons from her father, a magazine publisher, best-selling author and public speaker. Unlike Rick, Robin got the job done and enjoyed the process.

Trained to be Imperfect

What was the difference between these two traders? The reason that Robin is able to rise to the top is that Robin was trained to be imperfect. The emphasis is on getting the job done, not on getting it done perfectly. This goal provides Robin with the freedom to act, unhampered by the critical inner voice that saps creativity, risk-taking and self-confidence. This training in accomplishment, rather than in perfection, began when Robin's dad taught her the value of planning. He taught her that a plan should include the following:

1. Goals (the outcomes you are seeking)

2. Tasks (all of the actions required to accomplish your goals)

3. "Live-lines" (as opposed to deadlines, for all of these tasks)

4. Priorities (a list of what to do next)

5. Rewards (incentives for motivation)

6. Contingencies (what can go wrong as well as what can go right and what to do in each case)

Robin was taught to understand that there is always going to be another project beyond the project you are completing. For that reason, you should always give as much effort as necessary to each task within the time allotted to it. In following this strategy, you get the most done in the least time and your neurology gets accustomed to making it okay to not have everything perfect.

People who have trained themselves to get the job done within a predetermined plan, get a better outcome than the people who labor very hard to get one project done perfectly and are never able to accomplish their goals.

As a writer and publisher, Robin's father was profoundly influenced by the realization that the greatest works of literature were produced by the most prolific writers: Shakespeare, Tolstoy, and Dickens, to name a few. What endures, he told Robin, is their greatest efforts, but it is clear that they wrote and wrote and wrote, regardless of the outcome. Some worked and some did not. These writers strove for excellence, yes, but they were not paralyzed by the requirement of perfection. It was this lesson that Robin's father passed on to his daughter: set high standards and produce the best possible outcome within an allotted time frame, and then get busy and produce.

Where is Your Focus?

Notice how you feel when there is that small piece of food on someone's lip or between someone's teeth? Or how you feel when pictures are not straight on the wall.

If you have experienced this kind of discomfort, you will understand the discomfort of a perfectionist. So, what's going on? What is happening is that you have a belief or an idea of the way something *should* be, and your focus brings your attention to anything that does not fit that picture. Isn't it amazing that something else within the millions of potential points of focus does not attract your eye, but that one little piece of spinach between a person's teeth can grab all your attention?

Formula for the Perfection Trap:

Focus on the detail of a predetermined outcome and don't allow for any other possibilities. While you might get the outcome you want, you don't allow for other successful situations that can be equally satisfying.

Perfection Vs Perception

The key to our perfection predicament is in our perception of reality. Unfortunately, our perceptions are only as accurate as our core beliefs will allow. If you want to escape the perfection trap, you must consider your own perception of perfection when you look at others and consider the idea that there may be a better choice. These individuals are stuck in the perfection trap because their perceptions are based on their beliefs in the way things should be:

1. A young girl looks in the mirror and only sees fat when she is actually quite slim.

2. A composer hears an arrangement of his composition and is totally unsatisfied by the orchestra's performance although the audience and critics hail it as a great achievement.

3. A housewife makes a delectable dinner but feels that it does not meet her standards of taste.

4. A runner who has completed a marathon in a personal best time is not satisfied because he did not win the race.

5. A trader who makes good profits is unhappy with himself because there are still losses.

Just because you have an idea that something should be a certain way does not mean that another person will look at it in the same way. Therefore, universal acceptance of perfection cannot occur because perfection is only in the mind of the individual beholder. For example:

1. A professor once gave me a "C" on a paper. The same paper submitted to another professor received an "A" (don't ask). It was still the same paper.

2. Two traders are trading the same system: one trades it exactly the way he thinks it was meant to be traded while the other does the same thing with different results.

Formula for Getting Out of the Perfection Trap:

Look at the big picture, as well as the details, and choose a plan to make it okay to have the best possible outcome within the resources you presently have and reframe critical self-talk into supportive self-talk.

Conclusion

All too many traders are caught in the perfection trap by the critical voices of important people in their lives, internalized into their own inner self-talk. Afraid to make mistakes, these traders are stuck in a pattern of trying to be perfect while finding it difficult to deal with the uncertainties and risks inherent in trading. The result of this narrow focus on perfection can limit a trader's productivity or can create unnecessary tasks. What if he should make a mistake or take a loss? This fear of not being perfect can be paralyzing for these traders, forcing some to spend years perfecting a system they can never trade or never enjoying the rewards of any amount of profit.

The narrow focus of the perfectionist trader limits his ability to see the possibilities which exist for new solutions and different, even better outcomes. Next time you find yourself in the perfection trap, think from the perspective of how other positive movers and shakers might see your situation. Sometimes, it takes looking through someone else's eyes to discover possibilities.

Chapter 15

LEAVE THE HERD

So, you say you are a genuine, died-in-the-wool, card-carrying contrarian trader? Congratulations! You're the rarest of the rare, one of the natural wonders. The chances are, however, that you are really a "sometimes" contrarian, in which case, you have problems...

All of us are guided by the unique patterns in our behavior, thoughts and emotions that we have developed over time. Our neuro-networking systems are like little soldiers, waiting to take orders and do whatever is expected. When we feel the same feelings over and over again and behave the same way in response to a specific experience, our neuro-networking systems begin to anticipate our reactions. This anticipation creates the patterns by which we live. When these patterns are positive and supportive, they allow us to function smoothly and to do many things at once.

These automatic responses are deeply ingrained in our neurology, which is why, for example, it is so difficult for other people who have driven for many years with standard breaks to adjust to the newer, anti-lock brakes. Driving responses become automatic and unconscious because they require us to respond to similar situations over and over again. Many of the activities of our lives are controlled by these automatic responses, with trading being one of the most important. For better or worse, these unconscious patterns have an enormous influence on your trading results.

Decision-making Responses

Every trader develops a set of patterns in automatic logical and emotional responses which becomes his or her unconscious decision-making system. Positive or negative, these patterns give structure and direction to a person's work. If they arise from poorly conceived ideas or negative and self-destructive feelings and thoughts, the decisions that result will quickly lead a trader in the direction of loss and failure. If these patterns arise

119

from well-conceived ideas and positive, supportive feelings and thoughts, the decisions that result will lead a trader in the direction of success.

What happens, however, if these patterns are suddenly interrupted? Or worse yet, what happens if your pattern is a "sometimes" pattern? This means that your pattern is to do things one way most of the time and the opposite way sometimes, whenever a particular set of conditions takes place.

The Contrarian Trader

In the trading and investment world, there are two competing philosophical camps. The first camp subscribes to the notion that "the trend is your friend" and that you must identify the trend and ride it in the direction that it is going. A trend-rider is an integral part of the crowd, sensing its direction and merging with it. There is a compelling logic to this philosophy because it works very well in the right context. Trend riders can do very well when they buy into a rising market.

The second camp subscribes to the notion that, in order to make real money, you must do what is contrary to the crowd. Thus, to be a contrarian in the markets means that you identify the trend and trade in the opposite direction, buying on widely perceived weakness and selling on widely perceived strength. There is a compelling logic to this philosophy, because it works very well in the right context. Contrarians can profit very nicely by catching the trend as it breaks in the opposite direction, leaving the crowd on the wrong side of the move.

The problem with being a contrarian is that maintaining the contrarian response is difficult for most people, even when they believe in its value and consciously attempt to put it into effect. When the crowd is busily buying or when the crowd is wisely selling, common wisdom seems to defy common sense. When emotion is running high and the pull is very strong in one direction, few traders find anything appealing in the contrarian viewpoint and even the most die-hard contrarian must fight hard to maintain his opposition.

The Sometimes Contrarian Trader

Although most people cannot follow the contrarian path comfortably, a small minority of traders are contrarian by nature. They have always followed the beat of a different drummer, even among supposed contrarians. For example, Theo is a born contrarian. Like most children who are trying to show their independence, Theo said "no" to whatever suggestion was being imposed on him. Most children learn that going against the flow is too uncomfortable and generally give in to the pressure to follow everyone else. Not Theo, his contrarianism became the central response to any social or intellectual movement. In fact, his contrarianism was responsible for his successful career in trading and a generally successful life.

Theo's contrarian position served him well until there was a major shake up in his life: Theo's wife, Lettie, decided to leave him although he was a good provider and a generally good individual, his contrarian nature made it difficult for him to appreciate his wife's needs in their marriage. Despite the fact that Theo loved his wife, whenever he sensed that she needed him to respond in a certain way, he felt pushed and coerced. His contrary nature forced him to respond exactly opposite to her needs, thereby leaving his wife to feel hurt and unloved. When Lettie divorced Theo, his values underwent a major upheaval which forced him to do some soul searching and to change many of his ways. Although these changes made Theo a better person to live with, they also affected his contrarian thinking. As a result, his trading suffered.

What happened? Theo had conditioned his unconscious mind to a set of values and responses to market conditions that were highly contrary to the influence of other traders. His responses were so automatic that he no longer formed thoughts about his judgments and their consequences. When Theo consciously decided to respond differently to the people around him, everything changed.

Imagine Theo's mind as a big computer center with a storehouse of information which feeds back to him exactly the information that Theo gives it. Suppose that Theo had always given it information leading in a certain direction and suddenly presented it with information that led in a totally different direction. What do you think the new output would be like? Theo would probably get some very mixed messages. This is exactly what happened to him when he started to let others influence his thinking.

Another example of a contrarian trader who interrupted his pattern was Ray. As a successful trader whose income was consistent from year to year, he could almost predict what his income would be at the end of the year within a range of $25,000. Unfortunately, when the company for which he worked was bought out by another, stronger company, many of the high standards and rules set by the previous management changed. Ray had to make a decision whether to leave a lucrative client base and go elsewhere and start from scratch or compromise his standards. Ray decided to stay.

Ray attempted to comply with the demands of the new owners. Their ideas about the way he would trade in the future were in total opposition to the way he would normally trade. Naturally, this arrangement was doomed to fail. However, when Ray finally left and went to work for another firm, he was left with a conflicting decision making strategy.

The story for Al was completely different from our previous traders. Al was a contrarian at heart whose pattern had long been one of periodic, mixed messages. Raised in a strict home, Al's immediate response was to rebel against everything that other people required him to do. By the time he started school, he had become a contrarian in nearly every area of his life. He was especially strong in making decisions solve thorny and long-standing problems since he did not resort to tried and true solutions.

Whenever Al felt guilt or remorse, regardless of the circumstances, he resorted to a pattern of thinking that was accommodating to the human influences around him. Guilt made Al lose his self-confidence and his sense that he was morally and intellectually superior to others. Since he was trading with other people's money, whenever he would experience a loss for which he felt personally responsible, his trading would suffer terribly until he was able to regain his sense of confidence or until he was able to come to terms with the loss. The result of Al's periodic vacillations was that he would trade very successfully for many months, creating substantial profits and gains, only to give them all back and sometimes more, whenever he lost faith in himself.

Sometimes, contrarian traders are able to keep their independence alive as long as they are not exposed to outside influences. In Jack's case, he could function as a contrarian trader very successfully until he joined a small group of traders. His contrarian decision making was set upside down when he would hear his associates collectively urging on the market in one direction or another. And some contrarian traders are able to stay on track as long as they avoid specific influences that seem to have special associations for them. It could be a particular trader or analyst, or even a specific news source. Once exposed, these traders break with their patterns and lose all control over their trading.

The Fruits of Inconsistency

If contrarian thinking is working for your trading, this pattern, once established, is an important cornerstone to your trading. All trading methods and systems, regardless of how successful they are will create periodic losses. But, if the system is producing consistent, winning results over the long-term, then periodic losses should not result in inconsistent methods.

The result of periodic vacillation between a contrarian approach to trading and any other approach is to send your unconscious mind a set of mixed messages. When your neurology becomes confused, it cannot perform well and results suffer. This statement applies to every human endeavor. For example, I saw an interview once of an old, respected child psychologist who was asked what the secret to raising emotionally healthy children was. She replied, "Consistency!" When pressed, she said that even if a mother were consistently sad, or grim, or critical, a child would learn how to respond appropriately. But, if one day, a mother is all smiles and the next day she's enraged over the same set of circumstances, a child will become neurotic and unable to make appropriate choices or decisions. The same principle holds with a trader who sends his own inner child a mixed message: "one day we go against the herd and the next day we join it."

Making the Decision to be an "Always" Contrarian Trader

It is not written in stone that you must be a contrarian trader to succeed. What is written is that, to succeed, you cannot be a sometimes contrarian trader. For that reason, you must decide who you are and what kind of a trader you should be. Here is a strategy for discovering your own decision-making strategy:

1. Decide whether your decision-making strategy is bringing you the kind of results that you want in your trading?

2. If it is, then decide what criteria you use for making decisions. Are they based on going with the trend? Or, Are they based on going in opposition to the trend? Or, is it a combination of both under specific circumstances?

3. Once you are clear about your rules for going with or against the common trend, make yourself aware of anything that will influence you to go against your normal patterns. When you are aware of them, you can take steps to avoid these influences such as, newsletters, particular people, or company policy.

Conclusion

Consistency may be condemned as the hobgoblin of little minds, but if the consistent patterns that are established have produced long-term results, then hobgoblins it is! These patterns are broken at a trader's peril, just the way athletes suddenly lose their performance edge when they break successful patterns. This is especially true of traders who have established contrarian practices in their trading. Since the contrarian stance is a difficult one to maintain a contrarian trader must know who he is and why. Then he must learn to identify and avoid the traps in his environment which are ready to trip him up and set him on the path to confusion and lost results.

It's okay to be human,

but prepare yourself for its

shortcomings.

Tip from the coach

Chapter 16

_____

SAVE THEMSELVES

How many traders would want to be rescued from impending disaster? Every one of them, right? Who would want to be destroyed if there were an alternative? Who would?

The truth is, that under certain circumstances, any or all of us would refuse help. In fact, traders who are heading for calamity often refuse to reach out for a lifeline when it is offered. The question is, why?

Too Far Gone to Care

When traders have taken too much of a beating physically and emotionally, something happens to their survival mechanism. It malfunctions. At that point, these traders actually don't want help. Help means work. The offer of help comes with the requirement that you do something, that you extend your hand, metaphorically. But, at the point when traders reach emotional and physical overload, doing anything is too much, even if it means not surviving. When very old people who are faced with loneliness and pain give up, we are not surprised. But, when productive, healthy, young and middle-aged traders with a spouse and children give up, we need to find out why.

How many traders actually reach this point of desperation and overwhelming power-lessness to handle their own rescue? Unfortunately, this unhappy condition occurs in the lives of countless traders; this "quiet desperation" afflicts many of our fellow travelers, as Henry David Thoreau observed a century ago.

"I'm sick and tired of those self help books, all those doctors, gurus, and everyone else who has given me advice all of my life. I just don't want to do it anymore and I just don't want to talk to any of them," Joanne said.

"Right, dear," Bill replied, as his wife went on.

"I know what you're going to tell me. I can do anything if I put my mind to it. But, I just don't want to do it anymore."

"I understand, dear," Bill responded automatically, as he focused harder on the front page of the sports section of the paper.

As a successful floor trader, Joanne had been the kind of person who always believed in doing whatever it took to be a success. She was a top student in school, and highly-motivated at everything she had ever tackled. But, lately she could not see the affirmations on the wall, nor would she pick up the self-help and motivational books in her library that were begging to be read.

The problem was larger than picking up a book for a little inspiration, though. Joanne was not willing to consider the prospect of picking up the phone and calling for help. She knew all of the answers better than most therapists. Unfortunately, she was so deeply buried in depression that even the thought of having to rebuild again was just too much. Although she was still making money in her trading, Joanne was heading for disaster.

I hate to admit that Joanne was one of my clients. But, she will be the first to admit that she had fallen off the wagon and didn't want to get up. Unfortunately, she is not the only trader who has gone through the same progression toward disaster.

When Marvin came for coaching, he had established a long-term success/failure pattern. Like many serious young traders, after coaching he did everything right. As a result, he attracted many bright opportunities, which resulted in success. However, with his new found success, Marvin's workload increased along with his level of stress. Rather than continue the good habits and attitudes which brought him success and protected him from disaster, Marvin chose the self-destructive palliatives of wine, women and song. Marvin is a disaster waiting to happen. However, not only does he know it, he actually longs for it.

What has happened to these fine traders that when they reached the brink of disaster they are unwilling to pull back, even if help is offered?

In Joanne's case, she had worked very hard to get where she was. The last ten years brought her success, but also brought her considerable stress. Each small loss, each minor assault on her self-esteem was not enough to stop her forward momentum. However, the accumulation of all the stresses finally wore Joanne down. She said, "I'm not dying from a gaping wound. I'm bleeding to death from a million little duck bites."

After each setback, Joanne knew exactly which steps to take in readjusting her attitudes and behaviors to pull herself out of trouble. She was a highly disciplined and intuitive person whose personal power was more than sufficient to the task. On some level Joanne was tired of the process of pulling herself out of a slump. It was an old routine and she wanted to move past the cycle, resenting its inevitability like taxes. She didn't have the spirit for it any more than she had the spirit for starting up a business all over again, despite the challenges and excitement it brings.

Like Metal for Endurance

The resilience of the die-hard trader is a lot like the resilience of certain metals that are alloyed to increase their tensile strength and flexibility. These metals can resist seemingly constant and endless stresses without the slightest sign of weakness. Then one day, the wing on an old plane falls off, the bridge collapses, or the tool suddenly snaps from metal fatigue. "Too much stress accumulates over time and the old system shuts down." "I dipped into the well one time too many and the well went dry." "There is nothing left to fight with." These are a brief sampling of the verbal analogies from traders who have been through this experience, when their metal is tested too many times and it finally lets go.

On the other hand, if the stresses are great enough, the metal can let go immediately. Engineers who thought steel-reinforced skyscrapers would withstand major quakes were alarmed when their models collapsed in recent tests. The steel joints, which turned out to be the weakest link, let go and everything toppled. For traders, the same principle can hold, as well. Traders, who think they are immune to stress, are rarely aware of their weakest link which can topple the entire structure if the stresses are great enough.

Enter the Rescuer

Fortunately, there is help for the trader who is heading for disaster. Enter the rescuer. However, this is not an ordinary rescuer, but one who understands the problem and is prepared to take over. This rescuer is not usually found in the yellow pages. Many formally trained psychotherapists, require a potential client to demonstrate a willingness to not only seek help, but to prove their commitment to their therapy. If the therapist does not call back, the potential patient may be expected to demonstrate commitment by taking action to reach the therapist and set up the first appointment. For the trader who is courting disaster and has reached the "point of overwhelm," this is virtually an impossible barrier to cross. This trader no longer cares if he survives. The effort required to "pursue" help is far too great.

Over the last several years, a woman in Canada has received national recognition for saving the lives of young anorexic teenagers who were poised on the brink of death. Typically arriving at her "home" will be a fifty-seven pound teenager who still thinks she is fat and knows that she will die if she doesn't eat. The hospitals will have given up despite every known effort to cajole, force-feed, support or instruct her.

And yet, once she enters this woman's home, this shattered young person will, over the space of months, regain the ability to eat and will gain considerable weight. Eventually, she will be able to go home and live a near normal life. How can this Canadian woman perform such miracles?

When It's Okay to be a Victim

This miracle-worker's secret, in her own words, is that she lets the sufferer understand that she will do everything and that the sufferer does not have to do anything. The dying anorexic is then free to let go of all responsibility and be a total victim, no cares, no worries, no responsibilities. All will be taken care of because the sufferer understands that this wonderful woman knows what must be done and is completely capable of doing it. In fact, there is no fear of the outcome because "everything will be taken care and everything will be okay."

The sense of relief for these patients is indescribable. The effort to keep control has become too terrible for them to maintain - just like it has for the trader in the "state of overwhelm." Their metal has been tested too long but, instead of collapsing altogether, a very strong but gentle hand has reached up and provided the support that keeps everything together. This process allows the overwhelmed patient or the overwhelmed trader to let go, without fear and without effort. Only then, can the person who is overwhelmed find the relief that he desperately needs and healing can slowly take place.

In our sophisticated world where personal responsibility is a prerequisite for personal growth, success and survival, there is actually a time when it is appropriate to be a victim. That time is when you reach the "point of overwhelm." At the stops along the way, taking personal responsibility is the appropriate action. But once the metal lets go, the energy required to put the pieces back together in a person's life is no longer there. All that is left is hopelessness, guilt, grief and resignation as well as a desire to let it all go up in flames. Instead of succumbing to disaster in this way, the overwhelmed trader needs to let go of all responsibility, sink slowly into a state of victim-hood, and, let the rescuer do the job.

Finding the Right Rescuer

For the rescue to take place, a number of vital conditions must exist. Most importantly, this process requires that the trader trust his or her rescuer completely and without question. For this reason, an ordinary person with an agenda, or impatience under the surface, cannot do it. For the young anorexic, the parents are usually too tormented by fear, grief, anger and frustration to be the rescuer. The rescuer need not be trained in any special way. However, the rescuer must be capable of convincing the victim that he or she knows what must be done, has the ability to do it, and can be trusted completely to do it right, so that the victim can let go and take the time to heal.

Who can perform this rescue for you if you need it? The best person is the one who loves you the most - your spouse, parent, or best friend. When these people take over the role and are equipped to do the job properly, they are the best rescuers possible. After all, no one else knows you like they do or has as much at stake in your survival. The problem comes when the people closest to you do not understand the role or are unable or unwilling to take on the role and do it right. When the stress that creates the overwhelm state is major and immediate, those around you are often more sympathetic and willing to do what has to be done. Unfortunately, the process of overwhelm too often results from a "million duck bites," which leave the people closest to you either unaware of the danger ahead or no longer sympathetic - even if they are capable of doing the job.

This point is graphically illustrated by the case of someone who loses his home from a hurricane and is overwhelmed with the loss. His friends and family collect around him in his hour of disaster, take care of him and perform the needed rescue. But what happens if this same individual is in imminent danger of losing that same home through foreclosure? His family and friends, have watched his financial woes develop from afar, and have distanced themselves. Even though his state of desperation is extreme and he is nearly suicidal, those closest to him may be farthest from offering a rescue.

It is often at this point of overwhelm in a trader's life that he calls for help. But this call for help often comes masked by so much cynicism, distrust and hopelessness that it is difficult to assess the actual need. If a trader is too exhausted emotionally and physically to catch the lifeline when offered, the process of providing the rescue by long-distance can be daunting. If no one in this trader's personal life can help, how can he trust someone he doesn't even know? So, he hesitates and throws up barriers, making the rescue nearly impossible. His skepticism causes him to test and keep testing. Unfortunately, only he knows the right answers. Then, after halfheartedly playing his hand, he suddenly lays his cards face down and concedes the game, daring you to have a real winning hand. He surrenders the last vestiges of control because, just as the young patient in Canada, he is finally convinced that he can safely let go and someone is there to put the pieces back together again.

Conclusion

The way out of impending disaster for a trader in emotional overwhelm is the rescuer who understands the situation. This rescuer must be absolutely trustworthy to do what has to be done and to relieve the trader of the need to make decisions, and take responsibility. In this state, a trader needs to be able to let go and be a completely dependent, helpless victim. This letting go can be very difficult for men and women who have valiantly held the course through losses and setbacks, trusting only themselves to take responsibility. Once the exhausted trader is relieved of the need to endure any more stress, rebuilding can begin.

SECTION III

Traders Who Feel...

You are the one who created the fear.

If it's not appropriate, let it go.

If you cannot, get help.

Tip from the coach

Chapter 17

FEAR

Are you afraid of failure? Are you afraid of success? If you are, then you have a lot of company. More than fifty percent of the hundreds of traders who have taken our fifteen-page, comprehensive psychological evaluation have trouble with the notion of making money. In this evaluation, they answer questions that are designed to clarify their feelings about success and failure.

At the very heart of a trader's ambition to succeed is the fear that either he might fail or that he might succeed. And many traders are afraid of both, a situation I call "the double whammy."

The Pain of Failure

The possibility of failure is a day-to-day reality for traders. Along with this possibility comes the ever-present fear of the pain that is associated with failure, which, for most traders, equals loss in the markets. The feelings associated with loss can also include the following fears:

- The fear of being found unworthy or incompetent
- The fear of no longer being accepted
- The fear of being wrong
- The fear of being dislocated and having to deal with the unknown

Because few of us are prepared to deal with painful feelings, even the most well-balanced traders from supportive homes and successful backgrounds are not immune to the effects of fear of failure on their lives. The pain of loss can mean the fear of losing present comfortable lifestyles, accumulated possessions, and the love and support of family members.

The Pain of Success

The fear of success can have as many root causes as the fear of failure. Even though success can mean the accumulation of more and better things, it can also threaten the things you've accumulated in the past that have meaning for you, as well as the activities of the people in your life. In addition, success can be associated with losses in the past, so that the prospect of success can create the fear of anticipated loss and pain.

The Pull of Our Roots

As the second son of immigrant parents, Ben had grown up in a close, ethnic Brooklyn neighborhood in which everyone on the block knew everyone else. His mother and father, Ruth and Max, had fled to America from Germany during the early years of World War II, bringing with them a strong work ethic and a determination to give their children the foundation for a prosperous future. After school Ben and his older brother, David, worked in the family delicatessen, which supported their family. Their parents, subscribed to a social dogma which required them to educate their children in order to "make them proud." For Ruth and Max to hold their heads up in public, their sons needed to go to top colleges, then become professionals and marry college-educated women of the same faith.

The Black Sheep

David, the older brother, had fulfilled the family expectations by being accepted into a top Eastern school, going to law school, and marrying an ambitious young woman of the same religious background. Unfortunately, Ben was not quite as well-prepared to fulfill the silent family contract as his older brother. Ben went to a state university where he met and married Linda, a beautiful and wealthy young woman. The fact that Linda's family was from a different religious and ethnic background, however, distressed poor Ruth and Max like a sore that would not heal. Although Ben was keenly aware of their disappointment, he was very much in love with Linda.

Then, to make matters worse, Ben announced to his parents that he had decided to become a gambler! Well, actually, Ben told them he was going to become a trader. But, to many people who are unfamiliar with the financial markets, trading is the same as gambling. Not only were Ruth and Max mortified, but Linda and her parents were deeply anxious about Ben's financial security. To alleviate their fears, Ben did everything he could to assure his parents, in-laws and young wife that he was approaching this under-taking with solid training and self-discipline. He promised that he would make a lot of money and that they would be very proud of him.

With so much pressure to succeed, Ben launched his trading career.

The Double Whammy Personified

It was not difficult for Ben to accept the fact that he was afraid of failing. Surrounded by pictures of his family on the walls and tabletops, Ben easily conceded that he could not bear to fail for fear of losing their love and respect and for fear of causing them financial embarrassment. The pain associated with failure was a strong motivating force to keep Ben on the straight and narrow path. But, sometimes, a string of losses creates too much fear for a trader to manage. At that point, he may find himself afraid to pull the trigger or second guessing his system. This fear explained some of the problems Ben was experiencing, but not all.

Eventually, Ben began to open up about his deep feelings of attachment for the life he lived as a boy because it represented someone else taking responsibility for him. Unlike David who was so eager to fulfill his parents' dreams for him, Ben needed the connection with community and that sense of security that comes with tradition. He enjoyed the closeness of the old neighborhood and the easy interactions of the struggling families who shared what little they had with each other. As Ben became more successful, he moved into a neighborhood in which families lived farther apart, not only in distance but in thinking. He sensed a lack of genuine caring and community in the new neighborhoods of the affluent.

The truth began to dawn on Ben as he talked. For him, success represented the loss of the things that gave him joy. The question that was lurking in the back of his mind was, what other goodies would success take away? Ben was being attacked from both directions. The double whammy.

Stuck in the Water

Traders will often experience inner conflicts, such as the need to stick to a discipline competing with the need to resist any form of control, or the desire for security competing with the desire for emotional drama. In each case, the result is the same. These conflicts bring the trader to a state of immobilization, which results in progressively more damaging losses.

For Ben and traders like him, the conflicting fears of failure and success are like being afraid to go forward as well as backward. The result is that you cannot move. Opportunities to make money are avoided while opportunities to take losses multiply. This perilous situation is the one in which Ben found himself.

In Ben's case, his set of competing fears did not neutralize each other. Instead, they built on each other's strength, much like a lethal storm surge builds on the crest of the waves from high tide. This double dose of fear can create so much free-floating anxiety in a trader that he can develop panic attacks, much like Ben began to experience. Since every action resulted in an unwanted outcome, Ben felt like he was ready to explode.

What increased the stress for Ben was that the people he needed to reach out to for understanding and support were the very ones who were creating the stress. Therefore, Ben was afraid that they would begin to see that something was wrong and this would lead to others knowing that he was not in control of his direction.

This dilemma was soon solved for Ben. Although he could conceal his financial troubles for a while, the panic attacks made it abundantly clear that something was seriously wrong. At his wife's urgings, Ben finally sought help.

Recognizing the Signs

Like Ben, many traders have complex motivations and competing emotions that muddy the water for them. Instead of seeing the cause of their problems, they are confused and confounded. Addressing one side of the conflict only increases the distress from the other side. How then can a trader recognize that he is dealing with a double whammy?

1. One of the telltale signs that a trader is afraid of both winning and losing is in the resistance his trading has to improving. When a trader has tried everything he knows how to do to improve his trading but his results will not budge, a strong possibility exists that he is working against a powerful inner conflict that is keeping him stalled.

2. Another possible sign is when a trader is reluctant to solve the problem or to even admit that a problem exists at all. When these two competing fears are dominant in a trader's life, it is difficult for a trader to look at them for fear of completely losing what little sense of control he has left. In addition, many traders are afraid to admit to either one of these fears for fear of opening up the issue of self-worth:

    - If I am afraid of losing, does that mean I am not certain of my worth or my abilities?

    - Or if I am afraid of success, does this mean that I am not worthy of success?

3. A third possible sign is when the level of emotional charge increases to an alarming degree so that anxiety levels are creating panic attacks, or when rage episodes or crying episodes are out of control. These distressing symptoms, which call for immediate and professional help, are often the result of internal conflicts which place an unbearable burden on the trader.

Taking the Wind out of the Whammy

Once you have decided that you are being sandbagged from both sides, what can you do to correct the situation or gain some leverage over these opposing forces?

1. The first step is to come to acknowledge that these competing fears and feelings exist in you. Many traders are afraid to acknowledge these fears for fear of bringing up the deeper issues of self-worth. However, these fears of both success and failure are the natural, normal responses to the complexities of our life experiences. Understanding these fears dispels the cloak of secrecy our subconscious uses to conceal these fears from us in order to protect us from further pain.

2. The second step is to weight the scales so heavily in favor of success that we give our subconscious minds enough ammunition to win the conflict that is raging inside us.

3. Then, take a look at the list of payoffs for failing. For each payoff, construct an argument that refutes the benefit, for example: In Ben's case, his desire to stay close to the old neighborhood is really an unrealistic, child's romanticism of what it was like. Would he really want to live in a one-bathroom, two-bedroom walk-up without central air-conditioning complete with roaches and rats?

4. Seek professional help if you are unable to resolve these issues by yourself, especially if you are dealing with pervasive anxiety or other negative emotional states.

Conclusion

Although many traders are dealing with the fear of failure or the fear of success, a combination of these fears can be paralyzing to a trader as they prevent him from using any positive strategies in his trading. These fears build upon each other, while very often concealing from the trader their actual origin. Nevertheless, this set of conflicting fears leaves signs for us to read. And best of all, successful strategies are available to take the wind out of the double whammy.

Chapter 18

_____

GREED

It is common knowledge that greed is one of the two great challenges a trader must conquer in order to succeed over the long haul. (The other challenge being fear.) Greed is what leads many people to trading in the first place, and for some it drives them to great heights of monetary success. Why, then, is greed considered one of the major downfalls of traders?

As defined by Webster's dictionary, greed is a selfish desire for more than one needs or deserves. By this definition, most average traders would fall into the greedy category because most traders have met their basic needs and are now seeking to meet their desires. But, to understand the problem of greed in trading, we have to look deeper than this definition. Here are definitions of trader's greed by those who warn against it in trading.

1. Traders holding trades for greater profits, disregarding prudent money management because they are not satisfied with the profits already in a trade.

2. Traders wanting to make money only for the sake of making money and not additionally for the many ways that money can benefit those around them.

3. Traders not having positive intentions for the use of money.

4. Traders who push for greater profits because they believe "I'm not successful unless I'm better than him."

5. Traders with an uncontrollable appetite for money.

6. Traders trying to get away with more then they feel they deserve.

You may or may not agree with these definitions of greed in trading, but interestingly, they all tend to beg the question:

139

**Even if you are successful in creating considerable wealth,
if your life in general is not successful, what is the point?**

Smoke Screen

Sid wanted to talk to someone. "I did it again," he said. "I gave back everything. I was looking forward to a $250,000 year-end bonus and now it's gone." Unfortunately, this event was part of an ongoing pattern in Sid's trading.

"I saw an opportunity and blew off risk management because I didn't want to give part of the profits away if I could have it all. I broke my rule that I would peel off part of the profits on the way up, and I'm back in the same old situation."

Contrary to appearances, Sid is not an undisciplined trader. In fact, he had been doing everything right. He had given up smoking, had limited his drinking, and was routinely exercising and eating right. If anything, he had pushed self-denial to its very limits by working 16 or more hours a day without giving himself any periodic breaks or rewards, "What are you doing now?" I asked. "I'm sitting here at my desk smoking a cigarette," he replied, "and I just want you to know that it feels great."

By denying himself positive pleasures and releases that would compensate him for the self-destructive pleasures he had given up, Sid's mind and body were pleading for a break. Like people who are working so hard that they desperately want to get sick so that they can stop and rest, Sid had broken loose of his harness and was out of control. "Interestingly enough," he said to me, "while I'm pissed, upset, and angry, there is a part of me that just doesn't give a damn and just wants to keep smoking this cigarette."

Another aspect of Sid's situation was that he had no goals for the end-of-year bonus money that he wanted. He had planned no prize at the end of the year for doing well for himself or for others. The money was desired for its own sake. Sid had not attached a continued goal along with the money that would inspire him to repeat his performance. He was working hard and denying himself pleasures without attaching meaningful rewards to his efforts, except for the monetary bonus.

Sid had made a choice. Instead of taking the path that is built by self-discipline with positive rewards, he had chosen the path that is built by greed and leads to self-destruction. Why? Because by going on the path of greed, Sid got to experience the excitement that he was missing in his life by neglecting to provide alternative pleasures and excitements.

At this point, Sid needed to distance himself from his situation and to refocus his energy. I instructed him to do the following: to sit in a bathtub with no water and no clothes on for a minimum of forty-five minutes, with a clock close at hand, and to really enjoy the experience of misery. And, of course, to get several much-needed lessons. He was to call me the following day.

140

"So," I asked the next morning, " how was the tub experience?"

"I didn't do the bathtub thing," he said, " but I took care of it in another way. I went out and got drunk and enjoyed the amorous attentions of a beautiful blonde. And I'm smoking like a chimney."

"How do you feel?" I asked. "I feel temporarily fine," he replied and then added, "When I don't, I'll do the bathtub thing." "Good," I said, but I suspect that when that happens, Sid will not be alone.

Creating a Balance

There is an important lesson here in greed management. In the past, whenever I had instructed Sid to take off weekends, to enjoy himself, to spend his money in a way that would enhance his life, his reply had been, "Don't have the time, don't have the money." When I had told him that he must follow the rule of money management so that he wouldn't get into trouble again, he told me, "Handled!" A trader whose life is balanced by hard work, self-discipline and the positive pleasures in life is not a good target for the lure of greed. Greed's most likely victims are the traders whose lives are missing the elements of meaning and balance. Positive goals and positive pleasures keep a trader on track with his self-discipline, following his rules of money management and living.

Todd, another trader with whom I worked, had a pattern of falling off the wagon and succumb-ing to greed whenever his energy fell below a certain level. As he worked himself into a state of exhaustion, he would be the very model of self-discipline and self-denial. Then, depleted of his reserves, he would find himself fantasizing about instantaneous riches as a trade took off. Like Sid, Todd would throw caution to the wind, as he took the (usually short) roller coaster ride up and then down. He confided to me that he knew what he was doing was self-destructive, but he did he not care. He actually longed for an experience that was defiant, destructive and totally wild.

Like Sid, Todd had a vulnerability that had to be constantly reinforced. Sid's vulnerability was his need for meaningful rewards and pleasurable releases. Todd's vulnerability was his need to protect himself physically and emotionally. Whenever Todd managed the stress in his life and took the time to build his physical and emotional strength, he escaped the constant challenges to his self-discipline. Once again, for a trader to withstand the lure of greed, he must keep his life in a state of equilibrium.

Prone to Greed

All traders are prone to greed, because all of us are capable of reaching a point in our emotional or physical state where we are susceptible to its seductive quality. But what is it that greed does to lure us into its grasp when we are so vulnerable? Greed, like all addictions, promises to fill up the empty places inside us, to make the discomfort go away. The moment you are aware that you have that empty place, you become susceptible to any number of addictions: to food, to gambling, to drugs, to alcohol, to stealing or shopping. That empty space is more likely to develop when you are in a low-energy state, either physically or emotionally. When you are in that low-energy state, the need you have at the time feels as though it can be satisfied by having more and more.

Of course, you can have an abundance of material things and not be greedy at all. Many wealthy people have accumulated great wealth without craving more and more because having money was not the issue. The personal devotion to a particular profession for which a person is eminently suited has created immense wealth for people like Michael Jordan and Steven Jobs. Success and wealth are not the issues in greed; the needing of more and more is the issue.

When people have the kind of negative energy associated with wanting more, of hoping, wanting, and pushing for something that is not there, a change takes place inside. Suddenly, logic and reasoning are no longer able to moderate destructive urges. At that moment, the only thing the individual wants is to have more. But, having more will not satisfy these cravings because what is really needed is not material things.

The Greediest Trader in the Pen

"Leo" is a high profile trader with an international reputation. In addition to his reputation as a market genius, he is considered to be a devoted father and husband, a pillar of his community and his church. For many years, he has capitalized on this reputation, attracting thousands of traders, wanna-be traders, and investors. The truth about Leo is that he is consumed with greed to a degree that would make the Devil himself blush. Over the years, to satisfy his greed, Leo has advanced from cutting corners to committing outright fraud. Emboldened by the inability of his victims to stop him legally or seek redress, he has used his stable of unethical lawyers to thwart the courts, the government, and his most trusted associates. He has cheated the people closest to him in the name of money. Having secreted millions of his ill-gotten dollars in foreign countries, he has even developed an escape plan that could be put into action on a moment's notice.

From the outside, it looks like Leo has gotten away with it, that the downside of greed has no sting for him. Unburdened by a conscience, he does not suffer the pangs of guilt and fear of discovery felt by ordinary individuals. A person who can so convincingly lie to others can also convince himself that he has done nothing wrong. But, there is always a price to pay for greed even for those traders who look like they are getting away with it.

The True Cost of Greed

Despite the fact that greed can generate the energy and passion to drive a trader to success, there is a price to be paid. When a trader is in that low-energy state that invites greed, an internal part of the trader's unconscious mind will strike out to get his attention by creating an emotional pain. This pain will always come in the form of a loss - - of money, health, love, self-esteem or respect. The loss of money will follow inevitably from a pattern of breaking trading rules as greed assumes control. In Leo's case, his trading results are actually mediocre. He is so insecure about his trading, due to his inability to stick to his rules or to trust himself, that he hires traders to trade for him. If he had to survive on his own trading, he would be broke in no time at all.

The other set of negative results from greed are the ones which affect the people in a trader's life who have been manipulated, deceived and cheated in his unbridled race to get more. In this area of his life, Leo has a tremendous number of people who would like to see him suffer retribution. So much negative energy focused on an individual can produce interesting results over time.

Nevertheless, there are those who still feel that Leo has gotten away with it in this lifetime. But, I find it hard to believe, having worked with traders for so long. Even though he is surrounded by all the money and things that he has, there is still not some place inside him that knows what he is and feels it.

Money and Energy

Money is not just inert paper or metal currency. It has a life of its own. Money carries either positive energy or negative energy. The positive energy from money brings relief from the human plagues of pain, sickness, hopelessness and discomfort. It brings education, enlightenment, and the elevation of the human spirit through beauty in art, music, architecture, etc. It seeks to spread its benefits around to wherever it can bring happiness. This good comes from a sense of abundance and a love of the process that made the money in the first place.

On the other hand, a trader who loves to trade and who is filled with a sense of completeness about himself and his life can make a great deal of money and not be possessed by it. And because this successful trader is not owned by his money, he uses it to create jobs for others as he hires them to support his business and home, and he shares it with those whose lives will be improved by it. The more he shares it and gives it away, the more he seems to bring into his life. This is abundance and good energy.

Conclusion

Greed is a double-edged sword for traders. While enabling a trade to cut a swath through the market jungle toward success, greed simultaneously sabotages a trader's efforts by cutting down the very self-disciplines, relationships and values that support trading and give meaning to success. All traders are vulnerable to greed if they reach that low state of emotional and/or physical energy that throws them out of balance and creates a feeling of need. At that moment, if the opportunity arises, a vulnerable trader can feel that having more, and needing more, will fill up that need. Like all addictions, greed can take over long before a trader realizes what has happened. The long-term results are loss in the markets, in relationships, in health, or in self-esteem. But the best defense for a trader against the temptations of greed is to create a balanced life that supports him physically, emotionally, and spiritually. Unlike the out-of-balance trader who trades from greed, a trader who trades from a sense of completeness accumulates positive energy, shares his success, and attracts more abundance to him.

Chapter 19

TOO MUCH

You are probably not a manic/depressive, so why are you acting like one?

Over the years, I have asked many traders this question and you may be asking yourself this question, too. The unique stresses that are placed on traders makes them particularly susceptible to wide emotional swings. I call these swings "The Emotional Volatility Trap."

The path into the "Emotional Volatility Trap" is a particularly easy one for traders because the unique demands of their professional lives tend to magnify the stresses they experience. The result is a pattern of extreme emotional outbursts and mood swings which cause them to live in a state of hyper-agitation. The smallest event or irritation can then cause them to lose not only control over their emotions but control over their trading as well. This loss of control causes them to try harder to correct their trading errors, thereby creating even more stress, which accelerates their downhill slide.

What are some of the signs?

1. Extreme emotional behavior, e.g., increased irritability, irrationality, impatience, gambling.

2. Dramatic negative changes in moods, thinking, attitudes, beliefs, values, habits.

3. Dramatic changes in health, e.g., colds, flu, pains, insomnia.

4. Feelings of being driven and/or always seem to be racing to catch up.

What causes these emotional extremes?

If you liken your mind and body to a bank account into which you deposit the accumulated assets of health, vitality, strength and energy, then everything you do or say or think will determine your daily balance. A substantial balance will provide you with the mental and physical assets needed to trade with a steady mind and complete emotional control.

On the other hand, if your physical/emotional bank account has been overdrawn by the continuous demands of stress and poor living habits or by the sudden, overwhelming withdrawals that come with major traumatic events, the penalty is what I call "The Emotional Volatility Trap." When this happens, you suddenly find yourself experiencing dramatic emotional extremes, as if you are on a roller coaster ride without a stop. For many traders, this means that at one minute they are in the throes of a violent emotional outburst of anger and the next moment, they are hunkered down in the throes of fear or despair. If they are not yelling in frustration, they are yelling for joy. The smallest thing can trigger these swings of emotion. While bystanders are aware of the inappropriateness of the reactions, the person who is playing them out cannot see what is happening. He can no longer take proactive steps. He is merely a reaction-machine.

Nick's Story

When Nick first started calling me, his hyperventilated stories were always accompanied by the dramatic emotional extremes of a trader who has fallen into the "Emotional Volatility Trap." Either he was ecstatic because he was certain he was on the road to riches or in the depths of depression because his trading world was turning against him.

Nick found his niche in life when he was taken on a school outing to the Chicago Board of Trade. Until then, Nick was an unchallenged student who stole book reports just to get by in school. After his introduction to the markets, his new passion for knowing more about the markets gave him an insatiable appetite for learning. He took on as many part-time jobs as he could so that he could buy the tools, equipment and study material to become a successful trader. As a senior in high school, he ran his trading profits from $2,000 up to $4,000 in one year. To Nick, graduation represented the freedom to live his dream full-time. Recognizing their son's talent, Nick's parents gave him the family savings to manage. When Nick tripled his trading capital in one year, the news spread rapidly. Soon, other family members and friends wanted to invest their money with him.

How did the dream become a nightmare?

From the beginning, when Nick found trading, he was driven to succeed. With each success, he felt even more pressure to do better. With such an intense focus on his goal, Nick gradually let go of all of the healthy interests in his life. Like many traders whose passion for trading begins to take over their lives, Nick had become obsessed.

In the morning, he would wake up at 6 a.m. and not go to sleep until 12 p.m. Most of this time was spent either trading or studying trading, while gobbling down pots of coffee lifted by nicotine- stained fingers. Even when he should have been sleeping, he very often ended up tossing and turning, thinking about the next day's trades. Nick was now trading out of his own apartment, and as a result, junk food was the preferred menu. Exercise was limited to his keystrokes on the computer of which there were many. On Friday night, he became the weekend warrior. His reward for the week was bragging about his trades while shooting tequila with beer chasers. He would follow this with the lady of the week-end. Nick was twenty-five going on forty. The result of all of this physical abuse was that Nick's trading began to suffer. He had always been able to rely on his trading results, but not any more. Suddenly, Nick lost faith in himself and in his system. When that happened, the warrior activity that characterized his weekends took over the week as well. Nick was in "The Emotional Volatility Trap," well overdrawn in his bank account of life and heading for mind and body bankruptcy.

When you feel vulnerable, you are more likely to be volatile.

Nick has lots of distinguished company.

There are many ways for a trader to fall into the emotional volatility trap. While Nick took the hard, straight path to trouble, Oscar landed in the trap by changing lanes. Oscar was a passionate person who had been obsessed with possessions from childhood. Oscar always had to have the most and the best. Fortunately, trading supported his obsessive lifestyle and he acted as if trading would give him an endless flow of money. For fifteen years, Oscar provided his family a very comfortable lifestyle, which required twenty-five thousand dollars a month to support. But floor trading is a young man's game and, even-tually, Oscar grew tired of standing on the floor. He was beginning to feel like he was in the center of a crowd of very loud and very large Wagnerian opera singers. He was convinced that his fellow floor traders would resort to any trick to create the smallest advantage in the pit. With his senses on overload, Oscar left the pit, not thinking of the consequences.

If Oscar had felt pressed and squeezed in the pit, he was now the proverbial lamb in the wolfish world of computer trading. He also felt the need to maintain his family's lifestyle, and he was afraid to show his fears even to himself. Finally, the inevitable came when he had to face his family and tell them that they would have to live on half the income. He didn't dare let them know that he probably could not even afford this sum. How was he going to produce the needed income immediately without an off-the-floor system that worked? Add fear, guilt and family upset... Oscar was now in "The Emotional Volatility Trap."

Both Oscar and Nick arrived in the trap by obvious means. Sometimes, however, the most unlikely traders fall into the trap because of a series of unexpected losses. Jeff was an exceptional money manager for ten years. He had a sharp memory and seemed to be able to do a multitude of tasks three times as fast and with more perception than the average person. He looked like the epitome of health. Everything in his life was working until last year when he hit the wall. It was his first losing year. He needed a rescuer, but he couldn't let anyone know about his desperation because he was the pillar for everyone around him. Jeff fell into "The Emotional Volatility Trap."

So what is this trap?

The Emotional Volatility Trap results from the build-up of negative influences on one's physical and mental health. This accumulation can come over a long period of time, or be triggered by one major event that affects all parts of one's life. When I looked through my files, I was surprised to realize that one in three clients was in "The Emotional Volatility Trap" when they called me.

Causes of being in an emotional mental trap:

1. No business plan

2. Not enough trading capital

3. Any sudden change in lifestyle, e.g., moving, additional people in your environment

4. Any serious loss, e.g., death, divorce, bankruptcy, property, investment

5. Any project where you have over extended yourself, e.g., opening a new business, building a house

6. Health problems for you or a loved one, e.g., accident, illness, feelings of insecurity

7. Relationship problems, e.g., separation, bad or non-communication, betrayal, unfulfilled expectations, incompetence, family or business disputes

8. Legal and IRS problems

9. Internal or external negative dialogue or information

Why do so many traders stay in the trap until it's too late?

Unfortunately, many traders who fall into this trap fail to take any positive action to pull themselves out of it. Without taking positive steps to counteract the problem, the situation continues to deteriorate until something happens to bring about a natural end to the cycle. Either the trader is washed out of the market for good or something catastrophic happens such as a serious illness or the end of a marriage. The trader is then forced to take action, but often, the damage is done. For that reason, it is important for traders to look at their reasons for not correcting the problem before it is too late.

The Excuses "E" and their Rebuttal "R":

E.　　I don't have enough money.

R.　　What will your finances look like if you lose your health?

E.　　I don't have enough time to deal with my emotions right now.

R.　　You'll have plenty of time when you have to give up everything, but will it be too late?

E.　　My family members feel threatened by me getting outside help, these problems should be kept inside the family.

R.　　Are you comfortable in telling them all of your personal issues, and do they have the ability to assist you in making the changes necessary to overcome these issues?

E.　　I can handle my own problems.

R.　　Can you make the changes necessary and follow through on a consistent long-term basis, or do you find that your enthusiasm wanes and you fall back into old habits? Do you give excuses for not handling your issues now?

E.　　There really isn't a problem. It is only temporary.

R.　　Your trading will be temporary if this problem is not addressed immediately.

E.　　Too many quacks out there are eager to take my money.

R.　　True, get references, ask for evidence of competence.

E.　　It is part of the territory.

R.　　True, and this is what washes out most traders.

Although the emotional roller coaster ride can be disabling to a trader's professional and personal life, I have seen many traders pull themselves out of this trap in an amazingly brief period of time, if they are determined to do so. This process requires a trader to take proactive steps on his behalf.

How to deal with the problems associated with emotional extremes:

1. Recognize that the problem exists and has serious consequences i.e., health, financial, relationship, etc.

151

2. If possible, let your family and friends assist you with handling part of your load.

3. Re-evaluate your life and realize what is bringing you stress. If you can't eliminate the cause of the stress directly, then find a way to deal with it or reduce it.

4. Change to a healthy lifestyle. Get extra sleep. If you cannot, take a relaxing hot bath or shower, read a fiction book, listen to a relaxation tape.

5. Eat healthy foods. All foods have energy values. In general, eat food that is not processed. Eliminate caffeine, alcohol, and stimulant drugs.

6. Exercise. Meditate every morning.

7. Cut all unnecessary activity from your schedule and prioritize.

8. Realize you might need professional assistance. When possible, work with someone who has experience helping traders.

Our three traders, Nick, Oscar, and Jeff, all took these same steps out of the volatility trap. Nick now drinks his beer without the chasers. He has a steady girlfriend, exercises regularly and takes relaxing vacations. Oscar found his true niche trading for a top firm and is making very good money and feeling a needed sense of security. Jeff has just recently started out on the path to paying back the deficits in his emotional bank account. Nevertheless, he is doing well in his trading.

Conclusion

Emotional Volatility is part of the game of trading. Unfortunately, far too many traders fail to take timely remedial action. They are afraid to lose even more control over their lives by acknowledging the problem and by placing their fate in the hands of others. Fortunately, the road out of the "Emotional Volatility Trap" can be a quick one. Positive results can be immediate once a trader acknowledges the problem and reduces the stresses in his life. Exercise, healthful eating and sleeping habits, and daily meditation are necessary to bring an emotionally volatile trader back into a state of balance.

Over the short run, the spurts of energy from this highly emotional state can appear to help a trader to focus and perform at sudden high levels. Over the long run, however, the trader who is balanced and calm will out-perform, out-trade and out-last the volatile trader.

Chapter 20

_____

OUT OF CONTROL

So, you want to control the markets?

That's understandable. You've got a lot of company. Having control would mean making unlimited profits while eliminating all losses - a great fantasy.

And you want to control your spouse, your children, your life, as well? That's understandable, too. Control over the people and other influences in your life would eliminate all risk, all pain and all need for compromise. Unfortunately, or fortunately, it does not work that way.

As a trader, the only thing you can control is yourself. The market is beyond the control of any single individual, even large players have gotten stung thinking they had control over a certain market. The problem of needing control comes as a result of being out of control. Until you know that the probabilities for your outcome are positive and you are secure in that knowledge, you are going to remain out of control. Then, having lost control over yourself, you will be wishing and grasping for control of things outside of yourself.

A Society Out-of-control

In Afghanistan, when the Taliban took over the country, it was a dramatic example of a people who needed and wanted control. These fundamentalist Muslim revolutionaries were insecure about their women who, unchecked by political and social sanctions, had advanced to a state of economic and emotional independence. Deeply threatened, these poorly educated and provincial people forced their women into a form of bondage. Women who were working as doctors, nurses, administrators, and managers were suddenly required to cover their bodies from head to toe. They were forbidden to leave their homes for outside activities. As a result, hospitals closed, orphanages were left in the care of children, and many of the institutions necessary to their society were shut down. This situation was created in the name of a religion whose founder would have repudiated both the means and the ends.

So, why did this happen? Isolated from the global mainstream, this group of people did not develop the resources of education, skills and abilities which would make them feel that they could trust the outcome to be in their favor without the use of force. So, the only way to run the government and maintain control was by brutalizing and demeaning other people. In the final outcome, of course, everyone lost. The Taliban, which stole control with their guns, was then forced to look over its shoulders for someone trying to steal their ill-gotten political control back from them.

From A to T

How does this situation in Afghanistan lead us to trading and making money in the markets? It is easy to see the loss of control in others and the desperate measures they take in order to regain a sense of control over their lives. It is far more difficult to see the process in ourselves. However, 20/20 self-vision is essential for success, since the emotional component of trading is a variable which can wreak so much havoc in a trading career. As soon as a trader thinks he needs to control the market and attempts to do so, he begins to lose money. His focus is diverted from his own expertise to a perceived opponent who has a personal vendetta against him. As a result, the trader's emotions overtake good judgment.

In This Corner: Trader Andy

Andy was attracted to trading for the unfortunate reason that he was interested in gambling. Since childhood, Andy had followed professional boxing. He was a regular at the ring, betting heavily on each match. Once he learned about trading, he saw the markets as a quick way to make an economic killing with little effort on his own. In school, Andy had never been interested in putting effort into his studies; because he was intelligent, his school work was easy for him. This pattern was reinforced many times over in his life, even in his gambling. So, with the expectation that he would win instantly in the markets, Andy placed his first few trades. To his surprise, sometimes he lost. In fact, Andy lost more than he won.

What happened next is also a common pattern. Andy developed a personal relationship with the market. The market became an opponent whom he attempted to dominate or outwit. Andy was convinced that his opponent was out to get him and when he lost, he saw it as proof. From his interest in boxing, he began to see the market as a giant boxer who had weaknesses and bad moves that he could exploit. On the other hand, his nemesis also had a long right hook and was capable of getting in some underhanded blows to the kidneys and the head. As time went by, Andy became obsessed with the idea that he was in a death struggle with a real opponent and not an inanimate aggregate of business activities. In the meantime, Andy was not working on himself and his skills to become an expert trader. Instead, he was spending his energy engaged in a personal battle to control his giant. He felt the only way he was going to beat this giant was with insider information. So, he followed the picks of the self-proclaimed experts. Naturally, he took some powerful blows which nearly catapulted him out of the ring altogether. When he finally concluded that he was over-matched, he took the situation personally and became enraged with a sense of powerlessness and victimization. Andy was truly out of control.

The "Control-freak"

In Andy's case, he came into trading without skills and never attempted to gain any. Instead, he attempted to control the markets and the outcome with the force of his personality. But, in Ian's case, his attempt to control the market was through a different avenue.

Ian came to trading from medicine, where having control seemed like a professional entitlement. As a highly skilled and respected doctor, he had maintained god-like control over his working world. Then, once he went home, he demanded complete control over the lives of his family. This control over others seemed natural to Ian, who came from a family in which his every move had been closely monitored and controlled by his parents. Not only had they chosen his profession for him, but they also held out the authority to veto his choice of friends, spouse, and residence. Once Ian was finally on his own, he took to the business of minding everyone's business like a duck to water. Ian was the consummate control freak.

The natural progression for a wealthy man like Ian was the need to micro-manage the investing of his money. Because no money manager could stand to work with him for very long and because Ian needed to have complete control, he moved inexorably to trading his own money in the markets.

Ian met his match in the markets. With so much education behind him, Ian assumed that he would be starting out at a much higher level than anyone else. In fact, aside from the fact that the mastery of a medical career requires a vast commitment of personal resources, medicine has nothing to do with trading. Ian did not take the time to master the rudimentary skills of trading as he had done for medicine. The result was that, to Ian's consternation, he discovered that he did not have control over the markets.

For Ian, whose entire life was constructed around the need to have control over everything, the thought of not having control was a very serious matter. But his way of gaining control was completely different than Andy's attempt to personalize the market in order to control it. Ian took the intellectual approach to controlling it. He decided that he would know everything there was to know about the market and about trading. So, he read everything that he could find, he studied and took courses and seminars, he learned how to design a system, and he subscribed to the finest newsletters and information sources. In typical fashion, he learned everything about the fulfillment of his orders so that he was assured of getting the most efficient trades. When Ian was done, he knew intellectually as much about trading as the best in the business.

Did Ian become a brilliantly successful trader? Of course not, at least not before we transformed his need to control the markets. For Ian, like so many traders with whom I have worked, losses meant he did not have control over every single outcome. When he eventually became too frightened of losses to invest, he sought out help.

Assessment for a Control Freak

Are you like Ian or Andy, trying desperately to gain control over the uncontrollable external world? A controlling person thinks that whatever is external to him has the potential of controlling him. This fear of being controlled forces the controlling person to feel deeply anxious and defensive. He or she tends to become either demanding and overpowering, on one hand, or manipulative, on the other. Regardless of the strategy, the result is the same. The controlling person acts from a fundamental insecurity, and decision making is driven by this insecurity.

Assess your behavior to see if you might have control issues that hold you back from your best results by asking yourself these questions:

1. Have I personalized the market so that I feel I have a relationship with it? And if so, do I feel that the market is my adversary?

2. Do I need others to do what I want regardless of their own needs or desires?

3. Do I feel anxious, uncomfortable or irritated in a situation where I feel that I have little or no control, even if the situation is pleasant?

Conclusion

If there is such a thing as control in trading, it comes from emotional stability, knowledge of the craft, and a methodology which will give you the best possible outcome. However, if you attempt to control the market by personalizing it, you will be fighting an opponent that does not exist, and you will lose. Andy never made it as a trader because he was unwilling to conquer his limiting patterns; while Ian, with all of his negative programming for control, was willing to face the real opponent to his success in the markets and conquer his need to control. The result is that Ian is now a successful trader.

Chapter 21

ISOLATED

"There are times I feel so alone," Jack said. Of all the traders I would expect to make this heart-wrenching confession, Jack is not one of them.

If you were to make a movie of Jack's life, it would be filled with scenes of him surrounded by the people in his life: his adoring wife and three children, his supportive parents, his many friends and associates and his wider associations in the community where he is regularly elected to head committees and organizations.

So, how can such a successful man whose life is full of supportive relationships feel alone? Jack is a trader.

What Creates Loneliness in a Trader?

The answer to the question lies in two, four-letter hyphenated words: *Draw-Down*, a phenomenon which is built into the business of professional trading. Just like the finest doctor who has to face the death of a patient, as a trader, you will eventually face a series of losses. Even the most accomplished trader can lose confidence during these draw-down periods.

In fact, for some very successful traders, draw-down can become an even greater psychological problem than for the struggling trader who frequently faces losses in the learning process. A successful trader like Jack, who has a limited exposure to draw-downs for extended periods, can find himself boxed in by his own success. His wife and children, accustomed to the good life, look to him as their invulnerable provider. In addition, he may enjoy a reputation among his trading associates as someone who is high on the trading pedestal. This leaves Jack and traders like him with the feeling of nowhere to go for support when the losses seem unending.

The Ugly *Draw-Down Beast*

Of course, a single loss will not affect the psychology of a seasoned trader. Even a brief series of losses will be shrugged off confidently with the statement, "This period of loss fits within the parameters of my trading rules." As the draw-down period continues, however, this ugly *Draw-Down Beast* seems to take on a life of its own. This psychological beast makes you question your ability as a trader as you think to yourself: "Maybe all of my success has been nothing but pure luck. Maybe I have lost the knack of trading." It is the feeling a great baseball player has when he does not know why he cannot hit the ball any longer.

Soon, the ugly *Draw-Down Beast* can make you begin to question your ability as a provider. This fear can eat away at you when you come home and face the family with their newest financial expectations or needs. And if the fear digs down deeply enough, you start to question the meaning of life itself. You have become a victim of the beast, and it does not care.

Strength Breeds Strength

Positivity is the wellspring of strength in your life, and once it starts flowing, it increases by building on itself. When you are feeling good about the world, it is easy to dwell on the positive influences around you. You are more likely to notice them, and you are always amazed that there are more positive influences to notice. Joy and aliveness expand in your life when you dwell on what is going right. People want to be the recipient of the feelings attached to these states of mind and will gravitate to you. If you throw a positive stone into the pool of life, positive waves will spread out in every direction.

Weakness Breeds Weakness

The opposite is true also. Weakness breeds weakness, as it feeds upon itself. If you throw a negative stone into the pool of life, negative waves spread out in every direction, multiplying as they go. Negativity is something that people want to hear about if they are in a negative state, too. And, when they are deeply stuck in their own negative self-indulgence, they will tolerate yours. The first reason for their support is that they will want you to indulge them in their own negative talk and thinking. Secondly, your negativity justifies their own, making them "right" in feeling the way they do. Those who are intimately concerned with your situation will often take on negative feelings, which forces you to deal with the ramifications of their own insecurities as well. As a result, this pooling of negative thoughts and energy increases your own negative state by adding new insecurities, fears, hostilities and weaknesses to your thinking.

When you are in a negative state, close friends, with the best intentions, will point out your good qualities and the blessings you have in your life. Instead of making you feel better, this leaves you with the unspoken "yes, but..." response in your mind. You tend to dismiss the truth of these positive statements because you are not able to hear them. Also, when you are dwelling on what is wrong in your life, you will feel that the negatives with which you are dealing outweigh the positives.

What you want at that moment is not to be told how good you are. What you really want is for someone to take charge and say, "Everything will be okay" so that you can feel that this individual has taken on your responsibility for creating a positive outcome. For a brief time you feel you do not have to be strong for everyone. This interlude of psychological regrouping gives you a chance to pick yourself up, dust yourself off, and gather psychological strength. When you are feeling positive and strong, you can carry the weight of your daily stresses and responsibilities effortlessly. When you are in a state of negativity, your sense of weakness and powerlessness grows until you feel that you can no longer carry these burdens without help. But what you need at this point, however, is not a rescuer, but a listening, understanding ear and the right kind of "kick-in-the-butt" to move you in a positive direction again.

Jack is Not Alone in his Loneliness

If Jack could feel comfortable expressing his feeling of loneliness to the other traders he knows, he would be surprised how many of them either feel the same way now or have felt that way before. For example, there is Harry. Harry is a bond trader who works for a small institution in Chicago. Harry has worked all his life to achieve a successful trading career and private life. His daily schedule is filled with a variety of the good things in life and is carefully balanced to support a good trading life. Nevertheless, Harry is still subject to the same feelings of loneliness as Jack.

Harry follows long-term trends which come up only a few times per year. You can well imagine that missing any one of these trends can be a real downer. Harry is surrounded by day traders who are constantly making trades with immediate feedback. One of the problems he had to overcome was tuning out the noise and action all around him so that he could focus on those few good trades. In doing so, he felt very alone in a room full of traders.

Sal is another example of a trader who felt very alone. Of course, Sal is anything but physically alone. He is a floor trader and a very good one at that. However, Sal comes home at night feeling that he has spent the day among people who are his competitors. Even though Sal is surrounded by other floor traders, he is working by himself, and therefore feels alone.

A year ago, Sal began experiencing a lack of energy and became less motivated to trade. Without telling anyone, he consulted a doctor. Sal was told that he was just experiencing stress and that he needed to learn how to manage stress better. Unfortunately, the doctor did not give him specific instructions. Sal was back in the pit the next day with only the consolation that he did not have a terminal illness.

As Sal felt increasingly vulnerable, he also felt alone. He was uncomfortable talking to anyone about his problem. Finally, he reached the breaking point and shared his feelings with one of his fellow traders who recommended working with a trader's coach. As a result, Sal is now able and willing to rebuild his health and energy through a regimen of exercise, rest, meditation and nutrition. As he regains his strength, he also feels less alone. Sal has developed a sensitivity in recognizing other traders who are experiencing the same signs of burnout and has reached out to offer his help. By helping others, he renews his commitment to helping himself.

Elements of Aloneness

As we have seen with these traders, there are elements of aloneness which are experienced by many traders. Trading requires a trader to compete in order to survive and thrive, thereby pitting one trader against every other trader. In addition, the types of personalities which are suited to trading are not those which are suited to sharing their feelings with others.

Three problems which are key to overcoming feelings of being alone are:

1. **Not being able to communicate**
   A trader may not be able to communicate his feelings for the reasons cited above: competition, family expectations, lack of a shared experience. On the other hand, a trader may not be able to communicate uncomfortable feelings because he has no experience, is afraid, or has great difficulty because of emotional blockage.

2. **Not being able to fully experience emotions**
   When strong emotions such as fear or loneliness surface during the working day, it is often very difficult to experience those feelings without jeopardizing the trader's ability to function. As a result, many traders learn to deny or repress their feelings, which causes them to be unable to completely experience their emotions. Unfortunately, these unexpressed and incomplete emotions accrue to the point where the trader cannot go on until he has dealt with them. Those who do not deal with their suppressed or repressed emotions will find that they will create situations that sabotage their good trading results.

3. **Not taking the right actions to take to snap out of the negative psychological trend**
   When people are in a negative psychological trend, they give themselves excuses for not taking the action that is necessary to snap out of these negative feelings. Virtually any activity which will naturally stop the flow of negative thought patterns will break the negative trend.

METHODS FOR HANDLING THE ALONENESS

The following exercises are simple, concrete and effective ways that traders can learn to handle their feelings of aloneness:

1. **Expressing Your Concerns**
   This series of steps is very helpful for a trader who has either been afraid to communicate his feelings or has been blocked for any reason:

   - Write or type out everything you need or want to say about what concerns you. This exercise is important practice in expressing feelings without the interference or blockage that occurs when you have to do it verbally aloud and/or face to face with another person. It also gives you the time to discover what your concerns are.

   - Read what you have completed. Delete all duplications and exaggerations. This exercise provides you with feedback so that you can gain an accurate picture of all of the issues of concern.

   - Decide what advice you would give someone you cared about with this same set of problems. (Interestingly enough, very often the one person who knows best how to advise you is you.) We all have in us the same wisdom of healing. We just have to remember to ask for the answers. Write down all of the actions you would advise. Decide which of these actions you can do right now. Then take action! (Once you take action, it leads to other actions, and you are back in control.)

2. **Completing Emotions**
   This series of steps is very helpful for a trader who has either been afraid to express or experience his emotions or has learned to block them:

   - Rent the saddest film you know. *Wuthering Heights* and *Love Story* work for me. A sad book will do, as well. Whether you watch a movie or read a book, do it in an atmosphere that allows you the freedom to express your feelings in any way you want.

   - Or, rent the funniest movie you know, such as *Same Time Next Year*. Perhaps, an evening with Billy Crystal or Robin Williams. Instead of expressing sad feelings, you could take an opportunity to fully express laughter and happiness.

The point of these two exercises is to give you opportunities to experience blocked feelings through the vehicle of a movie or a book without feeling inhibited by the presence of others or the stresses of your work. When you allow your emotions to start flowing, whether they are happy or sad ones, it often leads you to express the very emotions you have been repressing.

3.   **Taking Action**

Here are two actions traders can take which will break the pattern of aloneness thinking and behavior:

- **Call a stranger**

  Many organizations, churches and publicly funded agencies offer hot lines with people trained to listen to whatever you need to talk about. Tell the person on the phone that you need a listening ear and that you do not expect him or her to understand everything you have to say. Once you have said everything you want and need to say, and before you get any feedback from your listener, quickly say, "Thank you. That's what I needed," and hang up

- **Helping others less fortunate**

  Just as Sal, the stressed-out floor trader, found a way to share his new-found health regimen with other stressed floor traders, helping others is a proven way to bring relief from your own problems. Altruistic acts put our own lives into perspective, diminishing fears and highlighting our blessings. These acts of kindness provide a natural release for our emotions, creating a unique bond and closeness to the people we have helped.

- **Networking with groups**

  You can network with groups that meet regularly to discuss issues of concern that have nothing to do with trading in order to have the experience of expressing your thoughts and feelings openly. Look for such groups in the calendar section of your newspaper. In addition, attend seminars and workshops where the focus is on discussing and overcoming stress and sabotage in the trading workplace.

Conclusion

The loneliness of trading is a painful reality for traders, regardless of their level of success, their experience or their personal relationships. The stresses built into the profession of trading isolate traders from their natural, emotional supports and outlets. Large losses, competition, and the built-in psychological and physical demands of trading create a perfect climate for traders to learn how to repress their day-to-day feelings of fear, guilt, sadness, isolation and boredom in order to keep going. Unfortunately, it is this survival pattern of blocking and not communicating feelings which can make a trader feel estranged from the very people in his life who offer support. The financial ups and downs of trading can also create an aura of insecurity that prevents many traders from communicating to their spouses their fears and anxieties.

The only way out of this loneliness trap is for you to acknowledge the problem and find healthy, non-threatening ways to express those feelings and concerns, so that you do not feel so isolated from everyone around you.

Chapter 22

LOVE

The state of a trader's mind will determine his ability to perform at his personal best. There are temptations and pitfalls that can throw the most balanced trader off course.

At the beginning of last year, Jeff could have been described as the perfect trader. In the business for a dozen years, Jeff had developed a trading system which was perfectly suited to his trading style and needs. In addition, he had carefully nurtured a balance in his home life and his working life, which allowed him to trade unemotionally and very profitably. With a highly analytical background in finance and economics, Jeff was rarely swayed by appeals to his sense of greed or unbalanced by fear. Then, last summer, everything changed and Jeff was suddenly trading like an out-of-control gambler. It was neither greed nor fear that possessed him. It was more like being a person who is possessed by the wrong kind of love.

Agape

The world "love" in English can represent many things, such as the love of a friend, of a spouse, of a child, of the color blue, or of chocolate ice cream. We use the word love to cover the entire range of pleasurable feelings for all living and nonliving things, experiences, and concepts. However, in other languages, several different words can exist for love which separate one kind of love from another kind of love. For example, in the Greek language, several words exist for love, two of which lead to very different consequences.

The first of these words is *agape*. *Agape* is the kind of love which is the foundation of a good relationship. *Agape*, the cornerstone of human success and happiness, both personally and professionally, is the kind of love that is built from caring, from friendship, from adoration, and from all of those feelings and actions that build a strong relationship, lasting bond and commitment. At its very deepest expression, there is a selflessness to this love which inspires people to spend their lives in the service of mankind, and which inspires us to make selfless sacrifices.

Agape is the foundation of good relationships with our families, our friends, our communities, and, interestingly enough, with our careers. Traders who love the experience of being a trader in this way transfer this sense of security to building lasting, successful careers because they feel free to enjoy the process of trading. As a result, these traders love their business and are willing to make the day-to-day, minute-to-minute sacrifices that support their trading. And very importantly, a trader then has the strength and courage to keep his other emotions, such as fear and greed, in check. This kind of feeling keeps a trader in the business for the long haul, just as it keeps him in his personal relationships for the long haul. But, as powerful and sustaining as it is, *agape* is like everything else of value in this life. It cannot be taken for granted. Like freedom, its price is eternal vigilance.

Eros

Agape was the type of love that Jeff had for trading as well as for his wife and children. The deep caring he had for the parts of his life gave him the strength to keep it all in balance. However, when his wife, Jill, took the children East for the summer to help her father cope with her mother's terminal illness, Jeff's carefully balanced life fell apart. While Jill was gone, her divorced sister, Beth, came by the house to help Jeff. Her increasingly frequent visits were soon eagerly anticipated by the lonely and vulnerable trader. This new and potentially ruinous relationship awakened a sleeping gremlin in him. For Beth, Jeff did not feel the agape-type love that he felt for Jill. Instead, he was thrown into the passionate, obsessive, demanding, and selfish type of love that totally consumed him and led him to abandon all of his old self-disciplines. By mid-summer, Jeff found himself consumed by his insatiable appetite for his obsession.

Jeff was in the throes of the other Greek word for love, *eros.*

The word *eros* came from the ancient Greek god of love, Eros, son of Aphrodite. Eros was later identified with the Roman god Cupid, the impish, flying boy with the bow and arrows, who was thought to send his arrows through the hearts of the unsuspecting, turning them into lovesick suitors. It is interesting that the word cupid is the basis for the modern word "cupidity," meaning avarice and greed.

Unlike the essentially selfless love of *agape, eros* is an obsessive love that comes out of need instead of want. *Eros* comes from passion that ultimately brings tragedy. This unyielding passion turns us into the kind of people we don't want to be, bringing out the worst in us, and breathing life into parts of us that we never knew existed: raging possessiveness, reckless abandon, insatiable appetite for self-gratification, and an avariciousness and greediness for more of the same. While in the throes of *eros,* everything in the trader's life is out of control. Because everything is out of control, the trader finds himself constantly trying to control others and to control the markets as well.

While *agape* is the kind of love that keeps traders in business for the long haul, *eros* blinds them to the future. Instead, it brings out the gambler in them. Because its poison-tipped arrow inflames the latent greedy child in all of us, under the spell of *eros,* traders find themselves trying to take shortcuts, which cause losses to build, ultimately destroying everything.

By the time Jill returned with the children at the end of the summer, Jeff's newfound *eros* for Beth had spilled over into his trading. He was shocked and excited by the dizzying feelings he was suddenly experiencing and, like a person who has suddenly experienced his first shot of heroin, he was desperate to feel that way again. Out of control emotionally, Jeff was now trying to squeeze every drop of excitement out of trading, He no longer cared about the consequences while he rode the trading roller coaster to the end of the ride. Jill, who was devastated by the situation, fled, leaving Jeff to cool his jets or crash and burn. By the time Jeff called for help, his career was in flames.

If Jeff had begun his career in the *eros* zone, there would have been no story to tell. His trading career, like that of other traders who start in *eros* and never transform their consciousness, would have been short-lived. Nevertheless, the light from his career's impact with earth would have been dazzling. Sadly, it is a common occurrence for traders whose approach to trading has been *agape* for a long time to have a change in their lives throw them, unsuspecting, into the *eros* zone. However, not every trader to be undone by the wrong kind of love succumbs to *eros* because of a heated affair.

What are the other causes for this dangerous shift?

1.   **A major change**
      The careful balance of a successful trader's life can be undone by any major change that has nothing at all to do with trading. For example, a car accident can have the same impact on a trader, depending upon the seriousness of the crash and the individual trader's response to it. A friend who is a chiropractor has told me of many cases of accident victims whose lives go into chaos from an injury which the victim interprets as a major "break" with his life. Suddenly, these people start making dramatic and self-destructive changes in their lives.

      Another example is the fifty year old trader I worked with who had been jogging with his lifelong best friend on Thanksgiving when his friend suddenly collapsed and died of a coronary. Afterwards, the trader left his wife of twenty-five years, relocated to the beach, and started trading from his home there. He needed to divorce himself from as much responsibility as possible. Abandoning his self-disciplined approach to trading, he felt that his days were numbered and he had nothing to lose by flying by the seat of his pants. But what he was leaving was exactly the regimen that kept him successful. He was soon a victim of an undisciplined environment of raging emotions and passions. And this resulted in his nearly losing everything he had spent a life-time building up.

2. Chemical imbalance

Because *eros* appears to assert a powerful biochemical presence in the brain, as neurotransmitters that are like powerful drugs take over the control of the brain, changes in the biochemistry of the body can potentially have an effect on the situation. Taking drugs and stimulants as well as consuming adrenal-stimulating foods such as sugar and fats seem to trigger the creation of *eros* passion while a balanced nutrition seems to support agape devotion. A floor trader with whom I worked recently was thrown into this *eros* state by taking an asthma medicine which was a powerful adrenal stimulant. His emotional state, once steady and balanced, was suddenly characterized by passionate outbursts, emotional extremes and irrational thinking.

3. A large loss or a large profit

A steady and predictable result tends to support the same type of emotions and vice versa. At the same time, an unpredictable pattern of extremes seems to trigger the extremes of emotional responses, and vice versa. A good example of this is Nate, a fairly steady trader who flipped into the *eros* zone when he suddenly had a major win. The excitement and passion for trading that this unexpected result caused in him was so pronounced that his trading was catapulted out of its previous range of activity. Nate was in love with the feelings he had experienced with that tremendous success, and he desperately wanted to feel that way again and again. Of course, the opposite situation can also occur. In fact, large losses commonly trigger emotional instability which leaves a trader vulnerable to warps in his once level emotional surface. *Eros*, like a virus going around, finds fertile soil in these traders.

4. A mid-life crisis

Traders are particularly vulnerable to the temptations of *eros* in middle age. One morning, they wake up and realize that their lives are, indeed, finite. At this point, many traders who have gone along on a steady course, ask themselves, like Peggy Lee does in the old whiskey tune, "Is that all there is?" The answer comes back in the form of long hair, an earring, a tattoo and a new red sports car. Once on the road to the *eros* zone, the road begins to descend steeply.

5. Bad role models

We are all influenced by the role models we have absorbed in our lives, consciously or unconsciously. Positive role models that we have absorbed can guide us through dangerous waters without our being aware of it. Unfortunately, I have worked with traders whose own parents provided role models that were the very ones they fought against all of their lives. These traders promised themselves they would never abandon their own children and careers for an imprudent affair, only to relive the role in adulthood. The hurt experienced by a trader as a child is released later on in a replay of the original event in real time, played out by the victim as an adult. Thus goes their trading as well as their personal lives.

Staying Out of the *Eros* Zone: Eternal Vigilance

How can a trader protect himself from falling into this emotional trap?

1. **Recognize your own vulnerability**
   Notice what throws you off a balanced course. You can do this by recognizing situations that make you feel vulnerable and checking your physical and emotional levels every day. No one, however happy and settled they may be right at this moment, is forever immune to this trap. I have seen too many traders, who were convinced it could never happen to them, succumb to temptation and take the plunge. Once armed with the certainty that you are, in fact, human, you can then keep your eye on the distant horizon, on your goals and values, while watching out for the potholes immediately under foot. One strategy is to remind yourself continually that you are in this business and this relationship for the long haul.

2. **Visualize all of the ramifications of your actions**
   These visualizations include your loved ones and others that will be affected by your actions as well as yourself. If you need a reminder that all of your actions have consequences so that you cannot lull yourself into suspending disbelief, think of the movie, "Fatal Attraction."

3. **Model on successful trading careers**
   After recognizing individual models, notice what they have in common. This focus can give support to the path you have chosen.

4. **Consciously avoid situations and conditions that can leave you vulnerable**
   Before Billy Graham retired from traveling the preacher circuit, he was known to have someone inspect his hotel room before entering to protect himself from tabloid opportunists. By the same token, good traders check their mental and physical state before entering a trade. If they are not at optimal performance level, they do not take the trade.

Conclusion

Once a trader has entered the *eros* zone, the effect of the emotions he is feeling are drug-like in their control over him: they are addictive, powerful and pleasurable. Once he enters the "eros zone" he must be willing and able to rescue himself. Otherwise, the game has to be played out to its final and destructive end. The best overall strategy is to put into place a great defense based upon a conscious awareness of your goals, your values, your vulnerabilities and your current situation.

Chapter 23

_____

HAPPINESS

What does happiness have to do with being a successful trader? NOTHING it seems. In fact, successful trading and happiness may actually be in perpetual conflict.

Over the years, I have worked with many successful traders who were miserable, but only a handful of successful traders who were genuinely happy. Nearly all of the traders I have ever interviewed said they wanted happiness as their ultimate goal in life, while very few of them had actually achieved it.

Why is it so unusual to be both a successful trader and a happy trader? What is it about trading which makes it so difficult to sustain happiness? Is it possible to have it all?

The purpose of this chapter is to give traders a way to bring together their two primary goals of being successful and being happy. This seemingly impossible achievement is made even more significant for traders by the fact that, under the right conditions, happiness will not only support but promote successful trading. The few happy and successful traders I have known learned how to balance their trading psychology so they could have it all. And we can learn a lot from their experiences.

The Anxious Trader

The first major cause of unhappiness among traders is anxiety. Many successful traders spend all of their waking and even their sleeping hours worrying. Barry had elevated worrying to an art form. This successful trader came to one of the first seminars I ever presented on the "psychology of trading" seeking help for his anxiety. When he started out trading, Barry was very happy and fulfilled. Trading was exciting and challenging. Barry's early days of trading were like the early days of a romance, filled with happiness and the promise of future success. The more successful he became, the more he began to face the trading day with growing apprehension and worry. He was anything but the happy trader he had once been.

What caused this change? Inevitably, Barry experienced trading losses, and he began to translate those losses into a great deal of pain and blame. Despite the fact that Barry was an extremely good trader, he blamed himself for each loss as if it were a mistake he made even when he traded by his system's rules. Barry supported his family in a luxurious lifestyle, creating a comfortable and easy life for everyone but himself. He was now looking for either a cure to his misery or a way out.

Although there was no time to address Barry's underlying problem at the seminar he attended, I wanted to give him something that would effectively change his condition. The result was that I asked Barry to find a very uncomfortable place near his office to sit and contemplate all of his considerations, his negative thinking, his worries, and his self-condemnation.

This seemingly simple exercise came with a set of rules. First of all, Barry had to commit a certain amount of time each day for two weeks in which he would do nothing but feel miserable. And he had to promise to do whatever was necessary to maintain that feeling of misery. Barry called me two weeks later to report that he had decided to worry for a couple of hours the first few days. After all, he had thought, this was a short period of time compared to the sixteen hours a day during which he had been worrying.

Not long into this exercise, a pattern began to emerge: a continuous repetition of the same fears and anxieties played over and over again in his mind. Another observation, however, was hard for him to admit. Barry realized that he derived a measure of enjoyment out of worrying. He modeled his worry from his mother who took worrying "very seriously." When she died, he kept her alive in his mind by taking on the trait of her worrying. It was at this time that he started feeling anxious about his trading.

After the second two weeks, he called me again and reported, "I'm continuing the exercise even though I start laughing every time I look at that hard, marble bench in the park. Instead of keeping my mother's memory alive by worrying, I've started talking to her. I think she's spending time in the Bahamas because now she tells me 'Don't worry, be happy.' Now, I can't even maintain five minutes of worrying. I'm actually looking forward to a day of trading."

What happened to stop Barry from worrying? In classic Neuro-linguistic programming, Barry had interrupted a negative habit which was controlling his thinking. Every time he laughed, he interrupted the normal pattern which made it impossible to continue the reflexive habit of worrying.

Worry as a Way of Life for Traders

Barry's situation is one of the most classic patterns of unhappiness for successful traders. The reason for this problem is that trading comes with an inherent state of anxiety for many traders, because it continuously poses the threat of loss. Loss can represent different things to different traders, from loss of self-confidence to loss of everything a trader has. For this reason, the longer a trader trades, the more likely he will begin to worry. The more a trader has to lose, the deeper the level of anxiety may go. In fact, many successful traders convince themselves that constant worry is what keeps them from taking greater losses. So, worry becomes a habit for most traders, a pattern of reacting to reality, which then creates unhappiness.

A Way Out of Worry

Even if a trader is not aware of the causes of his anxiety and worry, he can take control over this major cause of unhappiness by doing just what Barry did: derailing the pattern of worrying. Once a trader recognizes the pattern and interrupts it by changing its normal course, he can put worry in the same category as grinding your teeth: a habit you can stop.

The Excitement Junkie

The second major cause of unhappiness for traders is the addiction to excitement. Unfortunately, this excitement is what soon gets them into trouble. Too many traders interpret their happiness as a function of how much excitement they get from trading. The need to feel excitement, however, causes traders to sabotage themselves in their trading, which leads to losses, which then leads to anxieties and negative emotional states. However, if those traders who are hooked on excitement can survive the transition to another basis for happiness, they can find the more subtle pleasures in a trading day:

- The joy which comes through the discovery of oneself through trading
- The satisfaction which comes from the lessons learned
- The fulfillment which comes from being disciplined
- The rewards which come from reaching your short and long-term goals
- The self-esteem which increases with running a successful business
- The enjoyment of the tasks in which you are involved during the trading day

The Conditional Trader

The third major cause of unhappiness for traders is setting conditions upon happiness. Successful traders are those who set high goals for their achievement. Once they reach one level of achievement, they set the next level of achievement as their goal. Unfortunately, inherent in this system is the cause of much unhappiness because happiness is always defined as the result of a set of conditions being met, i.e.:

- "I will only be happy if I have 100% return on my capital with no draw-downs"
- "I will only be happy when I am making $1,000,000 a year"
- "I will only be happy when I own a Ferrari and a pool"

The problem with these conditions is that they are moving targets, and assuming that you reach them, the nature of the human mind is that joy is fleeting. And soon, these conditions are replaced with new ones, so that happiness is something you will only experience in the future.

Therefore, if happiness for a trader comes with conditions, you may want to ask yourself these questions:

- What are the conditions which I have set before I can be happy?
- What are the conditions which my family has set for me before I can be happy?

What, then, really creates happiness if it is not meeting a set of conditions?

Whenever I work with traders, I ask them to experience an overview of their lives and find out what has made them feel the most fulfilled and happy. What they discover is that the special moments they create by themselves or with other people are what really makes life worthwhile and brings them the most happiness.

We have all experienced something that happened in the past which causes us to feel an extreme amount of pleasure or pain. If you can create that pleasure once, you can create it all the time. Think back to special moments in trading which created happiness in you. Then, think about what followed: was it a pat on the back that someone was going to give you? Was it the anticipation of buying a new toy? Was it the satisfaction of being able to say to the world: "I told you so," because you had been told you would never succeed as a trader?

Where are you focusing your attention? Your happiness depends upon it.

It is within your power, at any moment and regardless of circumstances, to feel happy or miserable depending upon where you choose to focus your attention.

Allen was a perfect example of a trader who had it all but was only aware of what he did not have in his life. None of Allen's friends could understand why such a successful trader was always miserable. To hear Allen tell it, his life was one, big pile of woe. He could list all of his shortcomings, his recent losses, mistakes and problems. Allen seemed to be unaware of the fact that he had a remarkable, devoted wife with three fine children and a brilliant career. He had his health, his parents and his friends. But, he chose to focus his attention on what he did not have.

One of the exercises Allen did was to vividly imagine his life after losing all of the blessings it provided him. Allen forced himself to experience in his imagination the loss of all the love, abundance and joy he actually did have and recreate in his mind a happy life without those conditions. This experience was a revelation for him. Not only did he realize how many conditions he had placed on happiness, but also how much of his mental energy he had focused on thoughts that created misery.

The Happy Trader Who Became a Successful Trader

Mark is one of the happiest and most fulfilled people I know. And believe it or not, he is a trader! However, he did not start out that way. Through the process of learning his profession, Mark always looked to the next condition as the state that would finally make him happy. "When I make a certain amount of money, when my wife doesn't have to work, when I have certain toys, when I can give to charity...then I will be happy." Unfortunately, Mark traded for eight years without reaching any of his goals. This meant, of course, that he was never happy as a trader. In fact, like many traders, Mark unconsciously believed that if he actually were happy, he would not become successful, because he feared that if he were happy, he would lose his competitive edge.

Eventually, though, Mark discovered the psychology of trading. As a result, he began to realize that for each condition there would always be another condition. If he wanted to enjoy life and be happy with trading and every other part of his life, he would have to learn to experience the joy of each moment: In other words, Mark would have to stop doing the following:

- Taking past negative events and putting them into the present moment

- Creating anxieties of the negative events that could happen in the future and putting them into the present moment

In order to be happy, Mark would have to open himself to the awareness of the good that was in his life in each moment. How he learned to do this was by heightening his senses to the good things in life or, as some people say, he learned to "stop and smell the roses."

When Mark was able to change his awareness, he discovered that he was able to enjoy the process of being a trader. This new appreciation of the minute-to-minute experiences of his trading day began to have an effect on Mark's performance. Instead of worrying about what had happened or what would happen, Mark's focus increased dramatically by focusing on what was actually happening. His awareness heightened with his sense of calm and peacefulness. And, Mark's trading profits increased in proportion. Suddenly, Mark surpassed all of the conditions which he had once set for his happiness. But instead of tiring of his achievements, he remained happy. Mark had learned to disconnect his happiness from his circumstances.

What Mark discovered is one of the best-kept secrets in trading. Not only is it possible to be happy and successful, but it is possible to increase your trading success through your happiness, if that happiness is the result of an expanded awareness rather than being attached to a set of conditions.

Happiness Index

Where is the focus of your thoughts and attention? What are the conditions you are placing on being happy? On a scale of 0 to 4, four being the highest amount of discomfort, rank each question with a number which indicates how relevant it is to your trading life:

1. I feel stress and tension which inhibit my good performance.

2. I never appreciate my accomplishments.

3. I feel that my work does not give value to the world.

4. I do not look forward to the work day.

5. Work takes over every aspect of my life.

6. I am obsessed with profits and I fear losses.

7. I have unrealistic expectations which bother me when they are not realized.

8. I trade for the wrong reasons, i.e., excitement and, as a result, I am on an emotional roller-coaster.

9. I am not disciplined and therefore do not experience the full value of my system.

Obviously, the higher the score the more likely you fit into my "Not Happy Trader" model.

Conclusion

Most traders have two goals -- Success and Happiness. The reasons that so few traders ever achieve these two goals simultaneously are because:

1. They worry constantly about losing in the markets.
2. They need to feel excitement, which tends to create losses.
3. They set conditions on their happiness.
4. They focus on what they do not yet have.

As traders become more successful, they have more to lose, more to worry about and more to achieve before they can become happy. Misery-thinking too often becomes a way of life for traders.

Yes, this potent combination of trader success and trader happiness is rare. That is because so few traders understand the underlying forces in their profession which work against their happiness as they propel themselves toward success. The story is different for those traders who learn how to break up their patterns of misery-thinking and let go of their conditions for happiness. Instead of focusing their attention on what they do not yet have, these traders focus their attention on each moment and on appreciating what they do have. The result of this transformation in thinking is a trader whose underlying happiness supports and improves his trading in ways he could never have imagined.

SECTION IV

Traders Who Take Right Action By…

Chapter 24

LEARNING TO FOCUS
ON THEIR TRADING AT WILL

I Just Can't do It

A young intern at a hospital was about to experience, for the first time, the act of cutting through a third-degree burn victim's skin. This procedure was necessary because the skin tightens painfully when it is burned. Disgust at the sight of the charred flesh made the young intern realize that he just could not do it. The doctor in charge of his training said, "YES YOU CAN. NOW FOCUS!" With all the strength he could muster, the intern pulled his thoughts together and focused on the task at hand. He reached down with his scalpel and then reality hit him a second time. He could not do it and backed away. This was one of the stories on an episode of the television series, "ER."

Like this young intern, traders are called upon to make trades which require them to forget about their fears and just focus. Unfortunately, far too many traders find that they cannot do it either.

How many times do you approach the point of pulling the trigger and focus on making that trade, but your focus shifts and you just cannot do it?

Focus Means Giving Total Attention to the Task at Hand

Thank goodness for the Beta state, when our brain is functioning between 15 and 20 cycles per minute. This is the state of mind in which we are capable of looking at the computer screen while answering the phone, while thinking about our son's hockey game, while eating a sandwich. This Beta state allows us to do many different things at the same time, and comes in very handy at various, demanding moments in our lives. Of course, this state has a downside to it as well. When we have several conflicting internal conversations going on while we are trying to put on a trade, we may well come to the realization, like our young intern, that we just cannot do it. As we volley between thoughts, we can wave good-bye to the trade. For this reason, the Beta state is not the appropriate state of mind for trading.

The appropriate state of mind for taking action in a trade is the Alpha state. In this state, you can focus your mind on a single thought to the exclusion of everything that is going on around you. You know that you are in the Alpha state when you are staring at something as someone asks a question, and in a daze you ask, "What?" In this state, the brain waves are functioning between 7 and 14 cycles per minute. There is no room for conflict at this moment, because there is not enough brain wave activity to support it. This state is also known as the "learning state" because the attention of the student is individually focused on the subject at hand. In this state, the mind achieves the focus that is required to carry out a difficult task without being distracted by competing thoughts.

What happens to your focus, however, if you have a pattern of internal negative dialogue, and you are negatively focused on the "what ifs?"

The "What If" Shoot-out

One of the major reasons for not being able to follow your rules is the collection of "what-ifs" that occupy your mind and create conflict. If your "what ifs" are not satisfied, they will draw all the focus of attention to them. You know the ones I mean.

- What if I lose?

- What if I don't have a wide enough stop?

- What if I'm risking too much or too little?

- What if I'm entering too soon?

- What if my system is not working?

- What if the trade keeps giving profits?

The way to shoot the "what-ifs" away is to write down an answer which your neurology can live with. For example, if your focus is being derailed by the question, "what if I lose," you can write down the answers:

- I have already assessed the amount of risk I am willing to absorb and I have put in the appropriate stop. I can, therefore, live with this loss.

- I will make up the loss another day.

188

- Losing is part of the business of trading. Everyone loses. The important thing is to limit the losses and make it up in the wins.

- It is just as valid to ask, "What if I win?" This trade is being guided by my system and my rules. Therefore, my preferred outcome will ultimately win.

If you already know the answer, you do not have to think about the question. "Easy for you to say," you are thinking. Well, the act of formulating the answers is the first step in laying to rest the questions.

George, the "What if" Specialist

George had so many "what ifs" in his life, I don't know how he got out of bed in the morning. Naturally, he was not married because he kept thinking, "What if I had to deal with a divorce?" He did not work for anyone because, "what if" they fired him? The only reason he started investing in the stock market was because he inherited numerous investments from his father. Unfortunately, this comfortable inheritance came with a new set of "what ifs":

- What if I sell the stocks too soon?

- What if I hold onto the stock and lose money?

Naturally, George would never get counseling for his problems because, "what if" it did not work? Instead, George reluctantly hired me as a part-time hourly coach, calling me up every time he got into trouble, asking for a quick and inexpensive fix. From our periodic conversations, I found out that George developed his "what-if" paranoia from his mother. She lost her first child when he was only two-years-old. When George came along, she was so excessively careful with him that he developed the constant fear about the negative consequences of any action he would take.

The result of being in this perpetual "what if" state for George is that he cannot pull the trigger. He can't get into the right trades and then can't get out of them. He can't follow his systems because he can never trust those systems. He can't make the small decisions and can't make the large ones either because his mind is constantly clouded with the divisive chatter of his conflicting inner voices. He can never get into a state of focus on the task at hand.

Accessing the Focus State on Purpose

Throughout the day, most traders come in and out of the focus state. Few of them, however, pay attention to the object of their focus. If all traders knew how to and remembered to call upon the right focus when they were making their trades, they would be trading at their peak performance state at all times. The top traders with whom I have worked and studied who are able to produce consistently high profits have learned how to maintain a state of focus when it is needed. If you would like to consciously create the focus state at will, here is a useful technique:

- While looking forward, pay attention to the back of the center of your head.

- Become aware of your peripheral vision while still directing your eyes forward.

- Now that you are aware of what you naturally do when you are focused on something, give your attention to the trade that you want to take.

If you have mentally rehearsed taking action immediately after recognizing your entering signal, action will be automatic.

An Environment for Getting Into Focus

Increasing focus often requires an environment that is conducive to focus. Once you are in the Alpha state, it does not seem to matter what is happening around you. However, getting into that state can be difficult if your environment and life are disorganized. It is important for you to maintain organization to support a focused state. However, an environment that is good for creating focus is different for everyone. Some people are bothered by even the slightest amount of noise and cannot get into the focus state unless there is total silence, while others do not allow distractions to get in the way of their focus.

A trader's social and emotional environment can have an equally chilling effect on a his ability to reach the focus state. If the office environment is rife with personal conflict, a trader may not be able to get his mind free to focus. Or if the environment at home is full of hostility or disruption, the trader may have his attention still on the problems at home when he should be focused on the trading tasks at hand. For this reason, it is important for you, as a trader, to set your personal world in order and do what is necessary so that the people in your life support you and your trading if you want to be successful in your business.

Another source of distraction can come from a trader's physical well-being. It can be impossible to reach the focus state if you are suffering physically from pain, exhaustion, discomfort or any number of physical irritants. The loss of focus is just another compelling reason for taking care of your health, exercising, eating right and getting proper rest.

The Beta State Overload

When a trader is overwhelmed by sensory input while in the high-brain-activity Beta state, he can suddenly find himself being thrust into the low-brain-activity Alpha state. However, when this happens, the result is not the kind of focus you want. Instead of an Alpha state in which the brain can focus exclusively on one thought or activity, the mind comes to a complete halt and the trader finds himself paralyzed into mental and physical inaction because his mind and body are focused on the negative part of the self. For this reason, it is not advisable to allow yourself to get into a situation in which you are being assaulted by too many demands upon your emotional and physical resources. Too much stress can create this state in a trader. When a trader is paralyzed by stress, he is no longer capable of getting into the focus state, even though he is technically in the Alpha state. At this point, he must remove the stresses and remove himself from the environment which is overwhelming him.

The Focus State and "Flow"

The focus state has also been described as the state of "flow" by industrial psychologists. Recent studies have demonstrated that individuals reach the flow state in which they stay in a condition of high concentration and productivity when they are challenged in exactly the right way. If the task at hand is boring, they cannot reach a state of "flow," nor can they reach that state when the task is too challenging or too difficult. The task must be challenging enough to force them to focus, without overwhelming them with uncertainty and exasperation. You can just hear the internal chatter starting up with a task that is too hard. Self-defeating ideas keep popping into their minds, just like the "what ifs":

- I can't do this, it's too hard.

- How am I ever going to do this, I'm going to fail?

- How can anyone expect me to do this?

A particularly dangerous pattern for many traders is that they start off making money and it feels very good. However, making money becomes easy for them. When this happens, they find themselves losing money in order to regain the challenge of trading because they need the stimulation of this excitement. Not only do they thrive on the excitement, but the excitement creates the challenge that puts them in a state of "flow" or focus. This pattern is reinforced by the fact that their focus, at first, is on making money, but the actual reward is excitement. When they continuously make money, the reward is no longer there. So, they have to lose money to get the reward, and in the process, their focus is lost.

Conclusion

Successful trading requires a trader to be able to enter and sustain a state of focus on the tasks at hand. This state allows a trader to identify the right trade, to stay with it as long as he needs to do so, and to exit the trade at the right time. The loss of focus at any point in this process is just as fatal to a trader as an Olympic high diver losing focus on the way down. For a trader, there are many reasons to lose focus. Both a trader's internal and external environment can create distractions that derail his focus. And finally, the perception of trading as either not challenging enough or too challenging can prevent a trader from entering a state of flow.

The good news for traders is that all of these impediments to achieving a state of focus are correctable. Personal problems can be addressed, stress can be reduced, bad health habits can be changed, interruptions can be minimized, etc. What is required is a commitment to recognize that the problem exists and to take the steps that are needed to correct it. Then, once the barriers to focus are eliminated, practice going into a state of focus so that you can focus on demand.

Choose your thinking:

past negative stories,

future negative stories,

or present positive thinking.

Remember - you are continually making

one of these choices.

Tip from the coach

_____

Chapter 25

LETTING GO OF THE PAST

Into-wishing or tragic-drama thinking will impact a trader's decisions. Trading in the moment without negative stories is the only way a trader can get the support he needs to follow his rules. You know the kind of thinking I am talking about:

- Everything comes in threes. This is going to be a good trade because two good things happened today.

- Better get out before the big boys hit my stop.

- I'm always in the opposite direction of the right move.

The Cassandra Syndrome

In Woody Allen's movie, "Mighty Aphrodite," the Greek gods watch and speculate about the outcome of a modern man's brush with Fate. The goddess Cassandra is full of fears for the future of the character Woody plays, creating tragic stories for him. As these stories are mirrored in his own fears, we see that he is a modern day Cassandra, consumed with dramatic and tragic foreboding. Having the benefit of distance from his situation, we see how funny it is; but Woody cannot because he is stuck in the moment with his own limited viewpoint and his own tendency toward gloomy predictions.

Like Woody Allen's character, many traders are Cassandras as they talk to themselves about what could possibly happen based on past losses or future expectations. Are you a trader in this trap?

Anthony grew up in a tough neighborhood in Philadelphia where the vulnerable were under constant assault by the petty criminals who lived nearby. His family, which was long accustomed to tragedy and victimization, would always assume the worst had happened.

If Anthony was late coming home from a date, his mother assumed he had been kidnapped, murdered, robbed or in an accident. It never occurred to her that the reason he was late was that he had been having a wonderful time. This belief in the worst possible outcome was part of an unwritten law about the nature of conversation in Anthony's world. People would dramatically retell the stories from their past in a verbal game of one-upmanship in which the most tragic story won. This form of thinking and speaking became an integral part of Anthony's world view.

When Anthony became a trader, he brought this pattern of thinking to his trading. These negative stories dampened Anthony's energy and passion for trading. Even more serious was the fact that it prevented Anthony from following his system. When the signals dictated that he should stay in the trade, Anthony would exit too soon because all he could think about were the losses that would occur. In fact, he had experienced losses when he first got into the business. However, these negative stories prevented him from trading with consistent stability.

In our private consultations, I pointed this problem out to Anthony and proceeded to use Neuro-linguistic programming that would eliminate this particular problem. What I did not anticipate was that this negative way of talking and thinking represented all of the things that meant home, family and familiarity to him. Anthony wanted to hold on to the essence of these things. Giving up this form of story-telling was not acceptable to Anthony on an unconscious level. He was trapped in the Cassandra syndrome.

Weighing the Payoffs

As easy as it is to transform a negative behavior from the past through neuro-linguistic programming, it is just as easy to reverse the change if the negative payoff is more important to the trader than the benefits of the change. What made Anthony so reluctant to let go of the past was the fact that his father had died when Anthony was young, leaving his mother to struggle raising him. She managed to support the two of them and send him to college. Anthony loved his mother and held her in such high esteem that he promised to buy her a home and take care of her. Unfortunately, she died before the opportunity came for him to fulfill his promise.

As Anthony and I started working together, I began to realize that his connection with his mother was more important to him than being a good trader. So, while neuro-linguistic programming works for many people, in order for it to work for Anthony, the follow-up was extremely important. He needed to change some of his associations in order to support a new habit of thinking positively in the moment.

The Trick is All in the Framing

For many years, I have known a gifted picture framer whose business has grown so large that she frames for major suppliers and buyers from all over the world. You can take a rather mediocre piece of art to her and when it is framed, it can look like a masterpiece.

Conversely, she has shown me great works that were badly framed so that you would not give them a second glance. The trick, she tells me, is in how you see the work and what you choose to emphasize in your choice of frames and mats.

Photographers do the same thing. In the darkroom, they can perform their own reframing of reality. If they are working from a large negative, they can select only the most interesting part of the shot and print it. The finished photograph will be a beautiful scene that was taken from a larger scene that had little to recommend it. The trick is in reframing your view of the scene in front of you. Just as Cassandras like Anthony focus only on the negative shots, there are traders who reframe their point of view to include the positive shots.

Brad grew up in a home where his grandfather was one of his caretakers. Granddad Stephan loved to tell stories about the past and Brad loved to listen. Granddad's stories consisted of highly exaggerated special moments that stirred up pleasurable emotions in Brad. These stories, which were part of the family's verbal history, were so infectious that the whole family would laugh and make fun of them in a pleasant way. When Granddad would talk about a future event, he would create a great deal of anticipation in such a way that it would be even more incredible when he reviewed it in the future.

With this experience in reframing, Brad entered trading with the idea that everything would not only be okay but everything would be exceptional. And that is the way it was for Brad. He chose to make the right decisions and to align himself with the right people. In his mind, there was just no thought that it could be otherwise.

While other people come to my seminar to overcome sabotage or to protect themselves from the sabotage traps in trading, Brad came to learn about the psychology of trading. As the most positive thinker I have met, Brad brought the level of the seminar to a different dimension. And the instructor, yours truly, as a result of this, re-learned a major lesson:

> While we talk about all of the traps and all of the things that can go wrong in trading, it is actually more important to direct our thinking to what can go right in our trading and go with the mindset of someone who is a winner like Brad!

The Icarus Traders

Many people come into trading with the idea that they are going to be multi-millionaires. This is only an idea and not a deeply rooted belief that is central to their being. These traders remind me of young Icarus who challenged the gods by attempting to fly to the sun. Realizing too late that his wings, which were made of wax, would melt, Icarus fell back to the earth and perished. Inherent in this story for me is the suspicion that if the wings had been an integral part of Icarus and not some artificial, vulnerable attachment, the gods would have felt more inclined to forgive his arrogance and let him succeed. The same principle holds in trading. Beliefs in great heights of success, which do not arise from a strong psychological foundation, will get you in the end. The ambitions of famous men

197

which were not supported by inner strength were the cause of their undoing. Richard Nixon and Jimmy Baker, for example, were Icarus men.

On the other hand, Poseidon, the Greek God of the Sea, was portrayed as understanding his own nature. Filled with a sense of power, he had infinite confidence in the outcome. And the outcome was always the one he determined it would be.

Not only must a trader be trading with a positive outcome, the positive story must have a basis in inner strength or he will be like young Icarus, overreaching his actual grasp. This inner strength can come from many different sources:

- a certain knowledge of the rightness of the outcome
- a total commitment to the outcome
- the knowledge that he has done everything to prepare for a positive outcome
- the repeated experience of having achieved the positive outcomes
- the belief that not only does he deserve to succeed but that success is inevitable

Reframing the Cassandra Trader's Stories

While Brad's mindset is unique, it is the norm among traders who are successful to think that the outcome will always be positive in the long run. Most traders lose because they have Anthony's mindset instead of Brad's. To help Anthony overcome his attachment to his Cassandra stories, we had to attach importance to the new way of thinking. The best way to do that was to link the new pattern to the most important thing in Anthony's life, his mother. This devoted mother did not want Anthony to buy her a house and support her in luxury. Instead, she wanted nothing more in life than to see her beloved son happy. She wanted him to be confident in what he did and to expand his horizons far beyond those which circumscribed her own life. Fulfilling her real dream was one way he could pay her back for all of the hardships she experienced to raise him. Once Anthony had connected his new, positive thinking to the fulfillment of his mother's dreams, there were fewer payoffs left in the old way of thinking, and Anthony could move forward with his life.

Like Anthony, the best way to stop the Cassandra stories is to connect your new thinking to something that is more important to you than the payoffs you get from your old negative thinking.

Here are some steps to help you reframe your thinking:

1. First, recognize the nature of all the stories you are telling yourself and be willing to give up the perception of those stories.

2. Surround yourself with people who talk positively and avoid those people who are stuck in the Cassandra stories.

3. Like the audience watching Woody Allen's movie, watch your own movie and others in life and find the humor in all of these negative tragic interpretations.

4. Attach something that you really want, like being a really good trader, to very positive thinking.

5. It is important to realize that while it sounds more beneficial to be a good trader than to be a victim, you must determine what the payoff is for the negative thinking. Write down the payoff of negative thinking and the payoff of positive thinking.

Conclusion

You don't have a choice about the past. However, you do have choices about your perception of the past and the future and the moment of now. How you are thinking in the moment of now will direct your trading results. Your thinking will either sabotage your trading results or assist you in making the right decisions.

Chapter 26

BEING CLEAR ABOUT WHAT THEY WANT

To be a successful trader, you must be able to trade the signals your system gives you. However, if there is any confusion or interference in the transmission of these signals, you will miss entries or get into trades too late. Unfortunately, many traders sabotage the flow of these trading signals when they give themselves mixed signals about their attitudes, beliefs, values and as a result, their feelings. These mixed signals create internal conflicts, which, in turn, cause traders to confuse signals they are getting from the outside world. Then, the right signals are lost in transmission while the wrong signals are taken.

A Trader With no Rules

"There are no rules. Rules are meant to be broken. Money isn't important," Lon said as he played out his new role as a recently divorced, go-with-the-flow bon vivant. While professing to believe in a Bohemian creed and lifestyle, Lon's actual goal was a capitalist's fantasy of skimming a healthy living from his trading while he toured the world with his laptop computer.

If Lon's battle plan, supported by years of study and practical application, was clear, the two sets of conflicting messages he was sending to his own internal troops would now prevent him from reaching his goal:

1. Lon's training as a trader had instilled in him the firm belief that a trader must follow his rules. Now, he was telling himself that rules are meant to be broken, and...

2. Lon was telling himself that money was the reward for trading well and that he wanted to live the kind of life that only money could bring. But, his newfound freedom from a painful past was telling him that the creation of wealth was a source of self-imposed suffering.

The Wrong Path

As a once highly disciplined businessman, Lon's indiscretion while on a trip ended his long and generally happy marriage. When his marriage ended, the stability that had anchored him to the disciplines of his life ended as well. He wallowed in guilt and sorrow, scattering his focus and shattering his life. While in this emotionally and intellectually unbalanced state, Lon concluded that the solution to his unhappiness was to jump into a new relationship and use trading as the means to quickly recoup his financial losses. The results were, predictably, a bad relationship leading to more insecurities about permanent relationships and substantial trading losses leading to more insecurities about money.

On the Road to Peace, Love, and Bad Trading

Although Lon managed to pull himself out of his emotional hole through a crash course in self-help techniques and New-Age metaphysics, he was still not making any money in his trading. What had made Lon successful in the past was his self-discipline, his willingness to follow his own rules and his reward was money. But now, Lon connected both his discipline of following rules and his goal of making money to the pain of his old life. Naturally, Lon's unconscious mind wanted to avoid further pain. That is why, suddenly, Lon found himself spouting his new self-defense doctrine: "Don't follow rules and find other rewards in life." As a result of these mixed messages and the conflicts created for Lon, he stared at his computer screen, frustrated, playing the hindsight game, and wondering why he couldn't pull the trigger at the right time.

Intersecting Conflict

Lon's worksheet presented a detailed and impressive set of criteria for taking signals and rules for entry. However, what Lon actually told himself as he watched the screen throughout the day was something quite different. "Look at that! If I'd been on the opposite side of those trades, I'd have made a bundle." "Hindsight" became Lon's middle name. While he had specific criteria for entering trades, the signal Lon gave his neural-networking was, "There are no rules. Rules are meant to be broken." And, while his conscious mind wanted to make money in trading, the message his neuro-networking was getting was, "Money is not very important." The result of this conflict was that Lon didn't have to worry about an excess of money burdening his life. Nor did he have to worry about rules in trading; If he continued this way, it would take him out of the markets.

Holding Back on the Accelerator

Neil is another trader who was missing signals and taking the wrong ones. Confronted with the final barrier to successful trading, Neil felt that he was inches away from being not only a consistently good trader, but a wizard. Yet, he found himself sitting in front of the screen, watching opportunity pass him by. Admittedly, during occasional moments of brilliance, he pulled the trigger at the right time and the right place. But, most of the time he sat and watched, cursing the screen and all its ancestors.

Neil had a good, tested system that would make a reasonable living if he followed it. But, Neil wanted to be a wizard. He knew that in order for this to happen, he would have to conquer the dark shadows of his own personality. Neil's ultimate goal was the *Holy Grail* of trading, his definition being oneness with universal consciousness. This oneness would give him the advantage of significantly increasing the probabilities of the right outcome in his trading. In other words, his intuition would be the added indicator that would make him a market wizard.

Neil knew what it was to be at the mastery level in other areas of his life. Before Neil began trading, he had demonstrated an ability to brilliantly improvise in the performing arts and in entrepreneurial business deals. This creative brilliance was what he wanted to realize in his trading.

However, a conflict existed in Neil's life regarding his goals. On the one hand, Neil was publicly espousing his desire to become a trading wizard. But, on the other hand, Neil was privately dealing with a fear of loss that was deeply imbedded in his psychology. The more diligently Neil worked toward achieving his goal of success and the farther he stretched himself in its pursuit, the closer he came to experiencing loss. The result of this terrible conflict was that Neil was not taking good signals. And like Lon, Neil came to believe that if he won, he lost, and if he lost, he won.

Monsters Lurking at Every Junction

Like most traders, the fear of loss for Neil was not limited to money. If you consider all the traumatic events in your life, you will realize that all of those events had to do with some kind of loss: the loss of self-esteem, of face, of love and friendship, of a wonderful life, of health, of independence and freedom. Metaphorically, there is a place inside of us where all losses are stored. When we are physically, emotionally or mentally in a depleted state, we retreat to that place. Then all the shadows of those losses and the fearful monsters that represent them sweep over us and leave us in an unresourceful state. Some of the losses traders are haunted by include:

- **The fear of being wrong**
- **The fear of losing money**
- **The fear of not being able to continue with trading**
- **The fear of not making it after so much work**

> **These types of fears and many more can put you in the depleted state where the unresourceful trading monster lurks.**

On the surface, Neil appeared to have everything in order in his life. No one would suspect that there were dark shadows that could effect his trading ability. His life seemed full, rich

203

and happy. But when we reach for the gold ring or the one area of excellence that we want the most, we have to stretch, to reach beyond the norm, or the carousel will just move on.

Shining Through

The movie, "Jerry McGuire," dramatized Neil's psychological issues. The viewer could easily focus on the love story, but the more poignant story and lesson can be found in the relationship between the sports agent, Jerry McGuire, and his client. Jerry McGuire was skilled and passionate in every part of his professional life, but had never felt the passion of true love in his personal life. On the other hand, Jerry's cynical, mercenary client, a talented football player, experienced love all around him at home but never found love in his heart for his sport. It took a life/death experience for love to blossom in Jerry's heart. And, it took the same experience for the love of the game to finally grow inside the football player. The mixed signals and the conflicts these men felt in their lives had brought both of their lives to a crashing stop until they spoke with one voice.

Triggering the Right Signals

The only way for the transmission of the right signals to get through is for the receiver (you, the trader) to be free of static and interference. This static comes from unresolved and unrecognized conflicts in the things you are saying to yourself about what you want, about how you feel, and where you are going. While the issues that Lon and Neil are dealing with can be very serious, the following steps are effective ways that you can clear some of the static that is inside your own receiver without professional assistance:

1. **Determine if what you say and what you do are in conflict**.
   By comparing your own behaviors with what you say, you may be able to uncover some of your own conflicts. For example, are you telling yourself and others that you are eager to be a successful trader, but you fail to gather the resources, knowledge and psychological strength it takes to follow your rules to become a successful trader?

2. **Compose a statement about the way you want things to be.**
   Visualize the behavior that you want to see yourself engaging in. Repeat this over and over until your unconscious creates in your reality the steps necessary to make it so.

3. **Acknowledge your fears**.
   What are your deepest fears? In your mind's eye, face each fear, asking the fear what it wants or what lessons it has to give you. Follow through on what you are willing to do or can give the fear so that it can transform itself into an ally.

4. Learn how to do contingency planning.

Contingency planning is one of the most effective tools for permitting you to receive the right signals and then act on them. Contingency planning consists of answering the following questions on paper: What do I expect to happen? If that happens, how should I respond? What is the best thing that can happen? How should I respond? What is the worst thing that can happen? How should I respond?

Conclusion

To be an effective trader you must be able to act on the signals your system gives you without having those signals garbled in the transmission. Unfortunately, when you give mixed signals to your own neurology about your feelings and goals, you set up a conflict in your mind, which interferes with the clear reception of your trading signals. These unclear signals and inner conflicts will then cause you to miss entries or enter too late. If you are not clear about what you want from your trading and how you feel about your trading, you will be unable to trade successfully. So, the first step out of these unintended results is to uncover the conflicts and inconsistencies in the way you are talking to yourself. Once you have acknowledged these conflicts, the second step is to give yourself the clear, mentally rehearsed signals for positive action based upon your new, unmixed goals. Once you master these two steps, you will empower your trading with a dynamic and winning momentum.

Chapter 27

_____

STICKING TO THEIR TRADING RULES

If traders are going to succeed over the long haul, they must follow their rules; and in order to do so, they must stay in a state of personal and emotional balance. This paradigm is the essence of my work with traders.

However, the sticking point with this strategy is that we are talking about results over time. Unfortunately, over the short term, things can happen quite differently. It is a fact that even the most carefully conceived and faithfully followed system will periodically create losses. And even more vexing is the fact that, sometimes, breaking your rules can result in significant wins.

This paradox was illustrated to me when I attended a Dow Jones Telerate Conference where I met the *Futures* magazine columnist, Gibbons Burke. In discussing the problem of keeping traders faithful to their rules, he pointed out to me how markets will sometimes reward bad habits. As a result, the experience of doing the wrong thing and winning reinforces doing the wrong thing again in the future. As we explored this phenomenon through examples of traders we knew who had fallen prey to this temptation, we talked about what happens to our neurology when doing something wrong turns out right:

> At first our minds are confused by the fact that as a result of breaking our rules, we have won. Our neurology concludes that it should encourage this behavior. Then conflict sets in. The part of you that wants to follow the rules next time is in direct opposition to the part that is saying, "Remember last time? We were positively rewarded when we went against our system. Are you sure you don't want to do that again?" This temptress part of you thinks it has a valid argument because it has solid evidence that by breaking the rules you can get positive results. Thus starts the beginning of a sabotage pattern that can be the demise of a good trader and his working system.

Fresh Out of the Gate

As a brand new trader, Derrick had purchased and tested his system and had attended a seminar on trading. He was confident about his system. However, he was not feeling confident about his ability to use the system. At the seminar, he met several traders who were very good traders. Impressed, Derrick wanted to learn from them and emulate them. Once he had returned home, he solicited advice from several of these "exceptional" traders. To his surprise, their advice ran counter to the positions he would take if he were following his system.

Now, Derrick, who was feeling unsure of himself, questioned, "Who am I, just starting out, to go against the advice of these exceptional traders?" So Derrick took the trade they suggested, and he had a positive outcome. This positive outcome produced positive reinforcement for Derrick to disregard his system and to follow the advice of these other traders. In the meantime, Derrick's system was producing signals to take trades. He was even less confidence in following his system even though he sees that if he had taken these trades, they would have produced positive results.

As Derrick distanced himself from his system, he relied more and more heavily on his trader friends, calling them up constantly to ask which way they were going to trade. Derrick had now become a thorn in their collective side. Unfortunately, out of these assists, he received a few more positive outcomes. By turning over his trading destiny to other traders while abandoning his own system and rules, Derrick had sold his soul.

Out to Pasture

Kevin has been in the business so long that his trading rules had whiskers. The unfortunate result of his vast experience was the fact that Kevin no longer really enjoy trading. Yes, he had all of the rewards that come with country club living and all of the symbols of success. And the process of arriving at this point in his life was a lot of fun. Nevertheless, Kevin was bored and looking around for something else to excite him.

One day, quite by accident, Kevin was so distracted that he was not paying attention and he broke one of his major trading rules. To his astonishment, the result was a bigger profit than he had seen in many years. Kevin was more excited than he had been in so long that he could not wait to repeat the experience. From that moment onward, Kevin was eager to break all of his trading rules, one after another, just to see what would happen. Strangely enough, he began to see dramatic profits. These new positive results fueled his passion for even more defiance. And his profits ballooned even more. Until, that is, he lost nearly everything he had.

Rules That Work

With as many people losing in the markets as there are, you must always keep in the forefront of your mind that certain rules work and others don't. In any business you must have a plan and stick to it. Sure, your periodic review is important; but in making any adjustments in a plan, you must have contingencies for all of the consequences of those changes. This gives your neurology the clear-cut message of how to proceed unconsciously. When your unconscious and conscious mind agree, there will be no conflicts that will get in the way of your following your rules.

1. If you believe that there is a change to be considered, go back to the original planning mode while continuing to follow your original rules. The only way you will trust your new rules through draw downs is when you have back tested them and see the rules work over the long haul.

2. If good results follow out of a bad decision, recognize that your error in changing your rules will cost you in the long run if you don't test it and make it part of your rules. You wouldn't reward a child who cheats on an exam, gets an "A" and doesn't get caught. Therefore, you must make it a rule not to enjoy an emotional high from getting away with doing the wrong thing.

3. Always take responsibility for making your own trading decisions. It's easy to be swayed, especially when you are insecure.

4. Get your emotional outlets from something other than trading.

5. Connect following your rules with something that has value to you so that following your rules is attached to the emotion of receiving the reward.

The Turn-around Trader

Brad was feeling guilty when he called to discuss his recent success in the market. Several years ago, he had taken a seminar on following your trader rules, but had recently found that he was having a great deal of success breaking his rules. What had started as an accident had turned out to be highly profitable for him. Fortunately, Brad was conscious enough of the danger he was in to seek out support before he made breaking his rules a way of life.

The first thing Brad did was analyze his past trading rules. Although he stuck to them consistently, his results had never been very impressive. Worse yet, he had never done the serious back-testing that would have given him a compelling reason for sticking with them. So, Brad simultaneously back-tested his old rules with his new rule breakers. As we had begun to suspect, Brad's new rule-breakers significantly outperformed his old rules over a significant period of time. This meant that Brad was able to adopt his new rule-breakers as "rules" that he would commit to following. And this time, Brad had a reason to stick with them, even through draw downs and slow periods.

Conclusion

Every trader is in danger of benefiting from doing the wrong thing. Usually we pay the price for breaking our rules. However, when we actually benefit over the short term, the message to our unconscious causes confusion and conflict. When this happens, we must have a system of trading rules that we believe in for the right reasons: We have tested them over time and they have demonstrated their reliability. When our rules cannot pass this test, we have to go back and find out if they can. And if they can't pass the test, we need to see if we should be turning our rule-breakers into our new rules that we commit to following.

Translate all your thoughts

to the thinking of someone who

believes in himself,

believes he can be successful and

believes that it is possible.

Tip from the coach

Chapter 28

_____

USING ONLY SUCCESS-SUPPORTING
SELF-TALK

Self-talk Controls Your Trading Destiny

Self-talk is that inner voice that interprets for you what is happening and how you feel about it. Your self-talk can be positive, optimistic and encouraging so that it gives you the energy and confidence to stay the course in the face of the most overwhelming odds. Unfortunately, most traders with whom I have worked, regardless of success, engage in negative self-talk, which results in their not achieving their ultimate potential.

Negative Self Talk is Destructive, Demoralizing and Depressing

So, why do you choose to engage in it? The short answer is because it is a habitual pattern. As humans, we like to confine ourselves to familiar patterns even when they are negative. The familiar is comfortable, predictable and, even when painful, it is what we know and expect. For traders, what is comfortable means that you do not have to risk failure in new territories. You can keep losing in areas in which you are familiar.

"I can't pull myself out of this mess," Larry said to me over the phone. Once an exceptional futures trader, Larry was desperate. "The harder I try, the deeper I get into a depressed state. All I think about is my horrible losses which creates more losses. And all I do is worry." After talking with Larry, it was clear that he was not exaggerating the seriousness of his situation. His self-talk was rapidly leading him to a deeper and deeper state of depression.

Larry's present unhappiness was in stark contrast to his early life. Raised in a wealthy and optimistic family, he was surrounded by comfort and love which gave him the ideal foundation for optimistic self-talk. He was a happy-go-lucky person until the tragic accident which tested his emotional strength and led him to this debilitating pattern of negative self-talk.

Self-talk is a Magnet Attracting the Energy it Transmits

Through our *Trader's Evaluation* (an evaluation of every aspect of a person's life and how it relates to trading), we have been conducting an ongoing study of the patterns of behaviors, attitudes, and past experiences that correlate with losses in the market. One section of this evaluation includes the specific entry and exit trading rules a trader must have in order to be successful. Another area has questions about self-talk, and another is about losses.

From this study, an obvious pattern has emerged that correlates losses in the market with negative self-talk. The correlation between having difficulty in following rules, negative self-talk, and losses is also very clear. These correlations are so strong that I would eagerly sell an option on someone scoring negatively in all of these three areas at the same time.

A pattern of negative self-talk can be started when a trader experiences a single traumatic loss or a series of losses. In Larry's case, he lost his wife and two-year-old son in an automobile accident. This tragedy repeated itself over and over in his mind until it consumed this once optimistic person and made him look negatively at every aspect of his life. Naturally, his trading performance began to suffer from his negative self-talk, as well. As Larry's self confidence was diminished by his pessimistic inner voice, he made stupid decisions in the markets. After long, painful months of debilitating inner pain, Larry finally decided to see a psychologist. Although therapy helped Larry cope with his personal loss, his patterns of fear in the markets persisted.

Are you Singing *The Trader's Blues*?

Traders who cannot pull the trigger or who exit too soon have their own special monologue which effectively sabotages their trading results. Their self-talk is all about their fears, their losses and their uncertainties. This was the sad tune Larry sang all day. Let's listen in on one of Larry's conversations with himself:

"There's a good entry, but, but maybe I should wait a little. I need for this to be perfect, oh ! # * lost it... oh what the ! # *, I'll enter here. #*! Suppose I'm wrong, I **should'a** taken it when it was at the best point of entry, I **could'a** been in a much better place for getting a bigger profit. Suppose I'm wrong. Maybe I should pull out now. I can't afford another loss. - - - - - ! # * I **would'a** made so much more if I had waited.

Does Larry's self-talk sound familiar to you? It should, since the majority of traders eventually defeat themselves with their own words. The results of this negative self-talk for Larry were, of course, losses. His negative thoughts created a lack of focus, self-

214

confidence and energy which, in turn, made it difficult to pull the trigger and to follow his system.

Should'a, Could'a, Would'a is *The Trader's Blues*

What Fuels Negative Self-talk?

1.   **Interpreted negative perceptions of your experiences in life**
      Larry blamed himself for the tragic accident. He had asked his wife to run an errand for him on a rainy day. His perception of the accident was that if he had not asked her to go, she and his son would still be alive today. Naturally, anyone would be challenged to endure the psychological pain that would come from a tragedy such as this.

2.   **Diminished psychological and physiological energy from stress and poor living habits**
      Larry suffered from diabetes since childhood, managing his sugar levels with one pill a day, until the accident. He was good at monitoring his food and exercise. Since the accident, however, his stress levels increased because he stopped taking care of himself, requiring him to increase the dosage. The discomfort he was feeling mentally and physically brought on continuous negative self-talk.

3.   **The influence of negative self-talk from significant others**
      Larry's family had been very positive in the way they talked. However, after the accident, Larry gravitated to people who had also suffered a major personal loss. Many of these people were emotionally stuck in their tragedies, unable to see the possibilities in life.

What are the Components of Self-talk?

1.   **Attitudes, Beliefs, Values, and Limiting Decisions**

      Attitudes   **How you interpret everything in life**
                             Larry's attitude about life had become deeply pessimistic. "Life is a tragedy waiting to happen."

      Beliefs   **What is true for you**
                             After the losses that followed the accident, Larry thought he might have to give up trading. He was beginning to believe that he would not be able to make it as a trader.

| Values | **The importance of things** |
| | The avoidance of pain was one of the limiting values which influenced every thought and action. So, what do you think Larry attracted into his life? |

| Limiting decisions | **Decisions you make to protect yourself** |
| | Larry made the decision on an unconscious level that, in order to avoid the pain of unexpected loss, he would take from himself before he would allow others to take from him. So, he initiated a pattern of making money only to immediately lose it all |

2. Past, Present and Future

| Past | Larry could only see the pain of his tragic loss. He could not see the incredible life he had lived up to his loss. |

| Present | Larry's view of the present was of being stuck in a pit of problems. |

| Future | If life could bring the kind of pain that Larry had just experienced, then more pain was on the way. He started to worry about the well-being of all the people he loved. |

Prince/Pauper Negative Self-talk has no Economic Boundaries

Even though Larry can count on a luxurious lifestyle for the rest of his life from his family's money and from the insurance settlement after the accident, his financial security does not guarantee him a life free of negative self-talk. There is always a next level of success even for someone who is very wealthy. The rewards from Larry's success in business were the approval of his father, his peers, and himself.

In fact, based upon my research, I have concluded that most people talk negatively to themselves a good part of the day. Even people who are judged by their peers to be successful often are mired in negative self-talk. This negative self-talk prevents them from being as happy as they could be, from enjoying the fruits of their success, and from achieving the level of success they could reach.

How to Overcome Negative Self-Talk

1.   Start writing down your self-talk, or record it on a cassette.

2. Listen to the familiar patterns, stories, and words.

3. List all of your excuses, your fears, and your limitations.

4. List the negative beliefs, attitudes, values, negative past experiences and decisions you have that are limiting.

5. Notice the negative past experiences that you dwell on. Notice the recurring problems and the problems that you feel you cannot overcome. Notice the nature of your fears about the future and what limits you from creating the future you would like to have.

6. Viewing all of the things you have written down from the perspective of a very optimistic or positive person, ask yourself:

   - What kind of self-talk would this positive person have?
   - How would he or she interpret things in a way that is positive and motivating?

   (If you cannot come up with all of the answers yourself, ask one or more people who are very positive how they would reinterpret some of your negative dialogue in new ways.)

7. Now that you know what positive self-talk sounds like and how to transform negative self-talk, write it down or dictate it on a tape recorder and notice how you feel about it.

   (You might find yourself uncomfortable in the beginning because the negative dialogue is very much a part of you. To break the pattern, you have to make a conscious decision to make better choices.)

8. Listen to or read your new dialogue every day until it becomes the real you.

   (If you cannot do it on your own, consider professional assistance.)

Larry's Swan Song

Larry agreed to tape his own self-talk and listen to it. Each day, Larry focused on his self-talk, listening for those comfortable but destructive messages of despair. He shared his self-talk with me, and I helped him with positive re-framing of his inner dialogue. Larry was highly motivated to change these destructive patterns because he had recently met a woman who made him want to regain control of his life. As his level of emotional energy rose, he found it possible to follow his trading rules and to pull the trigger once more. His level of self-discipline began to rise every day, until, within months, Larry was a new positive self. He made a choice to think about the good experiences in the past. This new positive attitude allowed him to have success in his trading and be happy in a new relationship.

Conclusion

Negative self-talk has limited the success of countless traders. The ease with which a trader can slip into the pattern of negative self-talk makes it difficult to see how destructive it can be. Most traders are surrounded with the potential causes for negative self-talk: losses and stress, as well as negative associates, friends, and family members. Then, once the pattern of negative self-talk is established, it feels comfortable and "right." Unfortunately, negative self-talk often becomes self-fulfilling. If a trader fears losses and talks to himself about these potential losses, he will likely cause them to occur. These actual losses, in turn, cause more negative self-talk.

The way out of this morass is relatively easy if the self-talk is not connected to deep-seated unresolved psychological issues, and if you are committed to changing your self-talk. The steps include observing, identifying, and transforming the negative self-talk into positive self-talk, and then rehearsing the new dialogue. At first, this process will feel uncomfortable, as if you are using muscles which have atrophied from lack of use. With commitment and attention to the process, rapid and wonderful results will occur, and your trading will reach levels of success you have never before experienced.

Chapter 29

————

BALANCING THEIR LIVES

If I were looking at your face in a crystal ball, what I would see is that you are capable of extraordinary success. You have everything you need to not only reach your goals but to surpass them. However, you pull yourself away from a high level of performance by indulging in negative self-talk, and other self-abusive behavior. You also complain about not having enough time. Right? As I continue to look into my crystal ball, I see that you have had days where everything went right and you showed the world what you could do. On these incredible days, you accomplished far beyond the activities you planned for the day. Your energy and spirits were high, your focus was clear, you made the right choices and you felt good about yourself. Life was a banquet of opportunity and possibilities. These are the days when you were in *The Performance Zone*.

Who Stole the Magic?

There are those of you who will look at your astrology charts and say the stars did it. There are those who will blame it on their employer, their wife or their broker. And, then there are those who chose to have a terrible day because the markets went against them. It is easy to justify a terrible day. But, what if you went into a day with the attitude that no matter what happened, it was going to be a great day? You can say, "but what if," and be right about all the possibilities of having a terrible day. But, where will it get you?

Now, I want you to stop and think about "anticipations" themselves. Isn't an anticipation just a fantasy of what could possibly happen in the future? And if that fantasy is played out dramatically in your mind, don't you get to experience the feelings of living that fantasy in the here-and-now? So, who is the only one who can steal your magic?

How Much Time is There in Time?

Most busy people are always wishing for more time because there never seems to be enough. Time is not the real issue. What busy people need instead is high quality energy to accomplish everything they want to complete within a period of time. If that is the case for you, try this exercise:

1. Take the time to think back to a specific day when nothing went right and it took you two to three times as long to complete your work. Notice the lack of enthusiasm and energy. Notice how you feel and where in your body, specifically, you feel it.

2. Now, I want you to take the time to develop in your mind's eye a visualization of a specific time when everything in your day went right. On this day, time multiplied itself. Notice the enthusiasm and energy you feel. Notice where the good feelings are located in your body.

In this exercise you are acquainting yourself with how and where your feelings reside.

At the Heart of Performance

Andrew was a top trader who learned to live his life in the performance zone until the year he decided to end his marriage. He knew he could overcome the difficulties of separation and divorce faster than it would take the average person, however, he did not anticipate how to deal with his wife's pain. Nevertheless, he was smart enough to lighten up on his trading and was able to still maintain good performance.

During the separation process, Andrew met a fascinating woman at a conference. The excitement he felt when he thought about her not only erased his pain, but sent him back to a high performance level. He became addicted to these thoughts as an escape from experiencing the pain from the divorce.

Then, time passed, the love relationship began to produce in Andrew mixed feelings of pleasure and pain. Temporarily, he fell into a slump in his trading. What made the difference? His high performance level thinking was caused by hopes, dreams, passions, and incredible expectations. His energy was at a high performance level because he connected everything he did with thoughts of how it would benefit their relationship. The low performance level was created by disappointments, sadness, and unfulfilled expectations. Wondering what his efforts were bringing him, Andrew lost his motivation for maintaining high performance. He did not want to give up his thoughts of pleasure even if it meant having to deal with the painful thoughts as well. Fortunately, he decided to seek help.

Choose Your Energy Source

When you make the choice for higher energy, you also make a choice for giving up habits and patterns. The choice most people take is to ignore the problem, because they do not want to work on the solution. For Andrew, who had overcome many psychological issues, it took a month of growing misery before he cried "uncle" and he was willing to do whatever it took to change his present direction.

Andrew was happy with the realization that he did not have to give up his relationship; but he did have to give up his choices with regard to how he thought about the relationship.

Making Better Choices

Ask yourself these questions to determine if you are diminishing your performance level:

1. Where are you directing your energy?

2. Are your choices of thoughts and action supporting or undermining you?

3. What words and actions have motivated you in the past that gave you a high level of energy and performance?

4. What choices could you make that would give you a high level of energy?

5. Are you willing to make those choices?

The Performance Path

A trader I worked with has a particular spiritual path he follows. There is one great teacher from whom he takes guidance which makes good sense to him. This trader joyously gives his time, energy and thoughts to this path and all it means to him. He lives most of his life in the performance zone, because he has found his purpose and this purpose is a constant motivator. He lives a vital, happy life, handling more tasks then the average person and he does it with an abundance of energy

For some traders, it's the markets themselves that provide them with energy. To find out what your passions are, what creates your performance zone, you only need to look at those moments in the past when you found multiple time within time and everything went in your direction.

However, if you say, "I haven't had those kind of moments," I would ask you to imagine that you were the kind of person who did experience those high energy moments and what it would be like. Do not be concerned that these projections of the future are only a fantasy. Fantasies can become a reality, and the truth is that you only have the moment of now and any projections of the future are a fantasy. So, create your fantasy. If you put enough detail into it, you will discover that it can and will become a reality, perhaps not in the exact form that you pictured it. However, with an expectation of the fantasy or something better, the experience will be real for you.

The wonderful thing about the imagination is that you get to experience the feelings of a future anticipation here and now just by making it a fantasy. Consequently, when you are looking for the performance zone, you must realize that its creation is within your reach by making a choice to have it in your thoughts now.

Sharing the Performance Zone

Often, a trader is in the performance zone because he shares his life with someone who helps him maintain the balance and energy he needs to sustain his high performance. When the relationship loses steam, the trader will suddenly find himself out of his zone.

Kevin was a homebody. He derived great pleasure from exploring his own property, from being in nature, and from surrounding himself with things that were familiar and comfortable to him. His wife, Jennifer, however, had a variety of interests. While she enjoyed Kevin's world of quiet beauty, she also enjoyed the cultural and artistic life of the city. Kevin was happy and contented working on his computer and at his trading all day and had no problem with Jennifer being with friends on those occasions when she needed to pursue her other interests. But Jennifer was beginning to feel discomfort in the fact that Kevin wouldn't share a part of her life that was very important to her. Her stress began to affect Kevin's quiet world and trading. It wasn't until Kevin was willing to open himself up and enjoy Jennifer's world on occasion that he could come back to his performance level.

Keeping up the Energy in Your Day

In addition to strategies that are meant to increase your physical energy such as exercising and eating well, what can you do to keep up the vitality to maintain your performance? During the trading day, you will periodically experience losses. By anticipating the pain you will feel when these losses occur and other spots that consume your time and energy, you can avoid the emotional plunges that take so much energy from you. Look to the rest of your day and the tasks that become a heavy weight on you because you don't like to do them. Or look to the evening that you spend with your spouse doing what he or she wants to do and consider it a wasted evening. Imagine that you were the kind of person who finds joy and enrichment in all of the tasks that you choose to do to reach a particular goal. Wouldn't you be more energized with taking the positive approach to a task rather than fighting that task all along the way?

The Performance Ring

One of the best known, most visible performance zones is a 15 foot square platform that is misnamed a ring. The competition which takes place in this performance zone pits the physical, psychological and intellectual skills of two individuals against each other in a near-death struggle. Interestingly, neither of the two competitors can stay in their performance zones by themselves.

At the beginning of the match, each boxer is at peak performance. These two great athletes have trained long and hard for this moment. They have pumped up their psyches with public proclamations of their prowess and threats against their opponents. At this moment, they are feeling no pain -- just adrenaline.

Then, the fight begins and the single most physically grueling athletic performance that is known to mankind commences. Minutes into the match, everything has changed. Both of these brilliantly conditioned performers are slipping imperceptibly out of their performance zones. By the middle of the match, each boxer begins to feel the pain of the blows he has taken. His arms and legs become tired. His spirits begin to sink, and he wants to let go. But, there in his corner is relief waiting -- a time-out. He sinks onto his chair and takes a needed 30 seconds of rest. Someone pours cool water over his face, someone else stitches up the cut over his eye and a voice coming from the one person who truly understands what is happening to him starts to give him words of encouragement, hope, support, and vital strategic information. Suddenly, the fighter notices that his body is lightening up and his spirits are coming back. He is ready to do battle again. He has taken a needed time out. This is an essential step in re-entering the performance zone.

The responsibility for reviving that hurting and exhausted fighter during the brief time-out lies with his coach. The boxer's coach is there to orchestrate the revival of the boxer and to guide him back into his performance zone. He must attend to the boxer's physical, psychological and technical needs because the boxer can no longer see what his weaknesses and strengths are. In fact, many times, the boxer really wants to give up in order to avoid further pain. At other times, a boxer has taken too much punishment and his coach needs to take the boxer out of the game against his will.

The Performance Zone and the Coach

I am frequently asked why traders need coaches and the answer is that they often do not need them at all. However, like a boxer in the ring, a trader can slip out of his performance zone without realizing it. Or he may know that his game is not up to speed, but he cannot see why. And sometimes, a trader knows why he is out of his performance zone, but he does not know how to get himself back into it. And occasionally, after taking a terrible beating in the trading ring, a trader simply needs someone in his corner to help soothe the pain and give comfort. A good coach knows what needs to be done and knows when a simple "time-out" is called for.

Conclusion

The performance zone is a unique state in which a trader is blessed with a combination of abundant psychological and physical energy. This high level of energy makes it possible for the trader to accomplish a great deal in a brief period of time, while doing everything exceptionally well. This high level of energy is often derived from imaginings, passions, good feelings and expectations. However, a trader can easily be derailed from his performance zone. Changes in his life and in his expectations can easily drain him of passion and energy and mire him in negative thoughts. Losses and disappointments can change the direction of his energy. Then, like the boxer in the ring who has lost his senses, a trader may need a coach in his corner to get him back into the zone.

SECTION V

Traders Who Face Challenges

Allow your neurology

to get used to energy shifts

that result from changes in your life.

So, either get out of the markets,

decrease the size of your trading or

tighten up on your money management.

Tip from the coach

Chapter 30

CHANGE

When the CBOT was about to change buildings, I received countless calls from floor traders reporting their concerns regarding their move to a new building and new floor. Some of their concerns were:

- Would the new pits be too large?

- Would people be able to see the orders being placed?

- Would the change in positioning of the pits and the traders within their pits upset their relationships to each other?

- Would traders from the smaller pits be able to see into the larger pits, especially into the US Bonds pit?

For other floor traders, the mere act of rearranging the pits spelled trouble. Haunting fears and questions kept invading their focus and impacting their performance equilibrium. These potential changes had put everything out of balance for these floor traders, and a loss of equilibrium is a serious matter for any trader.

Performance Equilibrium

When a trader has reached the point in his trading where he is achieving steady, sustainable and significant profits, he is in a state of performance equilibrium. This state requires a balancing act of constant, minute and unconscious shifts and adjustments to maintain it, much like those that we unconsciously and automatically make when we are driving a car.

However, the state of trading equilibrium also requires things to stay the same for the process to work. Change of any kind can knock your trading out of balance. Even change in the small things you take for granted can create a ripple effect that can alter the final outcome.

The Ripple Effect from Small Changes

Trading is performance and like all other performance arenas, the state of performance equilibrium is essential to reaching the desired results. For example, at the height of his career, a great baseball player went into a sudden hitting slump. No one could figure it out. He was deeply worried, his coaches were baffled, and his fans were getting restless, waiting for their great hitter to get back to his game. But, the harder he tried, the worse the results were. Then, one day, his wife, who always sat in the stands right behind him, told him that he didn't stand the way he used to stand. At first, he ignored her observation, but she insisted that she was right. Finally, he asked her to demonstrate. So, she came up behind him, positioned him the way he used to stand, and positioned his arm in the way he used to hold it. The change was so subtle that no one else had seen it. But the results were nothing short of miraculous. The fans got their great hitter back.

In *The Lost Land*, Michael Crichton's sequel to *Jurassic Park*, the author argued compellingly that the dinosaur's extinction did not have to be the result of a cataclysmic event. Instead, the most minute change at the bottom rung of the complex ecosystem that supported those monstrous animals could have done it. These small changes would have had ripple effects that would have eventually been as catastrophic as the half-mile-wide meteor that hit the Yucatan, which is currently credited with wiping out the dinosaurs. Thus, the power of subtle change on the end result.

For traders, subtle changes can have the same ripple effect. Wally, a floor trader I worked with, was under a lot of pressure. As a result, he began to experience back pain. His doctor instructed him to buy an expensive pair of shoes designed to give his back support. It never occurred to Wally that, as the soles wore down to reflect the shape of his foot, that their original benefits would be altered. The subtle change in the soles caused the redistribution of weight over Wally's knees which now were under new stress. This in turn created inflammation in his knees. The doctor now put him on a diet to reduce the weight on his knees, which in turn made Wally irritable and headachy. His trading was severely affected, putting Wally under far more stress than before.

Major Change

If minor or subtle change can result in the disruption of performance equilibrium, can you imagine the effect of major changes on a trader's performance? Whenever there is a change of any kind, our nervous system is effected. The effect will be directly proportional to the energy that is already invested in having things the way they are. For example, if you are deeply invested in a personal relationship, and the terms of that relationship suddenly change, you will feel the results deeply and your neurology will be greatly affected. But, the relationship you have with your newspaper delivery man who throws your newspaper at your driveway at 5:00 a.m. has little invested in it, so that changes in that relationship will have little effect on your neurology.

I have had to help many traders find their way back to a healthy trading career after the breakup of their marriages. The energy invested in these deep and long-term relationships is so great that consequences can be quite dramatic in all areas of a trader's life.

The Changes that Changes Bring

This connection between the energy invested in a relationship versus the energy released by a change in that relationship means that you can predict if the effects of a change will be minor discomfort or major discomfort. The neurological shift that results from a move to a new parking space will probably be perceived to be small. Of course, if the original parking space was a status-loaded perquisite or reward that was taken away, the result of the move to a less convenient space could be quite significant emotionally. The result could then be vague feelings of inadequacy, depression, anger, or resentment.

On the other hand, the neurological shift that results from a floor trader being moved from his position in the pit or from his entire pit being moved or radically changed is, by definition, very significant. The result could be overwhelming feelings of discomfort, anxiety, fear, and anger, as well as physical changes such as loss of appetite, insomnia, heart palpitations, high blood pressure, and an inability to cope with cold, noise, and any kind of stress.

Even when the trader convinces himself that he is making the adaptation well, he may not be aware of the increased level of stress he is experiencing from a particular change. Like any individual who is out of touch with his feelings, he may not associate the changes in his moods and physical well-being with the change he is dealing with. Or he may be aware of the fact that, all of a sudden, he is feeling a lot of emotions which he does not know how to handle. So, he denies there is a problem.

Change and the emotions it creates can be scary. Even people who have had to deal with a lot of change can still find themselves unable to cope with a new set of changes in an area in which they felt secure. One successful way of coping with change is to realize that when it happens, you can do something about it before it gets out of hand.

What can you do to minimize the discomfort that results from change?
You can:

    1. Realize that there is a loss of energy associated with change that is perceived as negative and that an imbalance will result. Once you realize this fact, you can be alert to recognize the signs of these changes in yourself.

2. Seek medical or professional help to cope with change, especially when you have a great deal of energy invested in the way things were.

3. Take a vacation and allow yourself to rest, recuperate and back off from working a full schedule. Take time to do good things for yourself: for example, have a massage, read a good book, go to the theater or a sporting event. Many traders work so hard and so long that they think they are invincible. These traders never take vacations. However, when these feelings come to the surface, these traders do not know how to deal with them and they do not have the mental or physical resources from which to draw.

From the Conscious to the Unconscious

If you were to drive in London knowing that you have to drive on the other side of the street, would you drive unconsciously and automatically, or would you be consciously aware? Everyone who has to make the adjustment of driving on a different side of the road finds himself consciously doing all of the things that were once automatic. You can even hear them talking to themselves. "Now, the white line needs to be to my right. And, OOPS, I have to go clockwise around that roundabout." This process is very stressful and takes a tremendous amount of energy.

In order for change to become automatic and comfortable, you must consciously make an effort to prepare your neurology for the change until your muscle and nerve response can be transferred over to the unconscious mind. Once this transfer takes place, it relieves the conscious mind to do the other tasks at hand.

This transformation from doing things in trading automatically to doing them consciously is frightening to traders because they don't understand what is really going on. In trading, just like in driving, the unconscious mind does things for you, freeing you to think and handle many tasks simultaneously. Now, with changes in your entire working environment, all of a sudden you have to put all of your energy on the conscious basis to deal with changes. This expenditure of energy doesn't allow you the freedom to see all of the other nuances that were available to you before.

When everything is new and you are working on the conscious level, you can't pick out the important things. You have to do deal with everything new all at once.

A Matter of Conscious Time Effort

The important thing to realize here is that, although you do not know how to deal with the new situation now, you will eventually master it and return to the state of automatic mastery. It's just a matter of consciously directing yourself, which is the best way to speed up time. This conscious time effort will take you from the state of being out of control to the state of being in control.

How is this state of being in-control best achieved? Over the years I have learned that when confronted with a new situation, you are often presented with a series of new concepts, all of which, on the surface, are very easy to understand. The problem is that you are often presented with so many new concepts to deal with at the same time that you are overwhelmed. For example, if you are learning how to deal with a new computer program, and you attend a course on it, in the space of a four-hour workshop, they will take you through the entire program. They will even give you tutorials that you can practice on the individual computer assigned to you. The problem is that by the end of the afternoon, you cannot remember a single thing you have learned. Your brain is smoking!

The secret to dealing with this stimulation overload is to master one small change at a time. Refuse to be pushed! Take each change at your own pace. This is the only way that each change will become part of your neurology so that it becomes automatic. When everything is new and you try to deal with it all, you will be overwhelmed with the stress caused by so much conscious effort. When you take control of change by taking it one small step at a time, mastering it, and then going on to the next step, you will be able to handle it. Sitting in a car on the driver's side, playing with the new instruments until you are comfortable with each one, and getting used to each change before you pull into traffic will allow you to drive without the overwhelming anxiety and stress that most people feel on their first venture out on an English roadway.

Conclusion

When we return to the traders in the pits who were confronted with change in their physical surroundings, we know that some of them adjusted quickly and some adapted slowly over time. Whether they were aware of it or not, most of them were affected by this change and experienced some kind of discomfort which caused them to be off their game for awhile. There were those traders who took a proactive approach by consciously easing up on their trading, making comfortable adjustments along the way as they took control each day. And then there were those who will talk about the good old days, never adjust and use the new building as an excuse to trade poorly. Fortunately, most were able to pull their trading back to its old level of performance after a period of adjustment with varying degrees of discomfort. So, how do you deal with change?

Chapter 31

_____

INCONSISTENCY

Lack of consistency is one of the traps that even the most dedicated and disciplined trader can fall into without warning. Many traders can maintain a routine of self-discipline for long periods of time without any sense of self-denial. As a result, these traders will experience very positive results in their trading. Then, something seems to snap in the system and the next thing the trader knows, he is out of control, having lost all of his healthy habits and all of his positive grounding. At this point, just trying to be more disciplined will not work. There is a reason that the trader is uprooting his career and it has nothing to do with discipline.

Falling off the Discipline Wagon

Jack's situation was very much like many other traders who fall off the discipline wagon after having been a highly disciplined, consistent trader. Jack had been in the business for over ten years and did not consider himself outstanding in any way. He said, "I make a comfortable living in this business and I'm not at the top and I'm not at the bottom. I'm just a middle of the road kind of guy." The fact that Jack has been able to make a comfortable living at trading does indeed put him into a special category since most traders are washed out of the business early on in their careers. A professional trader who makes a consistently good living at trading is actually an exceptional and successful trader.

For Jack, the routines of his trading life were carefully regulated by some kind of internal mechanism. He was awake every morning exactly at 6:30 without needing an alarm clock. He would immediately go to a room in his house, set up for exercising, and put in an hour workout on his machines. After showering, he meditated and ate a healthy breakfast with his wife and children. By 8:30, he was in his office, with ample time to review his strategies for the day.

Then, Jack found himself getting to work at 9:45, without having worked out, and having eaten a fast food breakfast. Suddenly, all of the good habits he had carefully established were gone. In their place appeared many of the self-destructive habits that Jack had learned to avoid, such as drinking with his buddies in the bar near his office after a trading day and failing to follow his money management rules. The effect on his trading was immediate, and his profitable trades dwindled while his losses began to mount.

What alarmed Jack, was the fact that he knew he needed to get back into his old habits, but he had no desire to do so. He was showing signs of trader burn-out without having done anything he was aware of to cause it. His life had been characterized by a lack of stress rather than an excess of stress. He had taken relaxing vacations, relieving stress and stimulating his senses. He was not aware of any feelings of boredom or lack of meaning in his life. In addition, his home life was solid and happy.

With all of this balance in his life, Jack had suddenly come unwound. Why?

TWO OPPOSING FORCES

The Emotional Rush of Surviving

One of the underlying realities of human life is the constant need to protect and insure our survival. When we solve problems related to our survival, we feel a tremendous relief and a renewed sense of the wonder of life. Our senses feel more alert and everything around us is more intense. This emotionally high experience can be so heady, so powerful that it has an addictive quality. For that reason, many people actually unconsciously create situations in which they can periodically recreate this rush of adrenaline, this sense of being truly alive. Tragedy queens who thrive on high drama and traders who create the extreme ups and downs in their trading are examples of the patterns people create in order to experience this addictive feeling.

The Need to Avoid Pain and Seek Comfort

Balancing the desire for the emotional rush of survival is the need to avoid pain and to seek comfort. This need is one of the most powerful motivators that we have. It is the quintessential survival mechanism. As we strive to avoid pain and seek comfort, we place ourselves in less and less risk of pain and destruction, thereby increasing the likelihood of our survival.

Everyone experiences the internal tug of these two opposing forces in their lives. The fact that we are not aware of the battle is because it is conducted on an unconscious level with one of these two forces having either achieved control, or balance is keeping the issue from surfacing. The state of this balancing act is a temporary one, since unforeseen events can suddenly topple the balance in favor of one side.

If a trader has had an experience which created a great, emotional surge, such as a terrible loss, with the accompanying feelings of relief and renewal that come with having survived the loss or overcome the threat or pain, he may have an unconscious pull to recreate those feelings. The memory of that experience can stay in his unconscious forever, burned in deeply, especially if the feelings from that experience are not fully experienced and resolved. The addictive quality of these feelings cannot be minimized in their influence on behavior.

In addition, the subconscious picture a trader may have of himself experiencing a tragedy and surviving it will also influence his idea of what his life is like and who he is. That picture can be a powerful unconscious motivator as well.

So, we have Jack, a trader who has learned to minimize risk, increase his comfort and nearly eliminate all pain from his life, suddenly creating a situation in which maximum pain is nearly inevitable. He is unconsciously swinging the balance in favor of the Emotional Rush side.

What will happen if Jack does not turn this situation around? He will probably create losses so major that he will be in danger of losing everything he has. He will be under tremendous pressure to pull out of a disaster. This pressure will inevitably translate to his family life and put a strain on his marriage.

Is it possible that this is exactly what Jack wants to happen at some level in his unconscious mind? The answer is, very likely. Somewhere in Jack's past lay the answer, and our job was to find that experience and neutralize its influence.

The Trigger to Jack's Undoing

Although Jack had created a highly stable life for himself and his family, he did not grow up in a very stable home. His father had a difficult time finding and keeping a job which could take care of the family. As a result, his parents were always embroiled in a war of words and actions. His mother packed up the children three times and took them to stay with her parents during Jack's childhood. After each separation, his father would re-unite them in their old house with a joyous reunion full of tears and emotional embraces. Jack never felt happier in his young life than he did at these moments. Unfortunately, the family's situation would always deteriorate until Jack and his family were once more focused on the fear that they would not survive.

Later, he promised himself that he would create a totally stable world for himself and his children. As a result, he studied how to create stability and discovered that discipline, good habits and consistency were the keys to stability and freedom from the worry about survival. Jack learned to love the feeling of safety and stability that his careful self-discipline provided. He never consciously thought about the process or even his goal of building stability. He simply sailed smoothly on the wave-free surface he had created for himself.

Then, a seemingly unrelated event triggered the old memory of instability and survival living. Jack's brother-in-law lost his job and had to go out of state to look for a new job, leaving his wife and their two children to live with her parents until he could call for them to join him. No one in his wife's family saw this event as a tragedy, but Jack was bothered by it more than anyone. When he saw his brother-in-law's children, he suddenly experienced feelings he had not felt for more than twenty five years. Shortly afterward, Jack began to lose focus and found himself breaking all of his own good habits.

At first, Jack refused to see any connection between his change of behavior and his brother-in-law's job search. However, once he explored his feelings about the effects of a major change on his brother-in-law's children, he began to feel the rush of feelings from his own childhood and the connection was suddenly clear.

What Jack had been missing in his life was that surge of intense feeling he felt after his family was reunited. He never wanted to feel the pain of loss or the intense fear of not having enough to survive again. But, he never felt that intense joy at having survived again, either. In his unconscious, the only way to feel that feeling again was to come back from great loss and disaster. If he lost everything and was separated from his wife and children, the joy he would feel when he had made it right again would be worth the cost.

The Self-Correcting Mechanism

If Jack did not stop his head long plunge, it was going to destroy his business and his family. He would have to rebuild his business to reunite his family. Then, he would experience two intense feelings he needed to feel. First, he would get to feel the inexplicable joy of bringing his family back together and of having rescued his world from the jaws of destruction. Second, he would feel an intense desire never to feel that uncomfortable or scared again. As a result, he would find himself adhering to his old, good habits like glue on a postage stamp.

Once Jack was back to his old, positive behavior, his story would appear to be resolved. Right? After all, the self-correcting mechanism would have brought Jack's situation back full circle and, Jack, now older and wiser, would be unlikely to ever repeat such a mistake. Right?

Wrong. Unfortunately, now the cycle is much more likely to repeat itself. Jack's old pattern has been reinforced in his adulthood, and the pull of those old, addictive feelings are now stronger than they have been for many years.

The unconscious mind does not care whether it creates chaos or pain as long as it continues to experience the emotional states that make us feel the way we want to or need to feel. For this reason, the unconscious mind will guide us into disaster if the intense relief of pain is the reward we seek. It will guide us to stability if the prolonged relief of pain is what we seek, as well. If we are addicted to that brief, intense burst of feeling joy, then we are likely to seek out the dramas. If we are attached to the sense of security and comfort, we will seek out the stability and disciplines that make it possible.

No Value Judgments

None of us is in the position to create the early conditions which will later affect our lives. If we are raised in stability, then we have a much better chance of recreating consistent stability in our trading. But if we are raised in instability, we will have many associations with pain and loss that will stay with us for the rest of our lives and continue to affect our trading. Once these associations are formed, we react in very predictable, but unconscious ways.

Many traders successfully learn to compensate for the instability and loss they have experienced in the past by adhering to positive and consistent disciplines. Unfortunately, there is always the risk of falling off the discipline wagon if they are not well prepared. The right trigger may occur to bring to the surface all of their old feelings and needs associated with earlier threats to their survival. Like Jack, they will find themselves falling off the discipline wagon and not understanding why. Poised for disaster, they will be unable to stop the fall.

Mastering Your Psychology

The only way to reinforce your wagon so that you are prepared for the potential threats to your self-discipline is to master your own psychology. I hear many traders talk about uncovering their own psychology and working with it. Often what this means is that they have read some excellent books on psychology or they have gone to a therapist and talked out problems they have. A trader may understand who his is and why he does what he does, but he may still be trapped in his old patterns regardless of his understanding. Instead of mastering his psychology, the trader is still a slave to it.

What must be done to master your psychology:

1. Identify those experiences in your life which were traumatic and which you man-aged to survive. Fully experience the feelings associated with this traumatic event.

2. Disassociate the traumatic experience with feelings of aliveness and joyful relief.

3. Create new associations with the traumatic experience to replace the old ones which neutralize the experience.

4. Identify peak experiences in your life which were positive, such as major achievements or milestones, and fully experience the positive feelings associated with these events. Or, imagine the peak experiences of your life which you are

aiming toward and fully experience them. Build up the emotional charge around these experiences so that you may feel that way whenever you think about these experiences.

This is the process we followed in helping Jack to disengage from the addictive lure of his old, tragic experiences. By the time we had finished, Jack had created associations of peak, emotional experiences with past achievements as well as new goals he developed. He no longer needed to create a tragedy to feel intensely alive and joyful. Now, Jack can maintain the consistency in his trading which is necessary for continued success. Instead of becoming a slave to the destructive pattern of roller-coaster extremes, Jack can continue to build on a solid foundation so that each year is an improvement upon the next.

Conclusion

Consistency is the cornerstone of successful trading. Consistency in effort and discipline predictably results in consistent gains. Highly disciplined traders, who have a background of instability or traumatic events in their past, are at risk of being derailed from their consistent track by a need to re-experience the intense, emotional relief and joy they associate with coming back from disaster. This vulnerability can be triggered by a current event or the memory of a past event, and send a trader into unexpected turbulence. The best defense against this vulnerability is for a trader to become the master of his own psychology. This can be done by identifying those experiences which were traumatic and which now are associated in his mind with the joy of coming through the event alive and intact or with the intense relief and feeling of being acutely alive. Once identified, these experiences must be neutralized by replacing the old, intense emotional associations with new ones. Then, the trader must re-program his mind to link intense and joyful feelings to his positive goals and life experiences. Once these steps are taken, the trader can get on with his life and his trading, in a consistently productive manner without fear of being sabotaged from within.

Every negative situation in your life has

to do with some kind of loss.

Find the lesson in the loss and

you transform it.

Tip from the coach

Chapter 32

LOSS

If you are a trader, you have experienced loss. The trick is in recovering from the loss -- quicker, stronger, wiser. The alternative is to become so frightened of future losses that it impairs your trading, creating bigger and more painful losses, or to become pessimistic and depressed, and lose confidence and hope.

Learning from Losses

Every trader has dealt with losses, whether they are trading-related or not. Loss is at the heart of every painful experience in our lives, even the smallest ones. If we reflect back on all of the traumas and difficulties of our life, it becomes clear that most of these events were related to a loss. For example, losing a race at school is indeed a loss, experiencing the death of someone you know is a loss of a relationship, and experiencing an embarrassing moment in front of others is painful because it results in a loss of self-esteem. Even when we make choices, such as moving to a new location or changing jobs, the result is the loss of familiar faces and experiences. When these events are thrust upon us, they are even more painful.

Losses Can be Lessons and Turning Points

There are a variety of ways that we can perceive losses. They can be stepping stones to major breakthroughs. Losses can result in an awakening of who or what we really are and can realign our values, so that we remember what is really important to us. Basically, losses can be lessons and turning points.

Although the painful experiences are always low moments in our lives at the time they occur, when we look back at some of the greatest joys and successes of our lives, they are often connected to a loss. If you look for the silver lining in a loss, in most cases you can find one.

For example, when Carrol O'Connor, who played Archie Bunker in "All in the Family," lost his adopted son to drugs, he turned his personal tragedy into a crusade against drugs. Everyone now benefits from his efforts. When John Walsh's six year old son was kidnapped and murdered, he left his successful career and created the television show, "America's Most Wanted," which has resulted in the capture of over 400 dangerous criminals. When "Superman," Christopher Reeves, lost the use of his arms and legs in an accident, he campaigned for the insurance industry to provide extended benefits to quad-riplegics. Only time will tell what good can come from the murder of Bill Cosby's only son, Ennis, who had overcome dyslexia to earn his graduate degree in special education from Columbia University.

By now, however, you are saying to yourself, "That's all very interesting, but what good can come from a loss in trading?" That's an excellent question, which comes with an equally excellent answer. When I have interviewed some of the best traders in the world, I always ask them about the roots of their great success. Nearly always, they say that a big loss caused them to make the transition from being a mediocre trader to doing what it takes to become a great trader.

Patterns of behavior continue indefinitely unless they are interrupted. What it takes to inte-rrupt a pattern is often something that gets our attention. For a trader, nothing gets his or her attention as completely as a major loss. If the pattern of expected trading performance is interrupted by a major loss, the trader has three positive options:

1. The first option is to look at his present methodology and make the decision to make some changes. In this scenario loss is then perceived as a lesson, an opp-ortunity to improve.

2. The second option is to treat losses as an important or necessary step in the achievement of his goals. For a trader, this mindset would have him res-ponding to a loss by saying to himself, "This loss is one more step toward getting the best possible overall outcome. Losses must happen on the way to gains. Therefore, this loss brings me one step closer to my next gain." This is particularly true for salesmen who know that they will receive a certain number of "no's" before they get a "yes."

3. The third option is to perceive a loss as proof that the negative thinking behind it is the cause, i.e., "trading is too difficult for me," or "it's hopeless," or "my system is no good," or "my life is all about failure and loss." Observing this could lead to a different choice and, therefore, a new positive direction.

The alternative is that losses can also mean, for some traders; retreating, submission to being a victim, or just plain giving up.

The Trader Who Loved and Lost, and Lost Again

For a very long time, Stu was unhappy in his marriage. Stu's wife, Alma, was an entrepreneur who started up one business after another, only to leave them for another project when things did not pay off immediately. Unfortunately, she aligned herself with highly questionable or inexperienced people, and got involved with "get-rich-quick" schemes. She borrowed from people without paying them back. Stu, who loved Alma deeply, was always there to pick up the pieces. Eventually, Alma began using Stu's name to guarantee her deals and his business checking account to cover her losses. Then, one day, after ten years of marriage, Stu came home to find both his home and his savings account empty. Alma had moved on.

What happened then to Stu's trading life is typical of what happens to traders when they experience a great loss in their personal life. Once a steady, successful trader, Stu began to experience a cascade of losses in his trading. Because of the inner stress with which Stu was dealing, he was not able to put together the two events in his mind. One reason was that Alma's pipe-dreams of great success had become, for Stu, the basis for his sense of security and support. Stu failed to realize that he had created his own basis of support through his resources and skills. With Alma gone, Stu felt as though the bottom of his world have given way, and his new insecurity made him question everything that he did. Instead of the confidence with which he had once traded, Stu now questioned his signals and his decisions. The result was the creation of ever-increasing losses.

Creating Anchors

When a major loss takes place in our lives, we tend to associate certain parts of the experience with the particular loss, and by extension, to all losses. These associations become anchors which are unconsciously tied to that experience. These anchors, when they recur in our lives, shoot us back immediately to the feelings and thoughts associated with the original experience. For example, when Patrick was a child, his father worked for a company that moved him on a regular basis. By the time Patrick had finally fit into his new school, made new friends, and started feeling successful in his new life, his entire world would come apart. It was time to move again. He lost everything he had worked hard to gain. The anchor for loss for Patrick was success and stability. As a trader, whenever his trading had reached a high, stable level of profit, Patrick became uncomfortable. Without knowing why on a conscious level, Patrick was waiting to lose it all. His unconscious mind would then complete the pattern by creating the losses he was expecting.

Anchors Away

If every painful loss we have ever had in our lives has its own anchors, we will soon be weighted down by negative anchors like Jacob Marley in a *"Christmas Carol"* who was eternally condemned to dragging around the ill-doings of his life. Nearly everything will remind us of losses and the painful feelings associated with them. Once those feelings take hold, we are in a state to create losses. What we must do is disconnect our current anchors from their old associations. But how can we do that?

1. First, you have to be aware of the things which you now associate with loss. If you think about it, you will be able to uncover these anchors - - they are the sights, the sounds, the things, the words, the smells which bring you down, which make you sad, which make you uncomfortable and you have no rational reason for these feelings. Another way to uncover them is to recreate in your mind's eye the losses that are painful to you and note the particular details that stand out for you. Which ones seem to represent the experience to you?

2. The next step is to uncouple these anchors so that they are not creating the feelings of loss each time you encounter them. This can be done by replacing these anchors with new associations. For example, if you associate December with losing money because you once lost a great deal of money in December and you find yourself repeating losses at that time of the year, you need to unlink that association. Close your eyes and imagine the most rewarding trade you can think of, one which will create a high charge of emotion in you. Now, imagine that trade taking place in December. For this process to work, you must imagine it vividly and the emotional charge must be very high. The more you repeat the process, the more effective this process will be for you.

3. The last step is to replace old negative anchors with new, positive ones. Think back to a time when something really inspired or motivated you - - the trading book you read, the trader you mentored, the big lesson you learned - - until you experience sensations that feel good. Then think of a one-word description that describes that feeling or emotion. Repetition is important to setting strong anchors, so that only your word description is enough to bring on the desired state.

Now that you have begun to uncouple your old loss-anchors, you will need to have a strategy for dealing with future losses that will allow you to use the loss as an opportunity to expand or grow rather than having the loss deplete you of your resources and strength. The fact that the loss occurred will not change. It happened, and there is no way to undo it. What will change will be your reaction to it. If you think of the loss as a connection with energy, you will realize that the greater the loss, the more powerful the energy that is generated. This energy has to be directed somewhere. Where will you direct this energy? Toward more losses or toward your well-being?

Where Are you Going to Put Your Focus?

If you expect to find a disaster, you will. If you look for an opportunity, you will find it as well. Your brain will focus on what you are interested in, what you value, and what you expect to happen. There is a famous experiment in psychology in which a cat's brain was hooked up to electrodes that register input from the cat's ear to his brain. A rhythmic beeping sound was then played which registered on the instruments as it occurred. The cat was clearly hearing the beeping sound. Then, they placed a mouse in a cage next to the cat. Although the beeping sound continued to play as before, it no longer registered on the instrument. The cat was no longer aware of the beeping sound. Clearly, his brain was occupied with more important matters. His focus was on the mouse.

Conclusion

This same principle of focus applies to our own neurology. If you focus on something, it will become your reality, crowding out the other realities around you. If your focus is on positive outcomes, you will have the intellectual and emotional energy to reach them. If your focus is on losses, you will direct your energies there. The tragic losses that befell Carrol O'Connor and Christopher Reeves released a tremendous amount of energy which these men focused on positive outcomes. And Bill Cosby is directing his energy toward making people laugh. When the energy from a tragic loss is used for positive change or positive outcomes, it can be used for healing from the loss. When that same energy is directed inwardly toward depression and pessimism, healing from the loss will not take place. Instead, that energy will persist, creating more losses.

Chapter 33

FAILURE

The **"will to succeed"** must be a part of a trader's developed skills in order for him/her to be able to maintain the motivation it takes to succeed. When the going gets rough and the markets seem to be whipping you at every turn, the only thing that will maintain the momentum to move on is a deep-seated "will." This "will" is a resource you have developed over the years as an anchor to push through what feels like a dark tunnel of uncertainty. Those traders who can visualize a light at the end of the tunnel as a prize worth any discomfort along the way will overcome the odds and make it to the top. But, even when this "will" is deep-seated, situations in life arise which appear to destroy this will altogether. These events can be overcome when you understand what it takes to create **"the will to succeed"** in the first place, what destroyed it along the way, and what it takes to get it back.

Roots of The Will to Succeed

"Will" is a very important resource in building success. Whether by genetics or some unexplainable reason, it has been observed by parents and doctors that some babies have a natural inclination towards being relentless in getting what they want. The natural inclination of most children is to give up as soon as things become too challenging, but a special handful of children will develop this tenacity from modeling a parent, teacher, mentor or peer by observing that it is a way of winning rewards. The most attractive incentives for a reward are the good feelings attached to the reward. As humans we are driven and motivated by anything that will make us feel good, and avoid things that will make us feel uncomfortable. There are varying degrees to what lengths a person will go to succeed in order to feel good. Those who will go the extra mile to get pleasure from a small accomplishment when they are young, even if it means feeling uncomfortable in the process, will be the ones who succeed far above the crowd when they are adults.

Lighting up My Life

One experience can set off a chain of willful behavior as a lifetime resource. When I was in the fourth grade my teacher offered, as a prize, a small flashlight for any student with perfect attendance for the year. My allowance could have bought that flashlight immediately. But, having a picture of everyone being proud of me and believing it was something achievable was the incentive that drove me to win. The only flash light earned was mine. I did not know at the time, but I also received two precious prizes for life: the resource of the "will to succeed" at anything that was important to me and an anchor of knowing I could.

Lost "Will"

Losing the will to win means that the individual's inner dialogue no longer includes the belief that the individual has the ability to win. The loss of will marks the death of the spirit, a loss of faith, a giving up of the passion to be motivated. This happens to many seniors when they stop believing in the possibilities of life.

Losing will is really another aspect of the grieving process. In the face of a loss too great to bear, the trader loses his will to win. The loss is perceived as the death of something precious and irreplaceable to the trader so there is no reason to continue the effort. Going on becomes a mechanical exercise. The body goes through the motions of living but the drive and the commitment to winning are all gone.

What is that loss which is too great to bear? Often it is the loss of the dream or the goal. Or maybe the loss is the end of the belief in one's self because something damaged that image. For a trader, sometimes a loss in the market is so great that it results in the loss of something else, something which symbolized for the trader his belief in his ability to win and in the very goal itself.

Losing Control

Ralph had a very successful career as a trader for ten years. With a "take charge, get the job done attitude," he always seemed to be in control of every situation. This made him successful at everything he undertook in his life, including trading. The one thing Ralph prided himself on the most was his ability to hold himself together under difficult conditions and come out on top. Although he was not the senior member of his family, everyone in the family looked to him to solve problems and challenges that would arise in their lives. Ralph's wife, Jill, was his most precious pride and joy in life. She was a Major in the military during "Desert Storm." When Jill returned from her assignment, Ralph noticed changes in Jill's personality and physical condition, although the military hospitals could find nothing abnormal relating to her assignment. She became sensitive to all minor problems and could not cope with everyday stress. When Ralph took her to private doctors, they said she was probably exposed to chemical warfare. The situation escalated until Jill asked for a divorce. For the first time, Ralph was not in control of the situation.

He felt helpless to do anything that made a difference: to help Jill with her mental and physical disorders and to keep her in the marriage. Ralph started losing confidence in himself as a person who could handle difficult situations. He took some heavy losses in the markets but, this time, he could not get back into the saddle.

Losing the Dream

Tom's situation was an example of the relationship between the loss of a dream and the death of the will to succeed. When Tom and his wife, Cathy, were building their life together, they bought a tract of land outside of the city. Slowly, as Tom made more and more money in the market, they built a house, section by section. This house became their dream house. It was the place their families met for holidays and the place their children brought their friends for long weekends. This house symbolized, for Tom, his achievements and the fulfillment of his dreams. When he came home at night, even though it was dark and late, Tom would wander around his property and gaze in reverence at his house in the dark. Last year, Tom had to sell his house to cover some serious losses. He and Cathy and the kids moved into town to a nice apartment and Tom resumed his trading, but the will to win was gone.

The optimistic, cheerleading voice inside Tom was silent. In its place was another voice. This was the voice of hopelessness and despair. This nagging voice told Tom that nothing mattered anymore, that there was no need to bother. After all, what was the point?

For other traders, the optimistic voice of belief in oneself and one's dreams is replaced with silence. The good feelings have been replaced with feelings too painful to bear, so that the brain turns off the switch. The monologue is silenced and the trader seems to feel nothing, care about nothing and go on like a machine. Since he no longer believes in his dream or goal and has lost faith in his ability to achieve it, he can not see the sense in the struggle.

Linking Pain and Loss With the Process

Many traders who begin their career loving the process of becoming a trader lose this feeling as a result of a series of losses. With these losses, a positive association becomes a negative one. Where trading used to be linked with pleasure, it is now linked with pain and loss.

Facing the Inevitable Transition

A transition of changing patterns of behavior is necessary to rebuild self-confidence. But, before you can take the first step, you must realize a serious problem exists. What makes one trader able to make the transition successfully while other traders face devastation just by facing the prospect of the transition? The extent of the loss, and more importantly, its meaning to the trader, will determine how difficult the transition will be. If the loss symbolizes the end of a trader's belief in himself or his goal, the transition will be

251

extremely difficult. Recovery and success result from positive self-talk and action. Pessimistic self-talk will create the loss of the will to win.

How To Rebuild the Will To Win

Set aside time for recovery. Usually when a trader is in an unresourceful state of mind, it is not easy to get him or her to commit to more than three days for recovery. Even a weekend feels like self-indulgence. Traders feel like they need to catch up and don't deserve the time off. The following is a quick fix. I would certainly recommend more time and professional assistance when possible. If you go through this weekend and the nagging problems still exist, please get help. Remember you are not the only one going through pain. You must also consider family, friends, and business associates.

WEEKEND "WILL" FIXER-UPPER

First Half, Day One: think of nothing but your losses while cleaning out the basement, the attic, your drawers and your closets.

Second Half, Day One: continue to organize the space in your life while thinking of what would happen if you continued thinking this way. It is important to be aware of the pain and the self-talk directing it. At the end of the first day, listen to a "motivational-possibility tape" before you go to sleep.

First Half, Day Two: write down all the events in your life in which you have succeeded in the past, what it took to make you succeed, and which of those resources (abilities, skills, etc.) are still available to your right now (my *"Treasure Diary for Creating Affluence"* is a good assistant to this end). Do this in a beautiful setting preferably outdoors.

Second Half, Day Two: plan your future by writing down how you will take action: Dream about a more effective outcome.

Before you go to bed, read a book about people who have come through difficulties and became successful. One book I would recommend is *"Tough Times Never Last, Tough People Do,"* by Dr. Robert Schuller.

Day Three: Make a list of everything you want and how you plan to get it and write that you deserve to be prosperous and happy. Plan ten immediate tasks that would make a difference. Write out all the times you have succeeded in the past and what made you succeed.

Conclusion

When a trader loses the will to win, to be successful, or even to trade at all, it is because he has lost the belief in himself and his ability to reach his goal of being successful. He may have lost faith in the value of reaching his goal at all. He even begins to associate the

252

process of trading with pain and loss. When this downward process is complete, the trader will ask himself: what is the point? And the answer will be: there is none. With the memories of failure all around him and intense pressure to make a comeback ever-present, a trader will have no room to decide what he really wants. He will have no room to complete his grieving, and he will have no incentive to do so.

But, there is a way back for a trader who has lost the will to win. He can regain his sense of control and desire by breaking the new associations of pain with his trading and replace them with those of pleasure and success. He can make choices by demanding the room to fail or to give up. He can set himself up for small successes, so he can rebuild his confidence in winning. He can seek out help and support and finally, he can re-create the inner voice that guides him towards his goal all the while, cheering him on.

What keeps the will going on is not only those underlying feelings and beliefs, but the internal monologue which keeps us in touch with those underlying feelings and beliefs. Inside the unconscious mind is the voice which says "I can do it, I'm excited and passionate about life and its possibilities and opportunities and I will succeed because I deserve to." This optimism in the face of obstacles, defeats, bad days and losses comes from moving away from uncomfortable feelings and moving towards good feelings. This message will be embellished with details of worthiness and past successes as well as pictures of your success and the powerful feelings of accomplishment.

SECTION VI

Traders Who Limit Success By…

Chapter 34

_____

NOT SAYING NO

The list of personal qualities required to build a successful trading career (or a successful career in any other area of the financial and investing world, for that matter) sometimes appears to be endless. However, one quality is always first on the list: self-discipline. Self-discipline is, in turn, also composed of many parts, the cornerstone of which is the ability to set limits.

Setting limits can be viewed in many ways - as an ability or an innate talent, as a gift, as a willingness or personal decision, an inner discipline, or even as a virtue to be developed through personal commitment. However you define the quality of setting limits, without it, success is either an elusive dream or a temporary condition. Furthermore, many people seem to have areas in their lives in which they can set limits and other areas in which they are incapable of setting limits. This dichotomy is often seen as the ability of a person to set limits in his professional life while being unable to set limits in his personal life. The entertainment industry supports this observation with an inexhaustible supply of fabulously successful stars who lost it all due to their inability or unwillingness to set limits on their personal indulgences.

Limits for Traders

In few commercial endeavors is the need to set limits more urgent than in trading. If a trader cannot or will not set limits in his trading, he will rapidly put himself out of business and lose everything he has spent years building. If he only periodically fails to set limits, he can produce the very same results, except it will take a bit longer.

If a trader maintains a strict policy of setting limits in his trading and then lets the pent-up steam escape wildly and uncontrollably in his personal life, the effects on his trading will eventually begin to appear in subtle and destructive ways.

There is no escape or easy way out from the need to set limits.

The Trader who Couldn't Say "No" (To Himself)

Few people have the opportunity to begin life in the kind of loving and supportive home environment in which Jon, a twenty-eight year old trader, was raised. His parents, both educated and successful people, were devoted to both Jon and his older brother, Jacob. In addition, Jon's grandparents were equally devoted and doting. As they grew up, Jon and Jacob were afforded every conceivable opportunity to grow, learn and experience life in a supportive and caring environment.

As expected, these two young men developed into attractive, educated, self-confident, hard-working human beings. Jon's older brother, Jacob, built a highly successful business and lives in a large, beautiful house surrounded by a loving wife and three small children. And last year, the younger brother, Jon, made over $500,000 as a committed, disciplined trader! For this handsome, young bachelor, his free time was filled with dates with the most beautiful and desirable young women in his New York suburb.

A Not-so-hidden Problem

Why then was Jon coming for counseling? What was wrong and why did his brother, Jacob, insist that Jon do something about it?

The most obvious sign that something was seriously wrong was the fact that Jon's income for this current year has plummeted to $50,000. On less than one-tenth of his last year's income, Jon does not have enough money on which to live after developing expensive tastes and building in major expenses. The second sign that something was wrong was that Jon has nothing tangible to show for all of the money he has made. He owns no home or condominium. He has no flashy cars or boats. His checking account is anemic and he has no savings or investment portfolio. In fact, he paid the government 50% of last year's income because he had done no planning for his financial security.

The third sign of trouble was that Jon had no girlfriend or long-term relationship. In fact, the longest relationship he has had with a woman lasted four weeks. He moves on to the next woman as fast as he can, calling himself the "Honeymoon King." His self-anointed title refers to his predilection for avoiding all commitments and entanglements before they can make any claims on his feelings while enjoying the excitement of the chase and the conquest.

And, finally, the last sign that Jon was in trouble, which was certainly the most serious and dramatic, was his long history of using and abusing almost every type of addictive drug, narcotic and illegal substance known. In addition, he is an "equal-opportunity self-abuser" who eats whatever junk food he wants and exercises on a schedule of total abstinence punctuated by periodic killer work-outs. By his own admission, Jon is withdrawing heavily from the stored-up health benefits of his youth.

The Lessons from Home

Where did this out-of-control behavior in an otherwise highly disciplined trader come from? The surprising answer is that this destructive behavior came from that same loving and supportive home life which produced such a set of happy and successful young men. As loving and supportive as Jon's parents were, they were also unwilling to set any limits for their younger son, Jon. By the time their second child had arrived, Jon's parents had effectively absorbed a culture and philosophy from the 1960's that was rooted in rebellion against authority, conventional behavior, and values. The net result was that Jon's parents never said "No" to their younger son.

Not only was Jon taught to set no limits for himself, he was encouraged to push through any limitations that may have been imposed on him by others. In fact, limitations of any kind posed a challenge to Jon. If something was off limits to him, he viewed it as an invitation to try it. Since his parents also encouraged him to explore and test everything, he felt that he had been given the green light to do this by the only people who counted in his life.

This attitude about testing boundaries and not setting limits provided an open invitation for Jon to start experimenting with drugs. The fact that his parents were also experimenting with drugs also made their use more attractive to him. By the time he had gone to college, he had tried nearly every drug that was available at that time. Although Jon believes himself to be in control of his drug usage, he is never very far from another hit on some addictive substance.

Jon's brother, Jacob, however, is a completely different story. As the first child, Jacob tended to be more conservative about everything, especially since his parents were more attentive to the behavior of the only child they had for two years. When Jon came along, however, his parents eased up any and all restrictions they had set for Jacob. Nevertheless, the pattern was set for Jacob, who learned elementary limit-setting early. As a result, Jacob does not have problems with self-indulgent or out-of-control behavior. He does not feel the need to rebel at home once he is freed from his self-imposed harness at work.

When Jon leaves his trading office, he feels an instantaneous need to indulge himself. He tests his appetites to see which one needs to be satisfied and then he is off to do whatever feels good, for as long as it feels good, and possibly a good deal longer. The result is that he finds himself nursing morning hangovers, popping antacid tablets from over eating rich and spicy foods, fighting off mood swings and exhaustion from drug abuse, and dealing with the aftershocks of his "drive-by love life."

It is also important to note that Jon's ability to set limits for himself seems to be getting worse and not better. Instead of learning to be more in control, Jon seems to be going in the opposite direction. Every time his brother says something to him about needing to set limits or say "No" to himself, Jon feels a rebellious need to push the envelope open a little further.

All of this has begun to affect Jon's trading. He isn't as sharp and focused as he used to be and needs to be. He doesn't have the energy he had two years ago. And worst of all, he finds it a little more difficult to stick to his trading rules than he used to. After all, how can he follow his trading rules when he doesn't follow rules in the rest of his life?

"Limits" Set you Free

Like Jon, many of us find it hard to say "No" to ourselves. The problem of setting limits has become a national, if not an international, issue for many people who are being raised in families and communities in which fewer and fewer limitations are being set on their behaviors and where personal responsibility is shifted onto someone else. If we go too far and something unpleasant results from it, the problem must have been someone else's fault. It is difficult to say "No" to yourself when there have been no external voices to internalize.

The omnipresence in our culture of commercial advertising, with its appeal to self-indulgence and immediate gratification, also sends a constant message to our unconscious minds that we need to have whatever we want whenever we want it. As a result, "limits" has become a dirty word for many people. No one ever won a popularity contest, or an election for that matter, by telling people they had to give something up they enjoyed or that they had to set limits on their spending or their pleasures.

The Rebound Effect

Another young trader named Chris also came from a family who loved and nurtured their children. However, Chris's experience of personal limits was at the opposite end of the spectrum from Jon's experience. Chris's father was a Methodist minister who strongly believed in self-denial and self-sacrifice as a means to Godliness. Although Chris's parents were kind and loving to him, they raised him to feel guilty if he allowed himself the slightest indulgence. The result was that, as an adult, Chris found himself vacillating between the extremes of self-denial and the periodic explosions of pent-up emotional need. These explosions were unpredictable and could occur in his trading as well as in his private life. Afterwards, Chris was guilt-ridden and on-the-wagon for long periods. During these self-control times, his trading flourished. Then, he would reach his threshold of self-denial and take major losses in his trading and his personal life.

The Golden Mean

Somewhere between the total self-indulgence of Jon and the total self-denial of Chris is a place where traders can find a balanced life that supports their trading and their personal lives. This place was described over three thousand years ago as the *Golden Mean*. The philosophical principle of finding a place that was in perfect balance between two extreme positions was one of the most important and enduring contributions of the *Golden Age of Greece*. In recent times, we have updated the principle as that place on the Laffer Curve where the means justify the end, where risk justifies reward, where resources expended balance out the resources created. For traders, this point of balance must be found between the need to be disciplined and the need to be emotionally fed. Too much denial creates a need for over-indulgence. Too much indulgence creates an obsessive self-loathing and self-denial. Neither of these extreme positions is healthy or productive.

How to Find your Trading Fulcrum

When two people of equal weight get on their respective ends of a seesaw, the balancing point is in the middle. The board rests perfectly balanced on the support that we call the fulcrum. The trick to long-term success in trading is to find that point that balances the seesaw of our lives. When one thing is out of kilter, it throws everything out of balance. Just as Jon's personal life eventually affected his trading life, any serious weakness in our personal lives will eventually cast a shadow on our professional lives and vice versa.

One of the most effective ways to put balance back into our limit-setting is to do the following:

1. Make a list of all the changes that would make you a better trader as well as a more fulfilled person.

2. Write down all the tasks it would take to become the best you can be.

3. Take one of those tasks that you know you can accomplish within a short period and complete it. Keep repeating step 3. You have learned to do the "trader's waltz."

Conclusion

The need to set limits in trading is an indispensable part of the self-discipline a trader must have to work his system and make consistent profits. The traders who cannot set limits on their trading wash out quickly. However, those traders who are able to impose a set of limits on their trading behaviors but not on their personal lives, run the great risk of throwing their trading lives out of balance as well. The only way out of this situation is to be consistent with what you say you will do and make it a habit to carry out those tasks. When you give the right signals to your neurology, it will be there to support you in good trading decisions.

Chapter 35

LISTENING TO VOICES FROM THE PAST

Have you ever blown a trade, missed a signal, bailed out too soon, ridden a trade to near extinction or badly miscalculated a market move and, afterward, said to yourself, "How could I have done that?" Maybe the answer is that you didn't do it, after all. Maybe it was someone else.

No, I'm not talking about a story out of the Twilight Zone. There are no alien body snatchers or escapees from the Lost Colony of Atlantis at work here. Nevertheless, the person who is actually calling the shots on your trading may not be you at all.

Whose Voice is That?

Bob waved his arms about dramatically as he explained the conflict that was going on inside him when making a trading decision. "This part of me," he said as he waved his right arm, "knows exactly what to do, wants to do it, and is very confident about making the right decisions. But this other part of me," he continued, now waving his left arm about, "keeps asking me, 'are you sure you are making the right decision?'"

As Bob continued to talk about the cautionary voice inside him, he added, "As I listen to this part of me, she keeps saying that I'm making bad choices." I stopped Bob and asked, "Who is she?" Bob looked at me, puzzled, unconscious of what he had just said. "What are you talking about?"

"You just said 'she,'" I told him.

At first Bob refused to believe me. As our conversation moved from trading to his personal life and from there to his childhood, Bob slowly began to realize that the "she" voice in his head was his mother's voice.

Bob's mother had been a doting and concerned mother who was a highly controlling individual. Afraid that Bob would make a mistake that would result in his harm, she questioned every step he took as a child. By the time Bob was a young adult, he found it difficult to make simple decisions without a painful interlude of back and forth indecision. Embarrassed by his constant vacillation, Bob had learned to conceal this process from the people around him. He became inured to the discomfort he experienced with each decision so that he wasn't even aware of the internal process for most decisions. In fact, if each trading decision was not associated with a potential and immediate loss, Bob would probably not have been aware that he was in a state of conflict with each trade.

Look Who's Talking

Surrounded by the trappings of luxury that came from the success of both his business and long-term trading careers, Justin, nevertheless, talked endlessly about when he would get rich, when it would all happen for him, and when he would become successful. And when Justin talked about being a trader, he also talked about when he would become a good trader. Justin was apparently unaware of his already-achieved success in the two professional arenas of his life.

Nothing this highly talented and accomplished man did was ever good enough to enjoy his own stamp of approval. When he talked about the problems in his trading, he described how he would not act on good signals because they were never good enough. As a result, Justin's success in trading was good, but not outstanding.

Where did this voice come from which was always telling Justin that his trading signals were never good enough? In fact, where did the voice come from that told him that nothing he did in his trading was ever good enough?

Once again, the answer to the mystery voice could be found in the trader's childhood. In Justin's case, he decided that the voice came from his father. As far as Justin's father had been concerned, nothing Justin had done was ever good enough. When Justin played on the basketball team, the fact that the team won had never satisfied his father. What mattered to this frustrated perfectionist was how many points his son had scored -- and it was never enough. In his schoolwork, Justin was never praised for his outstanding academic achievements but was criticized by his father for the minor areas in which he could do better.

Although Justin's father has been dead for over ten years, he lives in Justin's head, directing Justin's decisions, minimizing his achievements and reducing his life to a series of areas in which he will "one day" succeed. If Justin is not trading to his capacity, it is because he is not really trading at all. Look who's doing the self-talking. It sounds like Dad!

Internalizing the Nebbish

Like most of the major life-effecting decisions we make as children, deciding which voice we are going to internalize for the rest of our lives is not done consciously based upon our long-term goals, our true self interest, our values and our sense of reason. Instead, the loudest, most demanding and influential voice in our lives tends to elbow out the other small, positive voices of reason and moderation.

Why do we rarely internalize the joyful, optimistic, can-do voices? Perhaps it is because these positive voices do not need to control the sound stages of our lives as we are growing up. In any case, it seems to be a common phenomenon that the voices which have a strangle-hold on stalled-out traders are the nebbishes from our lives - like Bob's mother, the ceaselessly complaining, whining, limiting and fearful voices that take hold in our unconscious. And before we know it, the voice that we hear in our formative years becomes a voice in our own heads. The author of the original voice can die, but we unconsciously take over the job of keeping the voice alive and in control of us.

The Critical Legacy

Of course, the foreign voice that we internalize is not just a nebbish voice. It can be a critical voice -- like the voice of Justin's father. The problem with the critical voice is that its influence pervades our lives in more than just the way we place our trades. For example, that critical voice can be turned on others as well as ourselves. When that happens, we find ourselves criticizing in others the very things that our critical voice is criticizing in us.

This externalization of our own inner voice is what happened to Justin's father. Having been raised in a critical, unloving home, he internalized the critical voice of his parents. Then, when his son, Justin, was born, he saw his son as an extension of himself and felt the need to verbalize the very criticisms he directed against himself. (So, the voice that Justin was hearing, was not his own. It was not even his father's. It was his grandfather's voice!!!)

When Justin's father was growing up, he promised himself that he was not going to be like his parents. Unfortunately, by the time Justin was a teenager, Justin's father discovered, to his dismay, that he had become his parents without realizing it and he began to hear himself using his father's voice. It was the same criticizing and demeaning voice that had destroyed his achievements as a boy. This was the same process that had transformed the fearful voice of Bob's grandmother into her daughter's nagging and controlling voice.

Fortunately, the process is not destined to be repeated forever. Old, destructive patterns can be broken and positive new ones can replace them.

How to Break the Pattern?

When Justin and Bob learned to listen to their inner voices and they became aware of the influence their second-hand voices had on their trading, they both committed to breaking the patterns. The process for both men was the same. First they had to acknowledge that they had a negative voice in their heads that was not representing their best interests. Then they had to be willing to commit to changing the pattern. To do this, they had to be willing to look at the unresourceful messages and replace them with resourceful messages by one of the following means:

1. **Becoming a direct translator...**
   Both men had to learn how to become a translator. Each time they heard the fearful, controlling, whining, negative voice inside their head, they learned how to translate the message from a lethal message to a positive message. How? Just like a direct translator in the United Nations translates simultaneously into English as a foreigner is speaking, you must learn how to translate into positive language what the negative language is saying. This process is clearly not a direct, accurate translation of what is being said. However, when you get good at translating to yourself, you will feel you are suddenly understanding what is being said, as if the negative language was a foreign language to you. Then, eventually, you will translate without being aware of it. And finally, you will not need to translate at all.

2. **Acting as if...**
   Another effective way to overcome the effects of these foreign, negative voices is to ask yourself how you would behave if you were a positive thinker? And then do so. This is a very quick method to bring your trading behaviors into alignment with your best interests.

3. **Modeling on a star...**
   If you cannot imagine yourself acting in a positive way in contradiction to the negative internal voice, act like someone who does. Find a person who acts in the positive way you would like to follow, and model your behavior on his or hers.

Conclusion

When a trader asks himself, "How could I have done that?" the answer may be that he didn't. He was under the control of the voices from his past which hold his success captive in their limiting messages. These voices are the negative, unresourceful ones which came from the neediest, most frightened, persistent people around us. We eventually internalized these voices so they continue to tell us what to do. And, we externalized them as well, turning those same critical, fearful or negative messages on the people closest to us. The fastest and most effective way out of this self-imposed trap is to learn how to translate these negative messages into positive messages and to act as if we are already in the control of positive messages.

What you repress will surface

when you are in a vulnerable state.

Handle your issues

before they handle you.

Tip from the coach

Chapter 36

_____

REPRESSING PAST TRAUMAS

After working privately with traders for the last seven years, it still never fails to amaze me how an incident in a trader's childhood can determine whether or not it is okay for him to succeed. These childhood incidents, too painful to remember or acknowledge, are often "swept under the carpet" by sensitive and vulnerable people. While these experiences may be perfectly concealed within the trader's consciousness, the damaging psychological issues resulting from them will sabotage his ability to perform. As a result, his profits are swept under as well.

Often, in the course of a counseling session, obvious issues will come up in conversation about beliefs, values and attitudes which will prompt me to say, "Aha! This is where the trader is having a problem psychologically." Then, suddenly, in a casual voice, the trader will reveal to me the fact that he was molested as a child or abandoned by his family or forced to fend for himself at an early age. We think these issues should not affect our adult life because they happened long ago. Unfortunately, we may be grown up on the outside, but the child inside us is still alive and hurting. That wounded child in us needs to be healed and will create opportunities for us to overcome the pain he still feels. And what better place to get your attention than in your trading.

The Rotten Apple

Bruce was raised in an upper class family where the accepted tradition was to go to boarding school at a young age. As an adult, Bruce still remembers loving the estate on which he lived, running with the animals and playing in the forest. He loved playing games with his nanny and his little sister, and although the family gatherings were rather formal, he felt protected in the arms of his nurturing family. It was understood that he would go to a boarding school, and he looked forward to it as a new, fun experience. On the day after school began, the reality of his situation hit when there was no one to give this sensitive child a hug, a sign of love, or a nod of understanding at the right time. And to make matters worse, Bruce began to realize that he had become a target of ridicule and attack for certain older boys at the school.

Bruce's parents were both professional people who traveled a great deal, and when other children were able to go home for vacations and holidays, he was one of the few lonely children who stayed behind. It was during one of these unsupervised periods that this defenseless, young child was physically and emotionally exploited by an older boy.

Years later, when he became a trader, Bruce would have a need to sabotage his success after any big wins. A part of him felt unworthy because, as a child, he had felt that anyone who could not defend himself and who could allow himself to undergo such terrible abuse and exploitation was unworthy of success. As an adult, he very rarely looked back at this traumatic experience, but when he did, he saw it as one of those "childhood things" that many people had to undergo. He had read accounts of what other children had experienced, and he had seen talk shows interviewing adults who had had similar experiences. He understood that for many people this experience presented problems, but not for him.

In counseling, Bruce realized how important it was to transform the long-held and limiting beliefs and decisions he made as a child into beliefs that would allow him to keep his profits.

While this story may seem overly dramatic to some, you may be surprised to learn that it has been recounted to me in various forms by a number of clients. A great many people quietly go about their lives having swept the most devastating experiences under the rug. Unfortunately, until those experiences are dealt with properly, they produce deep scars which, like a scratch on a CD, forever damage and reshape the sound.

Unfortunately, it does not take this level of intense drama for a young person (or even for an older person) to feel unworthy of success based upon a specific incident. Even when we are consciously aware of an incident that could potentially diminish who or what we are, many of us still sweep these experiences under the rug. With it goes our full potential for success.

Jealousy in the Pot

Not all of the incidents which we ignore as adults are as obviously damaging as the ones that Bruce experienced. In fact, it is more likely that we will ignore the less obvious ones because we are more confident that they can do us no harm.

As a talented young trader, Will was continually sabotaging his trading. Unlike Bruce, Will had grown up in a closely-knit, supportive family in which the average things went wrong. He was an attractive young man, bright, with a good education. His parents loved each other and stayed together all of his life. He lived in a middle class home in which he was neither indulged nor deprived.

However, during a brief period in his childhood, two of Will's classmates sent him messages that were both subtle and terribly destructive. Jealous of this happy and attractive child, two children from abusive homes pestered Will with criticisms that were patently untrue: that he was stupid and ugly. Despite his parents' desperate attempts to counteract the effects of these attacks, Will's self-esteem was damaged. By fourth grade, he was a shadow of his earlier self. He had long-since stopped smiling. He hung his head as he walked to his classroom, afraid of what other children might say to him.

As an adult, Will did not even remember the barbs of these two classmates, and he certainly would not attribute his failure to thrive to their assault on his self-image as a child. It was only after attending a seminar, that Will was able to dredge up the memory and deal with its consequences.

Deep Fried

For Bruce and Will, the source of their problems was deep in their childhood. However, a trader can also be sweeping a current situation under the carpet which is affecting his trading. This was the case with Peter, a bulky and handsome trader of Scandinavian heritage. Peter came from a very conservative background, which is how he approached his trading. Up until the time that he met Maria, he was consistently steady in his trading and always made a good profit. In contrast to Peter's background, however, Maria came from a family where emotions ran very hot and volatile.

At first, Peter was overwhelmed by Maria's full-of-life attitude. After a while, however, he decided that he could use a little spice in his life. Unfortunately, Peter got a lot more than he bargained for. Peter did not see the downside of Maria's emotional extremes until he was married for six months. One night, she became extremely upset when he arrived home late for dinner. With a frying pan in her hand, she came after him and hit him over the head before he had a chance to react. Even though Maria stood only five foot two inches tall, with the frying pan in her hand, she became a giant.

Sadly, this attack was the first of many. They began sporadically, but increasingly became a pattern. Peter tried every conceivable way to stop the violence, including reasoning, debating, yelling, bargaining and threatening. Finally, as the situation continued to deteriorate, Peter considered approaching Maria's family for help. However, before he was able to do so, he discovered that Maria had already told them that Peter was slapping her around. As a result, Peter was severely beaten by Maria's brothers and warned he would be killed if he hit her again or if he left her. It was during this experience that Peter confirmed his suspicion that Maria's family was involved in organized crime. Maria's father would not tolerate anyone harming his little girl, even though the physical violence Maria committed on Peter originated from her own father's abuse of her. Peter was living his life on eggshells, not knowing what would set Maria off.

Needless to say, all of this drama was damaging Peter's performance as a trader. He would not acknowledge the fact that he was a battered husband, much less the connection between this situation and the problems he was having in his trading. When he finally spoke to me about the situation, he laughed about it nervously, as though he feared that I was going to ridicule him for it.

Before Peter could deal with the effects of his battering, he needed to reduce the danger he was in from both Maria and her father and brothers. As a result, we developed an elaborate scheme to prove to Maria's family that she was the one with the problem. Fortunately, Peter is now safely out of the marriage and trading well again. In fact, he heads the trading department where he works.

You do not have to be hit over the head with a frying pan to be battered. Emotional battering is just as serious as physical battering. The effects are equally damaging to your well-being. And so, many traders sweep under the carpet the fact that their personal problems affect their trading.

Making the Recipe Work

The nearly extinct art of homemaking used to include a complete spring cleaning. At the turn of the century, no self-respecting homemaker would have considered her house in working order until she had washed every piece of linen and drapery, dusted behind and under every piece of furniture and cleaned under every carpet in the house. Using this same recipe for a thorough self-cleaning, a persistent problem in your trading can be brought to light and eliminated. Here are the steps:

1. **Realize that you are actually doing it.**
   You are creating a problem in your trading and it is not the result of some outside force. If you are experiencing a pattern of negative results in your trading, obviously something is wrong.

2. **Eliminate causes which are obvious by asking the following:**

   - Have you developed a sound understanding of the nature of the markets and trading in order to compete in the markets?

   - Would your trading make money if you followed the rules of your system?

   - Are you following your own trading rules?

   - Are you sufficiently capitalized to trade?

   - Is there a definite pattern to your losses?

3. **Dig Deeper**
   Once you have eliminated all of the obvious problems which can undermine any attempts to succeed at trading, and you find that you are at a loss to

understand your consistent pattern of self-sabotage, you will need to dig deeper to find out what you have swept under the carpet. A good clue is a situation which was:

- Emotionally or physically painful at the time you experienced it.

- One which you are unwilling to deal with or have forgotten about.

- One which you just don't think is important anymore.

If you have not been able to uncover the source of the sabotage, or if you are unable to work your way through the problem on your own, the next step is to get professional help. The area of hidden sabotage is often one in which private counseling is in order. For most people, uncovering and dealing with hidden sabotage is as easy as performing open heart surgery on yourself.

Conclusion

Traumas and negative situations in our life will resurface when we are in a highly emotional state or when we are vulnerable in any way. As traders, any threat to our neurology's comfort allows our negative experiences to resurface. Then, without any apparent reason, we begin to lose control and make mistakes that lead to the very losses we are afraid of causing. A cycle of self-doubt and frustration with attending fear and more losses is put into place. And still the cause is unknown because it has been swept under the carpet.

Therefore, if you have a continuing pattern of sabotaging your efforts and the cause is not obvious to you, you are sweeping your profits under the carpet as well.

Epilogue

Did you feel some of the stories were about you? You are not alone. The stories I selected for this book are intended as lessons for you to prevent problems from arising, to recognize the issues you now need to handle and to suggest how to deal with them. Keep in mind, the traders with whom I work are committed to making changes, so they don't necessarily reflect the majority of traders who are unlikely to be successful in the business.

When I started working with private clients, I pretty much worked with anyone. Now, I will only work with people who I believe have what it takes to become successful. Since I cannot work individually with all of the traders who want personal coaching, the lessons taught in *Winning Edge 2* will provide you with some of the tools you need towards each new level of your success.

The goal of this book is to inspire you to create a balance in your life between the demands of your professional and your personal life. Not even a holy grail system can achieve results for a trader who has not handled his psychological issues over the long haul. Fear, greed, impatience, lack of planning and the biggest saboteur of all, stress, are lurking to undo potentially winning trades and traders. To underscore this truism, a trader called today to say that for his first ten years as a successful floor trader, he never gave a single thought to working on his psychology. Now, after a string of professional and personal losses, he is now broke, and reading everything he can find to help him put his life back together.

After your initial reading, reread the chapters you identified with as being areas you need to work on. Complete the exercises, even if you think you don't need to. Update your business plan and review your trading plan. Take care to balance all of the areas of your life. Make the decision that it is okay to be very successful while enjoying the process as you share your abundance with others.

Best wishes for a happy and prosperous life.

**Adrienne would like to thank
the following magazines and newsletters
that have published articles and interviews:**

Applied Derivatives Trading

Australian Financial Review

Bullish Review

Eynno Xphma

Fax Alert

Financial Trader

Futures Magazine

Global Investment Technology

Ladies Home Journal

MBH Newsletter

Money World

Swiss Commodities Review

Technical Analysis of Stocks and Commodities

The Bridge Trader

The Sentinel

The Individual Investor

The Technical Trader

Trading on Target Newsletter

Traders' Catalog and Resource Guide

Washington Post

Worth Magazine

OTHER SERVICES & PRODUCTS

From Adrienne Laris Toghraie

SERVICES

- **Private Consulting**   Remove the Barriers to Each Level of Success in Trading and All Areas of Your Life

- **Institutional & Corporate**   Increase Production, Trading Ability and Teamwork

SEMINARS

- **Trading on Target**   For Discipline & Overcoming Sabotage

- **The Winner's Edge**   Gain the Technical & Psychological Tools for Becoming a Successful Investor

- **Intuition/Discretionary**   Develop & Use Reliable Intuitive Indicators

- **Building a Capital & Client Base**   Build Sales, Increase Production

- **Creating Affluence**   Increase Resources & Balance Your Life

- **Enriching Life Seminar**   Build Success by Making Better Choices and Gain Control Over Your Life

PRODUCTS

Trading on Target Home Study Course

(can be purchased in packages, as individual products, or purchased as an entire course)

Traders' Secrets Package
- Traders' Secrets Book
- Evaluation & Consultation on Phone
- Stress Relief Cassette Album
- 1 year subscription to TOT Newsletter

The Winning Edge Package
- The Winning Edge I Book
- Discipline 1 CD
- Six Steps to Greater Success Video

The Discipline Package
- The Winning Edge 2 Book
- Discipline 2 Cassette Album
- Get A Life Book

Business Plan Package
- The Winning Edge 3 Book
- Business Plan
- Business Plan CD
- 1 year subscription to TOT Newsletter

Interview Package
- Trading on Target 1 Interview Cassette Album
- Trading on Target 2 Interview Cassette Album
- Dear Coach Book

The Winning Edge 4 Package
- The Winning Edge 4 Book
- Discipline 3 Cassette Album
- 1 year subscription to TOT Newsletter

For additional information please contact us. Be sure to ask about the savings available when you purchase one of our packages.

**Trading on Target
100 Lavewood Lane, Cary, NC 27511
Call (919) 851-8288 Fax (919) 851-9979
Website: tradingOnTarget.com
E-Mail Adrienne@TradingOnTarget.com**

Visit our Website at http://www.TradingOnTarget.com